EC-08

D1540533

Standard FORTRAN:
A Problem-Solving
Approach

Standard FORTRAN:
A Problem-Solving Approach

Laura G. Cooper Florida Agricultural and Mechanical University

Marilyn Z. Smith Florida State University

Houghton Mifflin Company · Boston

Atlanta

Dallas

Geneva, Illinois

Hopewell, New Jersey

Palo Alto

London

Copyright © 1973 by Houghton Mifflin Company. All rights reserved. No part of this work may be reproduced or transmitted in any form or by any means, electronic or mechanical, including photocopying and recording, or by any information storage or retrieval system, without permission in writing from the publisher.

Printed in the U.S.A.

Library of Congress Catalog Card Number: 72–4395

ISBN: 0–395–14028–5

Preface

This textbook is the result of five years of teaching experience in the field of computer programming languages at both the undergraduate and graduate levels. We have used several unique teaching concepts:

1. a problem-solving procedure that provides a step-by-step method for writing a program for the computer
2. presentation of the standard ANSI FORTRAN language that the major computer manufacturers follow
3. early presentation of basic material so that the student can write complete programs from the beginning of the course

For each problem in the text, we start the problem-solving procedure with a statement of the problem, then we develop a flowchart, and finally, we write FORTRAN language instructions for the sample problem. Most textbooks give a flowchart only in its final form for a sample problem, but we show the student how to analyze a problem and how to approach the development of the flowchart step-by-step. Then, we guide the student in writing the appropriate FORTRAN instructions corresponding to the steps developed in the flowchart.

Many students shy away from learning FORTRAN because in most books the sample problems are strictly math or science oriented. The numerous sample problems in our text are not restricted to any one area. We feel we have presented a balanced mixture of simple problems from the fields of business, the humanities, and science.

We have adhered strictly to the presentation of standard ANSI FORTRAN, because FORTRAN is a programming language with many dialects. One of its earliest forms was called FORTRAN II. As new commands were added to the language, it became known as FORTRAN IV. Other dialects were developed when various computer manufacturers inserted their own special features into the language. As a result, a program which works on one computer may not work on another one, because the second machine does not know the same dialect of FORTRAN as the first. To bring uniformity to the language, the American National Standards Institute (ANSI) has recommended a standard version of FORTRAN and has encouraged the major computer manufacturers to adopt it. By having a standard language, ANSI hopes to eliminate all the wasted hours spent converting a program for use on different computers. A person learning ANSI FORTRAN can transfer from one computer installation to another and can use the language immediately without studying a new dialect.

One of the main objectives of our text is to teach the student how to use the computer to solve problems. We believe the best way to accomplish this is to have the student write many programs starting with very simple ones. Therefore, we present enough of the basics of problem solving and the FORTRAN language so that the student should be able to write his first program by the end of the second week of classes, if not sooner. We have organized the book so that the student can learn in stages, always progressing from simple problems to more complex ones.

We approach the teaching of FORTRAN as if it were a foreign language. We introduce new elements of the language in a sample program and later explain the rules of grammar involved. The examples illustrate how to take the different parts of the language and combine them to solve problems. While programming is probably best learned from an instructor, we feel that the ambitious student who has access to a computer could teach himself using our text. We have kept the language of the book simple and free from computer jargon. In addition, we have included many exercises and program assignments to let the student practice using his FORTRAN. Some suggested topics for programs are: an elementary one after Chapter 6, one using single-subscripted variables, one using DØ loops, one on two- or three-dimensional arrays, and one on subprograms. Depending upon the length of the course and the number of credit hours involved, the assignments may be expanded or combined. The entire book can be covered in a one quarter or one semester course. But a two semester course would allow the student to have more practice on the advanced topics.

In our attempt to simplify the material for the beginning student, we have omitted several topics from the main portion of the book and have placed them in Chapter 13. These topics include such items as double precision variables, complex variables, logical variables, the E- and G-field specifications, and Hollerith constants. An individual may use the topics in this chapter whenever a need for them arises. He does not need to finish the first twelve chapters before reading Chapter 13.

Some special features in the text include a brief history of the computer and a discussion of basic computer concepts in Chapter 2. At the end of each chapter we present a list of terms with which the student should be familiar before proceeding to the next chapter. We have included a section on how to use the card punch and the drum control card. To help the student when he writes programs, we have included an appendix designed as a reference to all the ANSI FORTRAN statements discussed in the text. It gives the forms of each statement, the rules for using it, and a reference to the discussion or examples of the statement in the text.

Laura G. Cooper
Marilyn Z. Smith

Contents

Standard FORTRAN:
A Problem-Solving Approach

Chapter 1

Flowcharts

1.1 Introduction

It is unworthy of excellent men to lose hours like slaves in the labor of calculation which could safely be relegated to anyone else if machines were used.
Leibnitz

Computers can handle large amounts of information compiled by insurance companies, banks, the Census Bureau, and numerous other corporations. They also aid in solving lengthy mathematical problems which involve complex computations. Many familiar situations emphasize the importance of the speed of modern computers. Airline reservations, police investigations, intensive care in hospitals, and space rocketry are just a few examples in which people need an answer immediately and can obtain it from a computer.

Men and women would find some of the tasks mentioned above very tedious and time-consuming, but a computer could do them in a matter of seconds. A computer is similar to an adding machine, because it can do simple arithmetic. Although both a computer and an adding machine are tools and may be used to solve problems, differences do exist between these two machines. In an adding machine the operator enters each number and instruction manually. In order to total a series of numbers, the operator must key in the first number and press the add button, key in the second number and press the add button, key in the third number, and so on. No matter how fast the adding machine, it must wait for the operator to give it a new number and a new instruction (add, subtract, multiply, divide). On the other hand, to have a computer total a series of numbers, an operator submits all the numbers and all the instructions at one time. Then with all the instructions in hand, the computer can begin executing them.

1.2 Why Use a Flowchart?

Computers cannot think, but they are capable of performing many arithmetic calculations if they are told what kind of calculation to do and what numbers to use. A computer must receive detailed steps to follow in order to solve a specific problem. It is not enough to command a computer to "calculate my income tax" or "find me a date for Friday night." If a computer is to calculate income tax, it must know which numbers to add, which ones to subtract, and other details a person must know in order to compute the tax by hand. Any problem which a computer is to solve must be broken down into a series of steps that are carried out in some sort of logical order. Usually we first write these steps in the form of a **flowchart**: a diagram which tells from start to finish all the commands which the computer must execute to solve a problem. For the computer to carry out the commands described in the flowchart, we then must convert the commands into some form which the computer understands.

In addition to representing a logical solution to a problem, a flowchart is a means of communication among people who use computers. In understanding another person's method, his flowchart is easier to read than the detailed form which he has prepared for the computer. In each of the next sections we will examine a simple problem and develop a flowchart for solving it.

1

1.3 Flowcharting a Simple Payroll Problem

Suppose you work for the payroll department of a large corporation with over 2000 employees. You have a stack of cards containing one card for each employee. The information on the card is the employee's name, his hourly rate of pay, and the number of hours worked per week. Using this information you must compute each person's salary and write him a check. You have an assistant, who may be another person or a computer, write all the checks. Your job is to write down precise instructions on how to do the company's payroll and your assistant will carry out the instructions.

First, we need some place to start. In a flowchart we start by using the symbol and writing the word START inside. Now, there sits your assistant with a pen and a stack of employee payroll cards in front of him. What should he do next? Compute the salary? But how does he know which numbers to use? Wouldn't he have to get these numbers off the first card in the stack? Yes, he would. Therefore, our first instruction is to read a card and remember the name, the rate of pay, and hours worked. A flowchart has a special symbol for the instruction, "read a card," so that we do not have to write the command "read" inside. This flowchart symbol instructs your assistant to read three items from a single card: NAME, RATE, and HOURS.

Knowing RATE and HOURS, your assistant can then compute the salary which is RATE × HOURS. We place this command inside the diagram in the flowchart. The arrow (←) states that the value of the product of RATE and HOURS will be labeled SALARY. The use of the arrow is another way of saying that SALARY has just been computed.

What should be the next instruction? To write the check. The items which go on the check are NAME and SALARY. The symbol below signifies the write instruction. We do not need to say "write NAME and SALARY." Instead, the words NAME and SALARY inside this symbol signify that command.

We connect all the boxes to show that we proceed from one box to the next. Our instructions so far have written a check only for the first employee. In order to design our flowchart so that it will write a check for the second employee, we must repeat the instructions, as in Figure 1.1. If this flowchart is to show how to write checks for a company with over 2000 employees, it certainly would be a lengthy one. However, if we examine the flowchart in Figure 1.1, we see that it consists basically of three boxes which we would write repeatedly. We may shorten our flowchart considerably if we use a **loop**—that is, show that we wish to repeat three instructions for each employee. The flowchart in Figure 1.2 illustrates the loop.

Drawing a line from box 4 to just below the START box signifies that after your assistant writes the first check he goes back to the instruction to read the second card, to compute this man's salary, and to write him a check. Then he goes back to read the third card, compute salary, write the check, and continue. What stops the loop? The flowchart does not say. Of course, when no

Start

NAME, RATE, HOURS

SALARY ← RATE × HOURS

NAME, SALARY

employee cards remain, there are no more checks to write. We should include something in the flowchart to ask if your assistant has reached the last data card. If he has, then stop; otherwise, continue writing checks. Every flowchart should have a place to start and a way to stop. Figure 1.3 gives the complete flowchart.

Figure 1.1

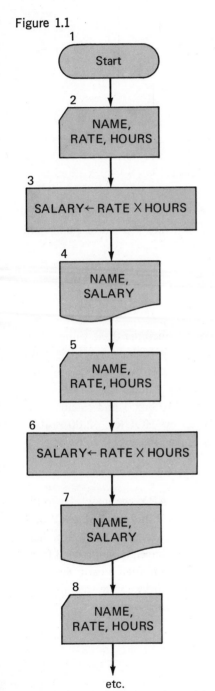

Figure 1.2   Figure 1.3

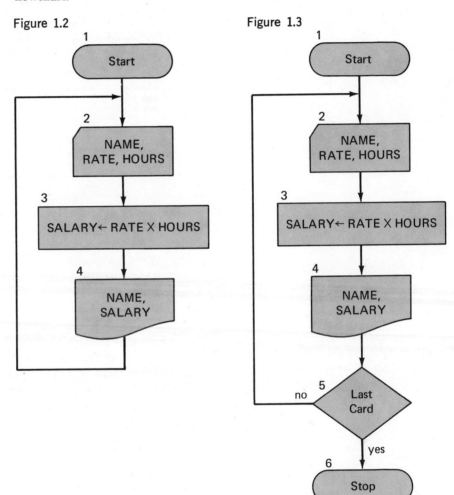

Notice several things about the flowchart in Figure 1.3. Box 5 asks the question: Is this the last card? It is not necessary to include the question mark in the flowchart box, because the diamond-shaped box represents a question. The question has two answers—yes and no—and the flowchart shows which direction to take and what to do whether the answer is yes or no. When we follow the flowchart, we proceed from box 1 to box 2 to box 3 to box 4. Then at box 5 there is a decision to make. We go either to box 2 or to box 6. The possible directions which we may take at a point of decision in a flowchart are called **branches.** The process of following one of these branches is called **branching.** Also note that lines connect all symbols and that the arrows indicate the order of the steps.

Now that we have written the flowchart, how can we be sure that it is correct? Our next step is to take some names and numbers which are employees' rates and hours worked and test the flowchart by hand to see if it will correctly produce the payroll. Is it necessary to use 2000 pieces of test data to check the flowchart? The amount of test data depends upon the problem. In this case, each data card contains the same type of information. Therefore, a flowchart which works for three or four pieces of data should work for any number of cards.

Suppose we have the three data cards shown in Figure 1.4.

Figure 1.4

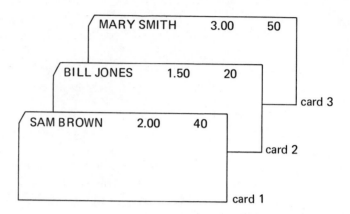

Referring to the flowchart in Figure 1.3, we see that the first command is to read NAME, RATE, and HOURS from a card. Take a piece of paper and write

     NAME = SAM BROWN
     RATE = 2.00
     HOURS = 40

With such a simple problem, we could probably remember these values without writing them. However, a good habit to develop is that of writing down everything read in or computed in a flowchart. As problems become more complicated, it is not always possible to remember every number.

After we read one card, we proceed from box 2 to box 3 and calculate the salary. Interpret this box as: multiply RATE by HOURS ($2.00 \times 40 = 80.00$), and call this number SALARY. This means that we should write

     SALARY = 80.00

When the flowchart says to write NAME and SALARY, we may refer to the worksheet to see that the NAME was SAM BROWN and his SALARY was 80.00. Knowing these items, we could write him a check. Then the flowchart asks if we have just processed the last card. Since we haven't, we proceed from flowchart box 5 to box 2 where we find the instruction to read a card. Since we have read the first test card and we cannot read it again, we may wish to cross it off. The card to read now is the second one. Instead of writing

     NAME = BILL JONES
     RATE = 1.50
     HOURS = 20

let us erase or scratch out the old values of NAME, RATE, and HOURS, and replace them with these new values.

     NAME = ~~SAM BROWN~~   BILL JONES
     RATE = ~~2.00~~   1.50
     HOURS = ~~40~~   20

Each name may have only one value at a time. Every time there is a new value, the old one is erased. This concept may not be very intuitive, but, in fact, it is the way computers work. We continue to compute RATE × HOURS (1.50 × 20 = 30.00) and replace the value of SALARY with this new value. The arrow (←) here indicates replacement, that is, replace the previous value of SALARY with 30.00. When we processed the first data card, the arrow told us to *compute* SALARY for the first time. Now that we are processing another data card and SALARY already has a value, the arrows means *replace* the former value of SALARY with a new one. In either case, whether the arrow means compute or replace, the arrow indicates that SALARY is to have a value.

SALARY = ~~80.00~~   30.00

We continue through the flowchart until we have written the check for MARY SMITH. Then, when the flowchart asks if we have processed the last card, the answer is yes and we stop.

There is an easy and convenient tabular method for analyzing a flowchart. We call this table listing a **trace.** Table 1.1 is a trace diagram of the wage problem. Note the following properties of the table:

1. For each step of the flowchart, one (and only one) line in the table is entered.
2. Since some values remain unchanged during several steps, we do not copy them down each time. In other words, in step 2, the values for NAME, RATE, and HOURS are still: SAM BROWN, 2.00, and 40; but we do not copy them over. However, in step 5 NAME becomes BILL JONES and no longer is SAM BROWN. At this point, when we have a new value for NAME, we may wish to cross off the old value.

The flowchart seems to work because it has produced the correct answers. But remember that a flowchart is the first step toward having the computer solve a problem for us, because the instructions in the flowchart are the same ones which we will give to the computer to tell it how to do the problem.

Table 1.1 Trace Diagram of Wage Problem

Step No.	Flow-chart Box No.	Variables				Test	Output (Write)
		Name	Rate	Hours	Salary	Last card	
1	2	Sam Brown	2.00	40			
2	3				80 = (2.00)(40)		
3	4						Sam Brown 80.00
4	5					no	
5	2	Bill Jones	1.50	20			
6	3				30 = (1.50)(20)		
7	4						Bill Jones 30.00
8	5					no	
9	2	Mary Smith	3.00	50			
10	3				150 = (3.00)(50)		
11	4						Mary Smith 150.00
12	5					yes	
13	6						

1.4 A Flowchart to Decide If a Crate May Be Mailed

A warehouse manager has over 1000 crates which he wishes to mail, but the Post Office will accept the crates only if they are not too large. As each crate was filled, the packing manager assigned a number to the crate and measured its length, width, and height. He wrote the information about each crate on a separate card. The Post Office requires that the length of the longest side plus the distance around the other sides (girth) must be less than or equal to 72 inches. We wish to develop a procedure which will enable the warehouse manager to decide which crates he cannot mail.

Figure 1.5

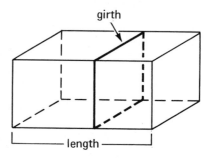

The information which we have consists of the crate code number and the lengths of the three sides. Let us label these items so that we may refer to them easily in the flowchart:

CODE—crate code number
SIDE1—length of the longest side
SIDE2—length of the second longest side
SIDE3—length of the shortest side

The main portion of the problem is to determine if SIDE1 + GIRTH is less than or equal to 72. If it is, the warehouse manager can mail the crate. If not, we should write a message saying that the crate "cannot be mailed." To write this in a flowchart diagram we have the following boxes in which the symbol $\le$ represents the words "less than or equal to."

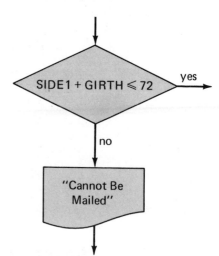

But how does the flowchart obtain a value for SIDE1 and a value for GIRTH? We must compute the GIRTH as 2(SIDE2 + SIDE3) before we may ask the question: Is SIDE1 + GIRTH $\le$ 72. Let us add this to the flowchart.

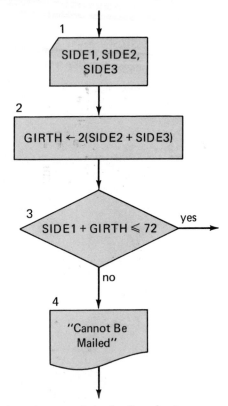

So far the flowchart seems to be progressing smoothly, but where do the values for SIDE1, SIDE2, and SIDE3 come from? They must be read from a card before they can be used. Therefore, we add this step to the flowchart.

Figure 1.6

So far, we have at least three loose ends in the flowchart:

1. Where do we START?
2. What do we do if SIDE1 + GIRTH is less than or equal to 72?
3. Where do we proceed after writing "cannot be mailed"?

We want to begin the flowchart by reading a card. If $SIDE1 + GIRTH \leqq$ 72, the warehouse manager can mail the crate, and we should proceed to check the next crate. If he cannot mail the crate, we should write the message and then proceed to check the next crate. By making the flowchart loop back to box 2, we can go on to process the next crate. This addition to the flowchart in Figure 1.6 appears in Figure 1.7

Figure 1.7

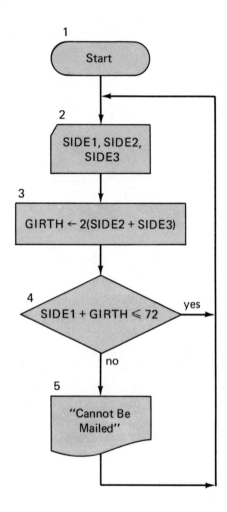

Let us now examine the flowchart in Figure 1.7. It seems to be complete, but there are several places where we could improve it. Consider the message which the computer writes. It does not say which crate cannot be mailed. Since each crate was numbered, we should write that number along with the message. To show in the flowchart that we want to write the specific words "cannot be mailed" they are enclosed in quotation marks. To show that we want to write the crate code number, we will include the word CODE in the flowchart write box. This means that the *value* of CODE will be written and not the letters CODE. If we wish to write the crate code number, first we must read it in along with the lengths of the sides.

A second improvement in the flowchart would be a way to stop the process. Our flowchart loops continually expecting a new card each time. At some point no cards will remain. What can we use to stop the loop in the flowchart? We could ask if the last card has been read, as in Figure 1.3. However, if we wish to convert this flowchart into a form which a computer can understand, there is no way for us to tell the computer to check for the last data card. When a computer reads a card, it cannot tell if that card is the first one, the last one, or any other one. However, we can insert a special card at the end of the card deck. If this card contained a number unlike any of the numbers in the data deck, then we could look for this card. When we find it, we would know that we had come to the end of the card deck. This special card is called a **dummy data card,** because it is not part of the actual data deck, but it signals the end of the data card deck.

What kind of dummy data card could we use in this flowchart? Since the crates would be numbered 1, 2, 3, and so on, our dummy card could contain a zero value for CODE. The complete flowchart appears in Figure 1.8.

Figure 1.8

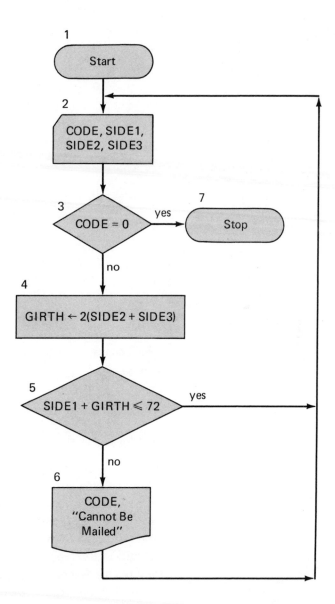

Exercise

Suppose the warehouse manager has the following four data cards:

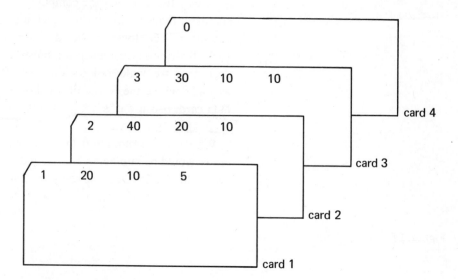

Construct a trace diagram of the flowchart in Figure 1.8 using these data cards. Your trace table headings should look like the following:

Step No.	Flow-chart Box No.	Variables					Test		Output (Write)
		Code	Side1	Side2	Side3	Girth	Code=0	Side1+Girth≤72	

1.5 Summary of Flowchart Symbols

A flowchart is an effective way of representing the solution to a problem. If a flowchart is going to be useful, the author should draw it so that someone else can understand it. This means that everyone should use the same symbol to represent the same command. For example, the diamond asks a question and the oval says either to start or stop. If we saw a flowchart in which ovals represented questions and diamonds represented starting, we would have to relearn the meaning of these symbols. In this section we will discuss those symbols suggested by the American National Standards Institute (ANSI) which apply to the scope of this text.

Rules for the Use of Flowcharts

1. A flowchart should have a place to *start* and a place to *stop*.
2. A line should connect every symbol in a flowchart to another symbol. If the size of the page prohibits the connection of two symbols, use the connector symbol. We will give an example of this later.
3. Do not cross lines on a flowchart.
4. Normally the direction of movement from one flowchart box to another is from top to bottom and from left to right. Use arrows on the connecting lines to show that the direction is from bottom to top or from right to left. Arrows may be used on all connecting lines to point out explicitly the direction of the flow.
5. Sentences, symbols, or words may be used inside the flowchart boxes.
6. The arrow (←) denotes replacement.
7. Use quotation marks around a message that will be written out.

Punched Card	*Read Cards*
Document (Printer)	*Write*
Input/Output	*Reading or Writing of Info.*
Processing	*Command to be carried out*
Decision	*? with a yes or no answer*
Predefined Process	
Preparation	

Input and Output Symbols

This symbol could represent either the reading of information from a punched card or the punching of information onto a card. Therefore, to avoid confusion we could include the word READ or PUNCH inside the flowchart box. However, in this text we will use this symbol exclusively for reading cards and will omit the word READ from the flowchart.

In this text we use the document symbol to represent the writing of information on the printer. In general, this symbol could represent either the reading or writing of a document.

This symbol represents the reading or writing of information. I/O is generally used as an abbreviation for Input/Output.

Instruction Symbols

This symbol represents a command which is to be carried out.

This symbol denotes a question which may have the answer yes or no (true or false, etc.). There should be two or more lines coming from the symbol to represent the possible alternatives.

This symbol represents a process consisting of one or more commands which are specified elsewhere (for example, in another flowchart).

We use this symbol for steps which are not part of determining the final results but which must be included to make the flowchart procedure work.

Connecting Symbols

These lines connect the symbols in a flowchart and indicate the direction of flow. Note that a horizontal line without an arrow indicates a flow from left to right, and that a vertical line without an arrow indicates a flow from top to bottom.

The symbol below usually contains a number or letter and connects two portions of a flowchart which cannot be physically joined by lines. For example,

	left to right
	right to left
	top to bottom
	bottom to top

Connector

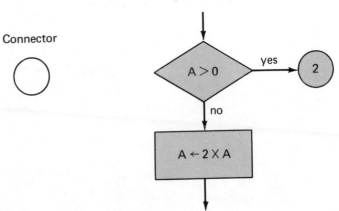

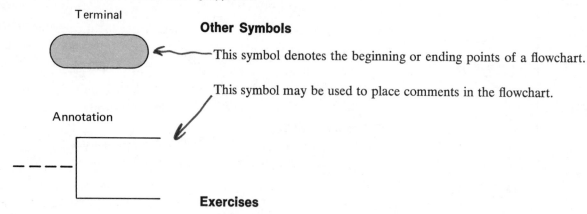

Terminal

Annotation

Other Symbols

This symbol denotes the beginning or ending points of a flowchart.

This symbol may be used to place comments in the flowchart.

Exercises

1. The employee records for a construction firm with over 800 employees are kept on cards. For each employee there is one card which contains his name, his hourly wage, and the number of hours worked per week. Write a flowchart which will compute each person's salary and will pay double time (twice the hourly wage) for any hours worked over 40. Some employees may have worked more than 40 hours and some may have worked less than 40 hours. Your flowchart should include a test to see whether or not a person receives overtime. Then write the person's name and salary on a check.

   For example, if the rate is $2.00 and a person works 50 hours, he should receive $2.00 × 40 = $80.00 for regular salary plus 2 × $2.00 × 10 = $40.00 for overtime = $120.00 salary. Yet, a person working 30 hours at $3.00 an hour should receive 30 × $3.00 = $90.00 salary. Check your flowchart with these numbers to see if it works correctly.

2. Modify the flowchart in exercise 1 so that social security is deducted from the employee's gross pay. The deduction is calculated as 5.2 percent of the gross pay. Write the gross pay, amount of social security deduction, net pay (gross pay minus the deduction), and employee's name on the check.

3. In the sample problem of section 1.4, suppose that you do not know whether SIDE1, SIDE2, or SIDE3 is the largest. Modify the flowchart in Figure 1.8 so that it will determine the largest side and will use the two remaining sides for the girth.

4. Each employee's payroll card contains his name, hourly rate of pay, hours worked, and a code. This code is either a 1, 2, or 3 and tells whether or not he belongs to the company's group insurance plan. If the code is 1, the employee should have $2.68 deducted from his salary for individual insurance coverage. A code of 2 means that $5.23 should be deducted for the family insurance plan. A code of 3 means that the employee does not belong to the insurance group. Write a flowchart which will compute each employee's salary (do not calculate any overtime pay), deduct for insurance where necessary, and write a check for each person. The information on the check should include the employee's name, gross salary, amount deducted (if nothing is deducted the amount should be zero), and take-home pay.

5. You are given a stack of cards from a bank. The first card contains an account number, the person's name, and his current checking account balance. All other cards in the stack contain a number and a code. If the code is a

"C," then the amount on the card is a check and should be deducted from the balance. If the code is a "D," then the amount is a deposit and should be added to the balance. Write a flowchart which will process this account's monthly transactions and will calculate and print its new balance. You may assume that the balance never goes below zero.

6. Data cards are available for a group of prospective basketball players. Each data card contains a player's name, a value for height in inches (H), and weight in pounds (W). The coach wants a list of the names, heights, and weights of those who are 72 inches and over but who weigh less than 250 pounds. Several of his beginning assistants submitted a flowchart to help him with the problem. Tell the coach why the flowcharts are wrong and give him a correct flowchart which incorporates the best features from each.

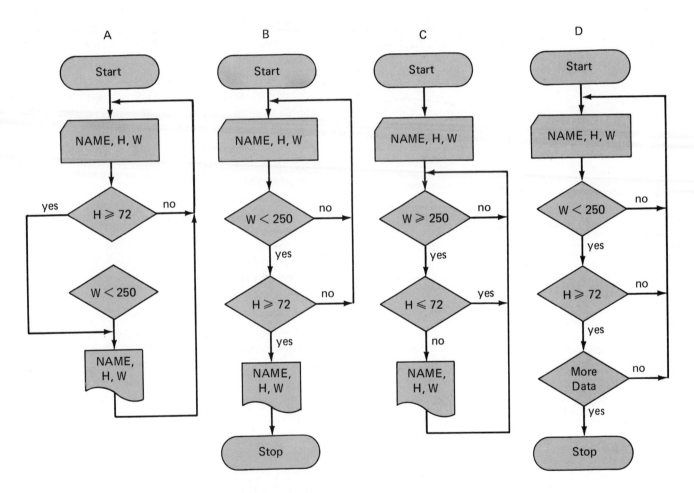

Special Terms

1. *branch*
2. *branching*
3. *dummy data card*
4. *flowchart*
5. *I/O*
6. *loop*
7. *replacement*
8. *trace*

Chapter 2

Computer Concepts

2.1 Introduction

Although many students quickly learn how to use a computer, they actually have little knowledge about the development of these modern machines. In this chapter we present a brief historical development of computers and introduce some important computer concepts and terminology. We feel that a general knowledge about computers will help the student judge what can actually be accomplished with the aid of these machines.

A computer, in a general sense, is a device which can accept information, perform calculations or manipulate material, and then produce results. Computers are classified according to the way they receive the information. An **analog computer** accepts continuous physical quantities such as voltage or the turning of a dial. An everyday example of an analog device to measure time is the continuous movement of the second hand on a clock. In a **digital computer** the information is not given in a continuous form, but as a series of separate and distinct symbols (beads, fingers, letters, digits, combinations of zeros and ones, and so forth). A simple example of a digital computing device is the abacus. With modern electronic computers it is possible to combine a digital and an analog computer to form one single device which is called a **hybrid computer.** In this text we will refer only to a digital computer.

2.2 Historical Background*

Computers do not have a long history. In 1822, the English mathematician Charles Babbage designed the first machine that embodied some of the features now found in modern computers. The Analytic Engine, as Babbage called it, had three parts: a place to store numbers, a place to do calculations, and a control unit to take numbers from the storage area and perform operations in a given order. After more than 40 years of work, Babbage never completed his machine because of inadequate machining techniques.

In 1886 when Herman Hollerith, a statistician and inventor, was working on information collected in the United States Census of 1880, he developed a system for representing data on punched cards. The machines that Hollerith developed for these cards used electricity to sense the holes in a card and in this manner could count the data from the census. Later, others developed machines which could reproduce punched cards, sort, collate, and even tabulate data. Removable plug-boards controlled the function of these machines. The task performed by a particular machine depended upon the way wires were connected into the plug-board.

The development of the early computing machines was due to the interest of scientists in a machine that could help them in tedious mathematical calculations. When Vannevar Bush wanted a machine to solve differential equations, he developed something which became the first general purpose analog computer. The machine, completed in 1930, was entirely mechanical and had

---

* This section may be omitted.

no electrical parts except a motor. Each number in this computer was represented by a certain number of turns of a rotating shaft. The Bell Telephone Laboratories completed the first automatic digital computer in 1939. Named the Complex Computer, it was built to do the tedious arithmetic of complex numbers, which were used by Bell's electrical engineers in analyzing electrical circuits.

For the next 30 years computers finally developed in full force. The new technological discoveries of these years were able to support the ideas of scientists and engineers in the construction and design of computers.

The MARK I computer, built by Professor Howard Aiken of Harvard University during the early 1940s, was the largest electromechanical computer ever constructed. The MARK I computer, completed in 1944, was the first machine that actually embodied some of the principles of the Analytical Engine as they were conceived by Babbage a hundred years before. Meanwhile, at the University of Pennsylvania, Professors J. Eckert and J. Mauchly were working on the first electronic computer. Their ENIAC computer, completed in 1946, was a much faster machine than other mechanical computers, but it contained 18,000 vacuum tubes, almost all of which had to function simultaneously. Rumors say that the lights in Philadelphia dimmed when the ENIAC was turned on.

The ENIAC was still difficult to use because engineers had to wire the instructions for each new task. Because this rewiring was so time-consuming, the idea was developed of being able to submit the instructions to the computer in the same form in which the data values were submitted (that is, on punched cards).

Professor John von Neumann proposed the concept of a stored program—engineers would no longer wire instructions into the computer, because the computer would store them with the data in its storage area. The first computer to actually use the stored program concept was completed in 1949 at Cambridge University in England. The stored program concept was indeed an important one which was quickly incorporated in the design of the new computers.

In the 1950s technological advances in components and design occurred so rapidly that computers were often outdated before they could be built. Although the early computers were designed for scientific calculations, the idea was soon evident that computers could also be used for data processing—handling large amounts of data. For example, large payrolls, insurance records, credit card accounts, and income tax returns are data processing tasks.

The development of transistors was another revolutionary mark in computer technology. These small electrical components, which produced very little heat, replaced vacuum tubes. Although the transistor was invented in 1948, it was not used in computers until 1954, and it actually made its impact in the manufacturing of the computers in the late 1950s and early 1960s.

The improvements made to computers in the 1960s were mainly in design. Computers became larger and operated with greater speed and efficiency. To utilize these large machines efficiently, many people had to share the same computer. Some users worked at the site of the computer. Others used remote terminals which were connected to the computer by communication lines. The concept of many people utilizing a computer at the same time is called **time-sharing.** Although each person has access to the computer, he pays only for the actual time the machine takes to do his work. In future computer developments, we will probably find that time-sharing and the use of remote terminals will have a predominant role.

2.3 Design of a Basic Digital Computer

A modern digital computer system consists of four basic physical parts:

1. input devices
2. output devices
3. memory or storage unit
4. central processing unit (CPU): control and arithmetic/logic sections

Figure 2.1 is a simple diagram of a computer.

Figure 2.1 Simple Diagram of a Computer

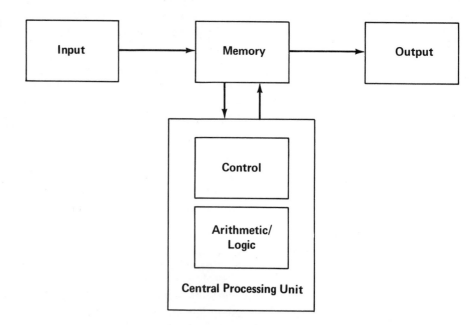

Input is any information coming into the computer. **Input devices** are the machines which accept this information. We can input numbers, letters, or instructions to the computer. Unfortunately, computers cannot process numbers and instructions written on paper, but they can handle different patterns of electrical impulses which represent numbers and instructions. Several input media, and corresponding input devices, have been designed to communicate with a computer. In a punched card, like the one pictured in Figure 2.2, the pres-

Figure 2.2 A Punched Card

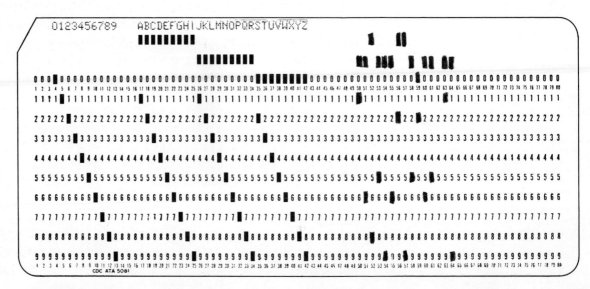

ence of a hole or combination of holes represents a character. When information is on punched cards, the input device is a card reader. If the information is on a magnetic tape, magnetic spots represent the characters, as depicted in Figure 2.3. The input device used for reading magnetic tapes is called a tape drive, such as the one in Figure 2.4, and it works on the same principle as a home tape recorder. Other commonly used input modes are punched paper tape, light pens, teletype, and magnetic ink.

Figure 2.3 Character Coding on a Magnetic Tape

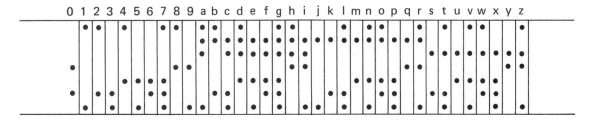

Output is any information coming out of the computer. **Output devices** are used for returning this information. Traditionally, the most common output device is a line printer, as shown in Figure 2.5. The name describes the fact that these printers are capable of printing lines on continuous paper forms. Another type of output is punched cards, produced by a punch device. Similarly, tape drives can generate magnetic tapes. Other commonly used output modes are punched paper tape, teletype, and cathode ray tube.

Figure 2.4 Tape Drive

The **memory** or **storage unit** keeps information. A computer's storage unit is composed of numerous cells, each one called a **memory location,** where numbers or instructions may be stored. Each location has a number called an **address.** A computer's memory locations are similar to post office boxes and the computer's addresses correspond to the numbers on the post office boxes. Each location has a different address so that the computer can tell them apart. Unlike a post office box, a memory location may contain one and only one piece of information—either an instruction or a data item. For example, suppose we store the number 5 in location 107 and the instruction "ADD 4 TO 3" in location 613. We can illustrate this as

107 | 5 |

613 | ADD 4 TO 3 |

Figure 2.5   Printer

If we now decide to store the number 3 in location 107, the computer will erase the 5 and replace it with the 3. Pictorially this is

107 ⟨ 3 ⟩

The control and arithmetic/logic sections comprise the **central processing unit,** or **CPU.** The control portion of the central processing unit has the ability to coordinate the various tasks within the computer system, such as transmitting information in and out of memory or sequencing the order of instructions to be performed. The arithmetic section performs additions, subtractions, multiplications, and divisions, and the logic section performs comparisons such as "Is INCOME greater than 1000?"

2.4 Communication with a Computer

People are able to communicate with each other when they speak the same language. Similarly, we say that a person speaks or understands a computer language when he can communicate with a computer. The relationship between a person and a computer is one in which the person will always be telling the computer what to do. We must distinguish between those things that a computer can and cannot do. We may tell a computer to "add 3 and 4," but we cannot tell it to "cook hot-dogs for Friday night."

An **instruction** is a command which the computer can carry out. The set of instructions belonging to a particular computer is called its **machine language,** which for most computers is entirely numeric. For example, 21 could represent the operation "add" and 22 could represent the operation "subtract." Using a machine language does not come naturally to people who are already familiar with the word "add" or the symbol "+." Since each computer has its specific machine language, learning a machine language is like learning a native dialect. Other languages have been developed that are relatively easy to learn and that are not specific to one computer. These languages use familiar symbols and words to represent instructions. They are called **symbolic languages** and are usually related to a particular kind of problem. Some examples are: COBOL, *CO*mmon *B*usiness *O*riented *L*anguage; ALGOL, *ALGO*rithmic *L*anguage; and FORTRAN, *FOR*mula *TRAN*slation. We will study the use of the FORTRAN language.

A **program** is the organized sequence of instructions to be carried out by the computer in solving a particular task. The computer cannot do anything without a person, or **programmer,** to write these instructions.

Although it is easier to learn programming with the use of symbolic languages, a computer cannot execute instructions written in a symbolic language. The computer is capable only of carrying out instructions in its own machine language. A **compiler** is a special program which performs this intermediate step of translating a symbolic language instruction into a machine language instruction. Before translating any instructions a compiler checks them to see if all the grammatical rules of the language have been followed. If any errors have been made, the compiler will not generate any machine language instructions. After a program has been compiled, the computer performs the instructions in machine language, and we say that the computer **executes** the program.

When referring to the program written in a symbolic language, we may also use the term **source program.** The **object program** is a machine language program which is the result of compiling the source program. The following diagram, in Figure 2.6, illustrates the concepts discussed above.

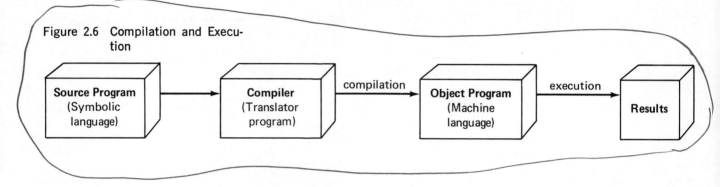

Figure 2.6 Compilation and Execution

Special Terms

1. *address*
2. *compiler*
3. *CPU*
4. *digital computer*
5. *execution*
6. *input*
7. *instruction*
8. *memory location*
9. *object program*
10. *output*
11. *source program*
12. *storage*

Chapter 3

Problem-Solving Procedure

3.1 Flowchart of the Procedure

A computer can only follow directions; it cannot think. Therefore, we must have a systematic procedure for the solution of any problem given to a computer. Figure 3.1 shows a flowchart of a general problem-solving procedure that we can apply to any problem.

Let us examine each step in the flowchart.

Figure 3.1 Flowchart of Problem-Solving Procedure

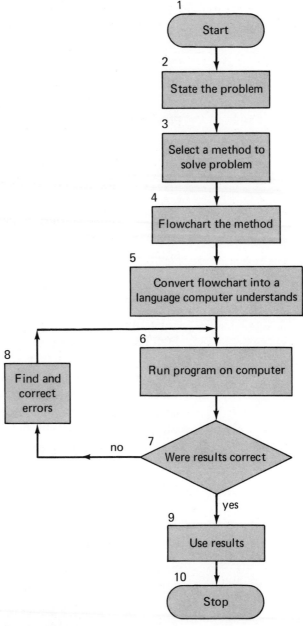

State the Problem

The statement of the problem should include what information we know, what we want to calculate, and what results we wish to obtain. We must understand the problem thoroughly before we can proceed to solve it. If the statement is not clear, then we should revise it until it is clear. For computer problems the statement should also include the form of the input and output data.

Select a Method To Solve the Problem

Since the computer can only follow directions, we must find an applicable method for the solution of the problem. The method must be one which we can convert into individual steps and commands which the computer can execute.

This step is generally the most difficult. In some cases we may have only one method which we can employ. In other cases we may have many methods. In still other cases we must create our own method. And in some instances we may find that no method will work. The computer cannot select a method or create a method or tell whether a method exists to solve the problem. It can only find a solution after a programmer has told it what steps to perform in order to arrive at the solution.

Flowchart the Method

To flowchart the problem, we break down the method into steps which the computer can perform, including the input of necessary data and the output of the results. We then convert these steps into a flowchart diagram which makes it easier to see the process involved. The diagram helps to check our logic—to see if all boxes are connected properly, and if there is a beginning and an end. After writing the flowchart, we choose some sample data and make a trace of the flowchart.

Convert Flowchart into a Language Computer Understands

For this text, the conversion means translating the flowchart into ANSI FORTRAN. There are many versions of the FORTRAN language, but not every option will work on all computers. To bring uniformity to the language, the American National Standards Institute (ANSI) has recommended one version of FORTRAN and has encouraged major computer manufacturers to adopt it. The result is that a program which works on one computer should work on another one with little or no changes. Also, a person learning ANSI FORTRAN should be able to transfer from one computer installation to another without having to study a new dialect. Of course, computer manufacturers may still have special features of the FORTRAN language, but we will adhere strictly to ANSI FORTRAN.

Run Program on Computer

After the program is written, it is punched on cards and is submitted to the computer. When a program goes through a computer, we say that it is being **run.** Actually, running a program involves two steps. First the program is compiled and is checked for punctuation and grammatical (syntax) errors. If the compiler detects any errors, the run will stop and will not proceed to the next step, execution. Even though the computer executes a program, it may not be correct because of errors in card punching or in logic (errors in the design of the flowchart).

Were Results Correct

When a programmer tests a program to see if it works correctly, he should make up a small group of information (sample data) as input to the program. While the computer executes the program, the programmer should use the sample data and compute the correct answers. Then the programmer can check his answers against the computer's results. Even though the computer prints results, they may not be correct.

Find and Correct Errors

A program may not work because it contains errors and could not be compiled. These errors may be the result of mispunched cards or statements in the program which do not obey the rules of the FORTRAN language. A programmer must correct all the mistakes found by the compiler before the machine language version of the program can be executed. Still, the program may not produce the desired results because of errors in the data, in the logic, or in the conversion of the flowchart to FORTRAN. The flowchart should have been checked with the sample data before it was translated into FORTRAN. If the procedure in the flowchart was correct, we should then see if the flowchart was correctly converted into FORTRAN. If so, then we should examine our data deck to see if the numbers were punched correctly. Finally, we may need to go through each statement in the program and see how the computer executed it. We will discuss finding and correcting errors in more detail in Chapter 7.

Use Results

The way the results might be used depends entirely upon the problem. The answers may be meaningful to the programmer himself or to someone who hired the programmer. No matter who will be using the output, label all results carefully.

3.2 Sample Problem

The following sample problem will illustrate the use of the problem-solving procedure given in Figure 3.1.

State the Problem

Find the average of a series of test scores. Each card has one score punched on it. Each score is between 0 and 100. Print the average after it is computed.

Select a Method To Solve Problem

The following formula gives the average A of a set of numbers $x_1, x_2, \ldots, x_n$.

$$A = \frac{x_1 + x_2 + x_3 + \ldots + x_n}{n} = \frac{\sum_{i=1}^{n} x_i}{n}$$

By dividing the sum of the numbers by the number of items, we find the average of a group of numbers. There are at least two ways to implement this method. We could have the computer read all the scores, store them, and count the number of scores. Then we could add up all the scores and calculate the average. Or, to keep the computer from having to store all the scores, we could have it read one card at a time, accumulate the sum and total number of scores, and then calculate the average after the computer reads all the cards. We will use the second method.

Flowchart the Method

Figure 3.2 shows a basic flowchart for our method.

Figure 3.2 Basic Flowchart for Finding the Average of a Set of Numbers

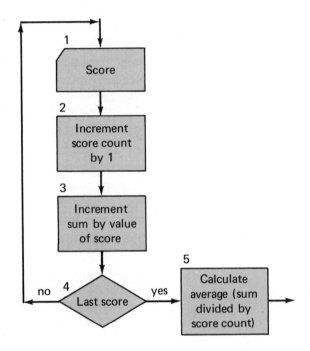

Before proceeding to the next step in our problem-solving procedure, let us discuss the flowchart in Figure 3.2. The computer reads a score from a card, increases the score count by 1 to show that it has read one more number, and then adds the score to the sum of the previous scores read. If that was the last score, the computer proceeds to calculate the average; otherwise, the computer returns to read another card.

The "last score" question in the flowchart cannot be used as one of the commands given to the computer. Instead, we will include a dummy data card in the deck and test for it in the flowchart. Since all the scores are positive, we could use a negative score on the dummy data card.

Once the flowchart's instructions are carried out, the computer will correctly accumulate the sum of the scores and count the number of scores. But what will happen after the very first card is read? The flowchart tells us to "increment score count by 1." This means we add 1 to the previous score count. But what was the previous score count? Our flowchart has not said. So that our flowchart will work correctly for the first card, the previous score count should be zero. This initialization (giving the first value to the score count) should be done outside of the loop so that the score count will be zero only once. Proceeding in the flowchart, we encounter the instruction "increment sum by value of score." Here again we have a problem for the very first score—what was the previous value of the sum? This sum should also be zero initially so that the computer will add the scores correctly. The score count and the sum are called **accumulators.** All accumulators should be preset with some initial value (usually with zero) before quantities are added to them. This is equivalent to clearing a cash register or an adding machine.

Also note that no provision is made for the output section. What is the purpose of calculating the average if we do not have it printed? Our next step is to print the average; and since nothing else needs to be done, the computer should stop. Figure 3.3 includes all the modifications to the basic flowchart.

Figure 3.3 Final Flowchart for Finding the Average of a Set of Numbers

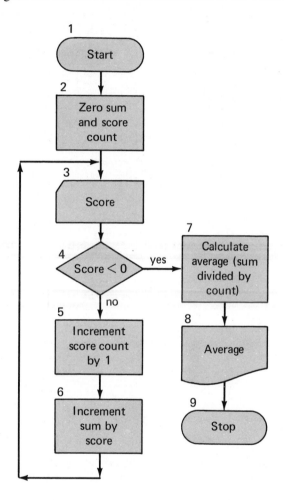

Convert Flowchart into a Language Computer Understands

In Figure 3.4 we present, written on a coding sheet, the FORTRAN program solution for our flowchart. We will not attempt to explain the statements here, because they will be covered in detail in following chapters. Try to see how the program corresponds to the flowchart. The lines beginning with a "C" are comment statements and in no way affect the computer's execution of the program. The coding sheet represents the 80 columns of a punch card, but some of the columns are not shown because of space limitations.

Run Program on Computer

In subsequent chapters we will discuss how to run a program on a computer and how to find and correct errors.

Figure 3.4 FORTRAN Program Solution for Sample Problem

C COMMENT					CONTINUATION	COMPUTING CENTER / FORTRAN	PROBLEM: / PROGRAMMER:		

```
C          ZERØ  SUM  AND  SCØRE  CØUNT
           SUM  =  0.0
           CØUNT  =  0.0
C          READ  SCØRE  FRØM  DATA  CARD
    10     READ  (5,20)  SCØRE
    20     FØRMAT  (F3.0)
C          TEST  FØR  NEGATIVE  SCØRE
           IF  (SCØRE  .LT.  0.0)  GØ  TØ  30
C          INCREMENT  SCØRE  CØUNT  BY  1
           CØUNT  =  CØUNT  +  1.0
C          INCREMENT  SUM  BY  SCØRE
           SUM  =  SUM  +  SCØRE
           GØ  TØ  10
C          CALCULATE  AVERAGE
    30     AVG  =  SUM  /  CØUNT
C          WRITE  THE  AVERAGE
           WRITE  (6,40)  AVG
    40     FØRMAT  (F10.2)
           STØP
           END
```

Chapter 4

Preparing Cards for the Computer

4.1 Hollerith Cards

The punched card is such a common input medium for the computer that we will use it exclusively in our sample problems. Frequently the card is called a **Hollerith card** after Herman Hollerith, its designer. Information on this card is recorded by one or more small rectangular punches in a column. The same principles of punching characters on cards applies to recording characters on magnetic tape or typing them on a teletype.

Figure 4.1 A Hollerith Card

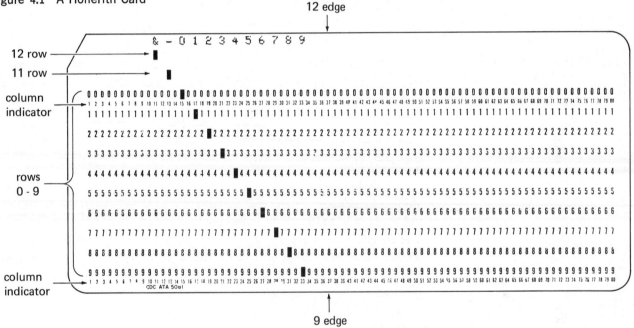

In Figure 4.1, we see that the columns are numbered 1 to 80 along the bottom and near the top of the card. There are 12 rows on a card. Rows 0 (zero) through 9 have their numbers printed on most cards. Rows 11 and 12 are in the area which is usually blank near the top of the card. The top edge of the card is referred to as the **12 edge,** and the bottom edge as the **9 edge.** The side of the card which contains the printed numbers is the **face.**

A **character** is any symbol that a machine can recognize. Characters are coded onto cards by using punches. Figure 4.1 shows a card with the ampersand, minus sign, and the ten numeric characters 0 through 9 punched. The ampersand is a punch in row 12 and is also called a 12 punch; the minus sign is a punch in row 11 and is called an 11 punch. The permissible characters in the ANSI Standard FORTRAN language are:

ten numeric characters: 0 through 9
twenty-six capital alphabetic characters: A to Z
eleven special characters: . , + $ * - / ( ) = blank

Figure 4.2 shows that the alphabetic characters are a combination of two punches in a column, and that most of the special characters are a combination of one, two, or three punches in a column.

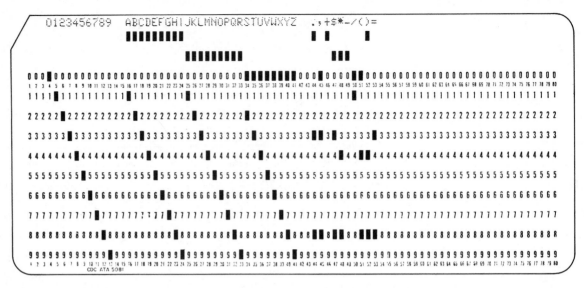

Figure 4.2   Permissible Characters in ANSI Standard FOR–TRAN Punched on a Hollerith Card

In writing the FORTRAN characters, we distinguish between the numeric 0 (zero) and the alphabetic O (oh), by slashing the letter O, making it Ø. We also differentiate the numeric 1 (one) from the alphabetic I and the numeric 2 (two) from the alphabetic Z. To denote a blank character, we use a lower case b, with or without a slash (b̸ or b). These distinctions between the handwritten characters are especially important if someone other than the programmer will punch the cards.

A complete deck of cards that we submit to a computer contains three groups of cards with special purposes: FORTRAN cards, data cards, and control cards. The **FORTRAN cards** contain FORTRAN language instructions. The complete set of cards which form a program is called either the **program deck** or the **source deck.** For most problems, the program will have **data cards,** or cards with data punched on them. The programmer also must tell the computer other information such as his name, account number, whether he wants the instructions compiled or executed; **control cards** contain this and similar types of information.

4.2 FORTRAN Cards

In FORTRAN, specific columns of the card are designated for the different parts which comprise a FORTRAN instruction.

FORTRAN Statement

FORTRAN statements are punched in columns 7 through 72, allowing a maximum of 66 columns per card for a FORTRAN statement. The compiler ignores blanks in a FORTRAN statement, but blanks should be used to improve readability. Instead of writing

AVG=SUM/CØUNT

we write

AVG = SUM / CØUNT

Usually each card contains one FORTRAN statement. If a FORTRAN statement is longer than 66 columns, the statement continues on subsequent cards.

Continuation

A FORTRAN character other than a blank or zero must be punched in column 6 to tell the compiler that the statement on this card is a continuation of the statement on the preceding card.[1] The character in column 6 is not part of the FORTRAN statement.

Statement Label

We have the option of labeling any FORTRAN statement with a statement number so that we may refer to it in other statements. Some FORTRAN statements must have a label; others do not require one. The label is an unsigned positive integer punched anywhere in columns 1 through 5. The compiled program will be more efficient if we do not label statements unnecessarily. But statements referred to in the program must have statement labels. The computer ignores leading zeros in a statement label.

Comment Statement

Comment statements identify the program, give details about the method used, and include the programmer's name. If the programmer wishes to insert comments in his program he punches a C in column 1 of each card containing comments. The message is written in columns 2 through 80. If the explanatory comment is too long to fit on one card, it may be continued to the next card. This card should also contain a C in column 1. Comment information appears in the listing of the program, but the FORTRAN compiler ignores it. To improve the appearance of the listing, the programmer may insert cards which are blank except for a C in column 1.

Identification Columns

The FORTRAN compiler always ignores columns 73 through 80. The programmer usually uses these columns for program identification or for numbering the cards in the deck.

In summary, the uses of the columns are:

Columns	Use
1	Contains a C for a comment
1–5	Statement label
6	Continuation
7–72	FORTRAN statement
73–80	Identification

Figure 3.4 illustrates a portion of a FORTRAN coding sheet. This printed form represents the 80 columns of a Hollerith card and indicates how the columns are used in writing a FORTRAN program. These forms aid the programmer in writing the instructions that will be punched.

[1] A given FORTRAN statement may extend to as many as 19 continuation cards on the IBM 360/370, CDC 6000 Series, and CYBER 70 computers.

4.3 Data Cards

A data card is a Hollerith card which contains information and which the program reads into the computer. Notice that, although a FORTRAN program uses data cards, the cards do not follow the same column designations of the FORTRAN instruction. Therefore, we may place data (words, names, numbers, and the like) anywhere in columns 1 through 80. In later sections, we will discuss more specifically how information on data cards and FORTRAN input instructions are related.

The following terms are frequently encountered when discussing data. A **field** is a unit of information. A **record** is a collection of one or more fields pertaining to the same subject. We define a **unit record of input** as a single card and a **unit record of output** as a line on the output page. The term **alphanumeric characters** refers to numbers and letters.

When we punch alphanumeric data in a field, we start with the leftmost column of the field. See Figure 4.3 with the name SAM L BROWN **left-adjusted** in the field 20–40. Numeric data is punched **right-adjusted** with the last digit in the rightmost column of the field. See Figure 4.3 with the number 1024 right-adjusted in the field 1–10, and the number 42.56 in the field 55–62.

Figure 4.3   Left-adjusted Alphanumeric Data and Right-adjusted Numeric Data

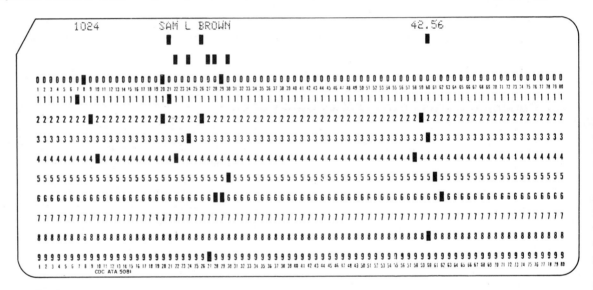

4.4 Control Cards

Special programs, called control programs, supervise the complex operations within a computer. Control programs contain the overall instructions for input-output operations, the receiving and sequencing of programs, and the order of processing information within the computer. We refer to the complete set of control programs as the **control system.** Among the special programs found in control systems are those that **compile** a symbolic language program into a machine language program; others cause the **execution** of the machine language program just generated by the compiler. Through a series of cards called **control cards** a programmer communicates with the control system of the computer. These cards will be specific for a particular computer installation, because they also provide accounting information. Check with your computer installation for details on the appropriate control cards for the computer you will use.

To run a program on a computer we must submit FORTRAN and data cards with the control cards. The arrangement of the cards in the deck is important because of the way the computer uses them. Usually, the control cards appear at the beginning of the deck followed by the FORTRAN program cards and the data cards. The order in which these cards are arranged is called the **deck set-up.** Figure 4.4 shows a sample deck set-up.

Figure 4.4 Sample Deck Set-up

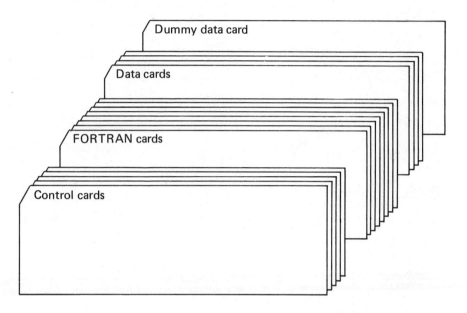

4.5 Punching Cards on the IBM 29 Card Punch

The diagram in Figure 4.6 indicates some of the features of an IBM 29 card punch. In reading this section, sit at an IBM 29 card punch so that you can verify the operations discussed.

The keyboard layout of a card punch is like a typewriter (see Figure 4.5), but there are no lowercase letters. The card punch is normally in alphabetic mode; in this mode, only the letters of the alphabet and the characters ' (*) − / , . will punch. With the NUMERIC key depressed, the card punch is in numeric mode; in this mode, only the numerals and the characters = , $. − + found in the upper positions of the keys will punch. The comma and the period may be punched in either alphabetic or numeric mode.

Figure 4.5

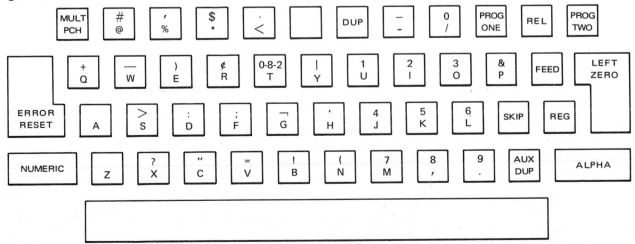

Figure 4.6 Close-up View of the
IBM 29 Card Punch

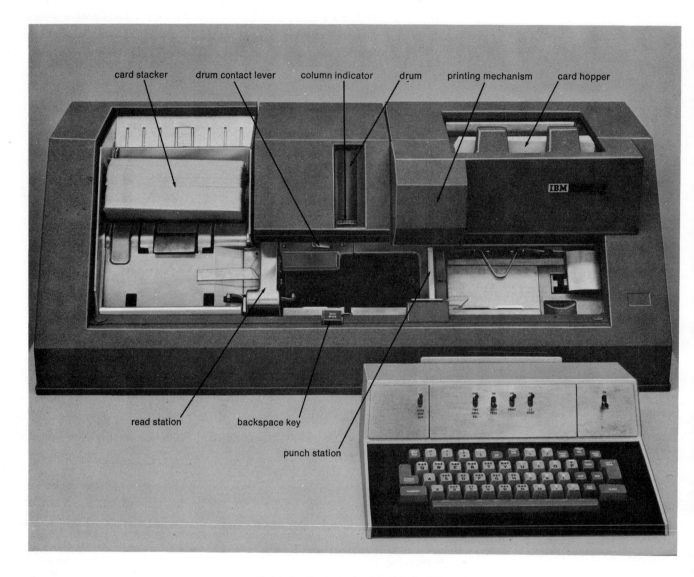

Some basic steps in operating a card punch machine are:

1. The table of the card punch should be empty. Throw away any material left by your predecessor.
2. The card hopper should contain a neat stack of unpunched cards. If not, get some fresh cards.
3. If the card punch is not on when you arrive, flip on the main switch, press REL and wait for the card punch to warm up.
4. Turn off AUTO FEED and AUTO DUP switches.
5. Press the FEED key to **feed** a card from the card hopper into the punch station.
6. Press the REG key to **register** the card in the punch station.
7. Each key you press punches one character in your card. Whenever you want to leave a column blank, press the space bar.
8. When you have finished punching a card, press the REL key to **release** that card. The card is now at the read station.
9. After releasing a card, you may feed the next. If you are through, clear out your cards by alternately pressing REG and REL. (It is faster to flip the CLEAR switch, if your card punch has one.)

Some keys of special use are:

MULT PCH Key

Use the MULT PCH (multi-punch) key when you need a special combination of punches in a column. For example, the code for end-of-information on the CDC 6400 is a 6–7–8–9 multipunched in column 1 (that is, holes in rows 6, 7, 8, and 9 all punched in column 1). To punch this, depress the MULT PCH key, press 6, press 7, press 8, press 9, release the MULT PCH key. The card punch is always in numeric mode during multi-punch.

DUP Key

When correcting cards, we do not always have to punch the entire card again. Instead, we may duplicate the correct portions and repunch only where we have made mistakes. To make minor corrections, place the incorrect card in the read station and feed a blank card into the punch station. Register the blank card. Hold down the DUP (duplicate) key until you get to an incorrect column. Punch the character you wanted. Duplicate some more if necessary. If there is no card in the duplicating station, you can use the DUP key for rapid spacing.

BACKSPACE Key and Column Indicator

The card punch machine also includes a column indicator and a backspace key. The column indicator can be seen at the bottom of the drum window which is located above the card read area. The column indicator shows what column is *to be punched* next. The backspace key is located directly below the drum. This key will backspace as long as it is held down. Note that both the card and the column indicator backspace.

AUTO FEED Switch

If you have many cards to punch, switch on the AUTO FEED. The FEED key should be pressed down twice so that there will be two cards in the punch station, and the first one will be ready to be punched. With AUTO FEED on, another card will feed automatically every time you press REL.

4.6 Drum Control Card for the Card Punch

Learning how to use a drum control card is not necessary for the beginning student. We suggest that you cover this section at a later time after you have had some practice in punching cards.

The card punch is normally in alphabetic mode. With a drum control card the mode of specific columns can be assigned. For example, in the FORTRAN statement we find that the type of information punched in columns 1–5 is always numeric. If we use a program control card and designate columns 1–5 to be numeric, then it is no longer necessary to depress the NUMERIC key when punching information in columns 1–5.

The punches in any given column of the control card determine how the card punch will act in that column. In designing the fields of a drum control card two things are important.

1. The column which begins a field must be designated.
2. The rest of the columns in the field must be punched according to the desired mode.

The meaning of the punches for the program control card are:

Punches To Indicate the Beginning of a Field

1 punch	Begin alphanumeric field
blank	Begin numeric field
11 punch [1]	Begin skip field
/ punch	Begin alphanumeric field to be duplicated automatically
0 punch	Begin numeric field to be duplicated automatically

Punches To Indicate the Remainder of the Field

A punch	Alphanumeric field
12 punch [2]	Numeric field

Examples of Field Definition

1 punch followed by A punches

The 1 indicates the beginning of an alphanumeric field and each column immediately following it that is punched with an A will be in alphanumeric mode.

blank followed by 12 punches

The blank indicates the beginning of a numeric field and each column immediately following it that is punched with a 12 punch will be in numeric mode.

11 punch followed by 12 punches

The 11 punch indicates the beginning of a field to be skipped and each column immediately following it that is punched with a 12 punch will be skipped.

/ punch followed by A punches

The / punch indicates the beginning of an alphanumeric field that is to be duplicated automatically. The A punches that immediately follow indicate the columns to be duplicated and that the columns punched with A are in alphanumeric mode. The duplication is made automatically from the card in the read station to the card in the punch station. This implies that for automatic duplication to be meaningful, some information must be punched first on a card that begins this cycle. Even when a card is released, any areas on the remainder of the card which are in automatic duplicate fields will be duplicated as the card is released.

0 punch followed by 12 punches

The 0 punch indicates the beginning of a numeric field that is to be dupli-

---

[1] Punch the minus sign (−) key to get an 11 punch.
[2] On most card punches the ampersand (&) key produces a 12 punch; on others the plus sign (+) key gives a 12 punch.

cated automatically. The 12 punches that immediately follow indicate the columns to be duplicated and that the columns punched with 12 are in numeric mode. A blank is considered an alphabetic character, not a numeric one. Therefore, the machine will not duplicate any blanks in a numeric field to be duplicated.

Instructions for Use of Drum Control Card

1. Turn ON the AUTO DUP and AUTO SKIP switch.
2. Disengage the contacts (star wheels) before removing the drum. Use the drum contact lever located below and to the left of the drum window.
3. The control card must be well fitted on the drum. Since it is easier to learn from a personal demonstration how to place the card on the drum, we will omit the description of this process.
4. Replace the drum.
5. Lower the contacts.
6. Any time the contacts are disengaged the action programmed in the control card is discontinued.
7. Depressing the NUM key or the ALPHA key on the card punch will override the specified mode of the program control card.

Program Control Card for a FORTRAN Statement

b&&&&&1AAAAAAAAAAAAA AAAAAAAAAAAA AAAAAAAAAAAA AAAAAAAAAAAA AAAAAAAAAAAA AAAAA—&&&&&&

Columns	1–6	indicate a numeric field
Columns	7–72	indicate an alphanumeric field
Columns	73–80	indicate a field to be skipped

If columns 73–80 are going to include some identification characters, this field could be programmed with automatic duplication.

If we wanted to punch a C for comments in column 1, then the alphabetic key (ALPHA key) on the keyboard must be depressed to override the numeric mode programmed in the control card.

Program Control Card for Sample Data

Suppose that we wish to punch the following data for a problem.

Columns	1–25	name
	26–30	identification number
	31–50	address
	51–60	columns to be skipped
	61–70	telephone number
	71–76	classification (alphabetic)
	77–80	department number, always the same

We would punch the program control card as follows:

1AAAAAAAAAAAAAAAAAAAAAAAAAb&&&&1 AAAAAAAAAAA AAAAAA—&&&&&&&&&b&&&&&&&&&1 AAAAA0&&&

Special Terms

1. *alphanumeric characters*
2. *character*
3. *comment*
4. *continuation*
5. *control cards*
6. *control system*
7. *data cards*
8. *deck set-up*
9. *face*
10. *field*
11. *FORTRAN cards*
12. *FORTRAN characters*
13. *Hollerith card*
14. *left-adjusted*
15. *9 edge*
16. *program deck*
17. *record*
18. *right-adjusted*
19. *source deck*
20. *statement label*
21. *12 edge*
22. *unit record of input*
23. *unit record of output*

Chapter 5

FORTRAN Expressions

5.1 FORTRAN Constants

When solving a problem, we often want to multiply a given number by a number read into the computer. Take, for example, our payroll problem. To pay an employee double time for working overtime, we must multiply the pay rate by two. In FORTRAN, we write this computation as RATE * 2.0. The number 2.0 is called a **constant** because it is explicitly stated in the expression. The RATE is a **variable** because it is named and its value is allowed to change. For one employee the RATE may be 2.00, for another 3.50, and 1.75 for a third.

FORTRAN has two major types of numeric constants: *integer* and *real*. An *integer* constant is written as a whole number without a decimal point. In the following examples of integer constants, 026 is the same as 26; the 0 does not change the value of the number.

$$-10$$
$$5$$
$$026$$
$$26$$
$$-1111$$
$$+7$$

A FORTRAN *real* constant may be a whole number or may contain a fractional part, but it is *always* written with a decimal point. Some examples of *real* constants are:

$$2.18735$$
$$5.$$
$$5.0$$
$$-.000618$$
$$358.7$$

The constant 5. has the same value as the constant 5.0; the zero is not necessary. However, the decimal point does make 5. and 5.0 *real* constants. Because a computer must remember where the decimal point belongs in a *real* constant, a computer will store a *real* constant in a manner different from the way it stores an *integer* constant. Although the *real* constant 5. and the *integer* constant 5 have the same numeric value, the computer will make a distinction between them, because they are stored differently.

A very small *real* constant, such as $-.000618$, or a very large *real* constant, such as 237000000.0, may be written in a different manner called E-notation, which is similar to scientific notation. The number $-.000618$ is equal to -6.18×10^{-4} in scientific notation and 237000000.0 equals 2.37×10^8. In FORTRAN the letter E replaces the value 10. Therefore -6.18×10^{-4} becomes $-6.18E-4$ in FORTRAN E-notation, and 2.37×10^8 becomes 2.37E8. The number following the E is the exponent of 10. To determine the value of a *real* constant written in E-notation, multiply the number preceding the E by $10^{exponent}$. Some examples of *real* constants in E-notation are listed below. See if you can determine their values.

$$-367.28E7 \qquad .125E+03$$
$$.216E-4 \qquad .31459E+2$$
$$3.8273E10 \qquad .10051E-13$$
$$-.1865E-4$$

Rules for Writing a FORTRAN Constant

1. A constant may be positive or negative. If negative, it must be preceded by a minus sign ($-$). No sign or a plus sign ($+$) means that a number is positive.
2. A constant may *not* contain any commas.
3. A constant may *not* contain a dollar sign ($).
4. An *integer* constant is written *without* a decimal point.
5. A *real* constant is written *with* a decimal point.
6. A *real* constant may be followed by the letter E and a power of 10.

The maximum and minimum sizes of constants depend upon the type of computer. Table 5.1 lists these values for several computers in use today.

Table 5.1 Value Range of Constants for Various Computers

	INTEGER		REAL	
Computer	Range	Number of Digits	Range	Number of Digits
IBM 360 IBM 370	$-(2^{31}-1)$ to $(2^{31}-1)$	10	-10^{75} to -10^{-78} 0 10^{-78} to 10^{75}	7
CDC 6000 Series CYBER 70	$-(2^{59}-1)$ to $(2^{59}-1)$	18	-10^{337} to -10^{-308} 0 10^{-308} to 10^{337}	15

5.2 FORTRAN Variables

A FORTRAN variable is a name whose value may change. One memory location is set aside for each different variable name in a program. The value stored in that location is the value of the variable. Pictorially we may think of memory as a number of boxes. Each box named contains some quantity. The names are used to distinguish one box from another. For example, Figure 5.1 tells us that PAY = 2.0, MAX = 17, and KODE = -1.

Figure 5.1

PAY	2.0
MAX	17
KODE	-1

The variables are PAY, MAX, and KODE and their respective values are 2.0, 17, and -1.

We say that a **variable is defined** when it is given a value. There are three ways of defining a variable:

1. reading its value from a card (tape, teletype, etc.)
2. assigning it a value in the program
3. computing its value in the program

As the program is executed, the values of the variables may change. Since only one value may be stored in a memory location, the new value replaces the value previously stored for the variable.

The choice of a particular variable name is up to the programmer. Usually he will choose a name which is related to the problem. For example, in a program which computes income tax we may find variables named GRØSPA (representing gross pay), TAXINC (for taxable income), NØDEP (number of dependents), and TAX. The programmer chooses the variable names, but they must obey certain rules.

To be an acceptable ANSI FORTRAN variable name:

1. A name must start with a letter.
2. A name must be no longer than 6 characters.
3. Except for the first character, a name may contain only the letters A–Z and the numerals 0–9; no special characters are allowed.

Variables are classified as *integer* variables or *real* variables because their values may be *integer* or *real*. An *integer* variable is one which begins with one of the letters I, J, K, L, M, or N. A *real* variable is a name which does *not* start with I, J, K, L, M, or N.

The following list gives examples of acceptable FORTRAN variable names which are classified by type (*integer* or *real*).

Variable	Type
INDEX	Integer
SALARY	Real
BIG	Real
K2	Integer
TOT10	Real
M	Integer

Exercises

1. Tell whether the following constants are *integer, real,* or not valid.

2.6312	+607813
7,168	6.078E05
−11	0,132E−7
−1.	0

2. Tell whether the following variables are *integer, real,* or not valid.

APPLE	1708A
JACK	MILE.
AVERAGE	TØTAL
2X	NØ

5.3 **Arithmetic Replacement Statement**

SALARY ← RATE × HOURS

In the flowchart box to the left, the arrow (←) denotes replacement; that is, replace the old value of SALARY by a new one, which is computed by multiplying RATE by HOURS. We convert this flowchart step to the FORTRAN statement:

SALARY = RATE * HØURS

The equal sign (=) in FORTRAN denotes replacement; the asterisk (*) is FORTRAN'S way of representing the multiplication operation. This statement is called an **arithmetic replacement statement.** The general form of this statement is

FORTRAN variable name = FORTRAN arithmetic expression

It is used to give a value to the variable on the left-hand side of the equal sign.

The simplest kind of arithmetic expression is a constant or a single variable. Examples of statements using these simple expressions are:

X = 7.38
ID = NUM

More complicated expressions may include calculations such as addition, subtraction, multiplication, division, or exponentiation (raising a number to a power). Different symbols in FORTRAN represent these operations:

Symbol	Operation
+	addition
−	subtraction (or negation)
*	multiplication
/	division
**	exponentiation

To instruct the computer to add A and B, we write A + B. To subtract A from B, we write B − A. To multiply A and B, we write A * B. Simply writing AB does not mean multiply A by B; in FORTRAN, AB is a new variable name. To multiply A by 3.0, 3.0 * A or A * 3.0 would work, but 3.0A or A3.0 would not. The compiler would try to interpret 3.0A and A3.0 as variable names and they are not valid ones. To square A, we write A**2; to cube B, we write B**3. We can instruct the computer to perform more complex computations by combining the simple expressions above. An example of this is A**2− C / D + B**3.

Rules for Forming an Arithmetic Expression

1. A simple arithmetic expression contains constants and/or variables separated by an arithmetic operation symbol. The simplest expression is a constant or variable.
2. Two operation symbols may *not* be written one after another in the expression. The two asterisks (**) representing exponentiation are considered one symbol.
3. An expression may begin with a plus sign or a minus sign, but no other operation symbol.
4. Other arithmetic expressions may be formed by enclosing a simple arithme-

tic expression in parentheses. This expression in parentheses may then be combined with other variables and/or constants and/or expressions in parentheses. The variables, constants, and expressions in parentheses must be separated by an arithmetic operation symbol. Frequently parentheses are introduced in order to compute the correct mathematical value of a formula.

5. All variables and/or constants in an expression must be *real* or all must be *integers*. There is one exception: the exponent of a *real* expression may be a *real* or *integer* expression. (See section 5.7 on mixed mode.)

Rules for Use of the Arithmetic Replacement Statement

1. The variable on the left-hand side of the equal sign must be a valid FORTRAN variable name. It may be a *real* variable or an *integer* variable.
2. The expression on the right-hand side of the equal sign must be a valid FORTRAN arithmetic expression. It may be an expression containing all *real* items or an expression containing all *integer* items.
3. All of the following are valid combinations in an arithmetic replacement statement.

$$\text{real name} = \text{real expression}$$
$$\text{real name} = \text{integer expression}$$
$$\text{integer name} = \text{integer expression}$$
$$\text{integer name} = \text{real expression}$$

The following arithmetic replacement statements are correct.

$$X = A + B * 3.0$$
$$Y = I / J$$
$$MAX = -MIN$$
$$M = P**2$$

Box 5 of the flowchart in Figure 3.3 appears to the left. Box 5 could also have been written like the box below it, which means add one to the current value of COUNT and make this number the new value of COUNT. This statement in FORTRAN is CØUNT = CØUNT + 1.0. The equal sign does not signify mathematical equality, for CØUNT = CØUNT +1.0 is not a valid mathematical equation, but it is an acceptable statement in FORTRAN. The equal sign means replace the value of the item on the left of the equal sign by the value computed on the right side. Therefore, there must be only one FORTRAN variable on the left-hand side of the equal sign. Mathematically, the two equations $A + B = C$ and $A = C - B$ are equivalent. In FORTRAN, $A = C - B$ is an acceptable statement, but $A + B = C$ would cause an error. The compiler would try to interpret the characters $A + B$ as one name; but since $A + B$ contains the plus sign, it is not a valid FORTRAN variable name. In general, when we examine a FORTRAN arithmetic replacement statement, we read the expression on the right-hand side of the equal sign to see what is being calculated and then look at the left-hand side to see where the value is being stored. When the computer executes the statement, it does two things:

1. evaluates the arithmetic expression
2. stores the value of the expression as the new value of the variable on the left-hand side of the equal sign

Throughout this process the computer remembers the mode (*integer* or *real*)

Increment
score
count by 1

COUNT ← COUNT + 1

of the results. If an *integer* value is to be stored under a *real* name, the value is converted to a *real* form before it is stored. If a *real* value was computed and is to be stored under an *integer* name, all decimal digits are dropped. For example, let I = 5, J = 2, A = 2.3, and B = 7.4.

X = A + B	results in X = 9.7
K = A + B	results in K = 9
M = I / J	results in M = 2
Y = I / J	results in Y = 2.0
Z = 5.0 / 2.0	results in Z = 2.5
N = 5.0 / 2.0	results in N = 2

5.4 Evaluation of Arithmetic Statements

When many operations are combined into one statement such as

$$VAL = A**2. - C / D + B**3.$$

how does the computer decide which operation to perform first? In evaluating the right-hand side of any arithmetic statement the computer scans from left to right performing some operations before others. The order of these operations is:

1. exponentiation
2. multiplication and division
3. addition and subtraction

Within the above order of operations, the computer assumes that multiplication and division are at the same level. Similarly, addition and subtraction are at the same level; but the computer performs them after all other operations. Evaluation of operations at the same level proceeds from left to right.[1] For example, VAL = A + B − C would be evaluated in the following order:

1. A + B is computed and the answer is saved.
2. Result of step 1 minus C is computed and the answer is saved.
3. Result of step 2 becomes the new value stored in VAL.

The operations of multiplication and division of the same order so they are performed from left to right. ANS = A / B * C would be evaluated in the following order:

1. A / B is computed and the answer is saved.
2. Result of step 1 times C is computed and the answer is saved.
3. Result of step 2 becomes the new value of ANS.

For a statement like WGT = A + B * C the order of evaluation would be:

1. B * C is computed and the answer is saved.
2. Result of step 1 plus A is computed and the answer is saved.
3. Result of step 2 becomes the new value of WGT.

Consider the statement

---

[1] In the CDC 6000 Series and CYBER 70 this rule is strictly enforced and A**B**C is evaluated as $(A^B)^C$ which equals A^{BC}. In the IBM 360/370 A**B**C is evaluated by computing B^C and then raising A to this power. In other words, this is A^{B^C}.

$$FCT = A * W - C / D + B**3.$$

Because exponentiation is performed before multiplication and division, and also before addition and subtraction, the statement would be evaluated in the following order:

1. B**3. is computed and the answer is saved.
2. A * W is computed and the answer is saved.
3. C / D is computed and the answer is saved.
4. Result of step 2 minus result of step 3 is computed and the answer is saved.
5. Result of step 4 plus result of step 1 is computed and the answer is saved.
6. Result of step 5 becomes the new value of FCT.

We will take several examples of FORTRAN arithmetic statements and evaluate them in the same way as the computer. If the right-hand side of the replacement statement contains all *real* constants and/or variables, the computation is performed so that every intermediate result is a *real* number. If the right-hand side contains all *integer* constants and/or variables, every intermediate value is an *integer*. For example, in the statement J = 7 / 4 the exact answer should be 1.75, but since 7 and 4 are integers, 1.75 is converted to an integer by removing the fractional part. Therefore, the result is J = 1. In *integer* arithmetic no answers are rounded. This process of dropping the fractional part of a result is called **truncation.**

In the examples in Table 5.2 A =12.0, B = 2.0, C = 3.0, D = 0.5, I = 2, J = 3, and M = −25.

Table 5.2 Evaluation of FORTRAN Arithmetic Replacement Statements

FORTRAN Arithmetic Statement	Value computed
a. X = A / B * C	X = 18.0
b. X = A / 5.0 + B * C	X = 8.4
c. Y = B + A / C	Y = 6.0
d. Z = A * B / C * D	Z = 4.0
e. M = I − J ** 3	M = −25
f. N = M + I / J	N = −25

We evaluated the arithmetic replacement statements in Table 5.2 in the following manner:

a. 1. A / B = 12.0 / 2.0 = 6.0
   2. 6.0 * C = 6.0 * 3.0 = 18.0
   3. X = 18.0

b. 1. A / 5.0 = 12.0 / 5.0 = 2.4
   2. B * C = 2.0 * 3.0 = 6.0
   3. 2.4 + 6.0 = 8.4
   4. X = 8.4

c. 1. A / C = 12.0 / 3.0 = 4.0
   2. B + 4.0 = 2.0 + 4.0 = 6.0
   3. Y = 6.0

d. 1. A * B = 12.0 * 2.0 = 24.0
   2. 24.0 / C = 24.0 / 3.0 = 8.0
   3. 8.0 * 0.5 = 4.0
   4. Z = 4.0

e. 1. $J**3 = 3^3 = 3*3*3 = 27$
   2. $I - 27 = 2 - 27 = -25$
   3. $M = -25$

f. 1. $I / J = 2 / 3 = 0$ (The answer is zero because I and J are *integers*. The correct arithmetic answer is 0.66666 . . . , but when the decimal part is truncated, the result is 0.)
   2. $M + 0 = -25 + 0 = -25$
   3. $N = -25$

Exercises

1. Evaluate the following FORTRAN statements. Use a decimal point to denote a real number.

   a. $A = 1 / 2 - 1$
   b. $BØY = 3 * 1 / 2$
   c. $I = 3 * 1 / 2$
   d. $I = 1. / 2. + 1.$
   e. $JØB = 1. / 2. * 3.$

2. Evaluate the following statements showing all intermediate results in the order that they are computed in the expression. Assume that M = 7, N = 4, K = 10, X = 18.0, Y = 2.0, and Z = 5.0.

   a. $GF = X - Z / Y**2.0 * 8.0$
   b. $E = Z * Y - X / 3.0 * Y + Z$
   c. $A = Y + 6.37$
   d. $B = Z / Y + .5$
   e. $C = Z**2.0 + 1.73$
   f. $IN = M + N / 3$
   g. $J = N * M + K$
   h. $AA = Y**3.0**Y$
   i. $L = K * N / 5 - M + 3$
   j. $VAL = X + .1E + 2$

5.5 Evaluation of Arithmetic Statements Containing Parentheses

To compute the correct mathematical value of an expression, we may use parentheses for grouping arithmetic symbols, variable names and constants. By the use of parentheses we can change the inherent hierarchy of operations. The computer carries out operations within parentheses first, starting with the innermost set of parentheses. However, within a set of parentheses the normal order of operations will take place. We will examine several statements and see how the computer would evaluate them. The statement

$$Y = B**(A + 3.0)$$

is evaluated in the following manner:

1. 3.0 is added to the value of A.
2. B is raised to the power of the value computed in step 1.
3. The result of step 2 is stored as the value of Y.

The statement

$$X = (2.0 * (A + B) - 3.0) / P$$

is evaluated in this way:

1. A and B are added.
2. The result of step 1 is multiplied by 2.0.
3. 3.0 is subtracted from the result of step 2.
4. The result of step 3 is divided by P.
5. The result of step 4 is stored as the value of X.

And, the replacement statement

$$I = (J1 + J2) / (K + M)$$

is evaluated in the following order:

1. J1 and J2 are added.
2. K and M are added.
3. The result of step 1 is divided by the result of step 2.
4. The result of step 3 is stored as the value of I.

Exercises

1. Evaluate the following statements showing all intermediate results in the order they are computed in the expression.

   a. AUG = (3. + 2.) / 2.
   b. PØW = 3.0**(7.0 − 5.0)
   c. SQR = (5.25 + 3.75)**.5
   d. DIV2 = 3689 / (5 − 3 * 2)
   e. LIM = (42 − 7) / (15 / 3)
   f. K = − (6 + 3 / 2)

   g. KØDE = (1 / 2 + 2)**4 + 1
   h. UP = (1. / 2.)**4 + 1.0
   i. FEM = 1. / 2.**4 − 1.
   j. L = (1. / 2.) ** (4 − 1)
   k. MAXX = (1. / 2. + 2.)**2 − 6.

2. Identify the constants and the variables in the following FORTRAN statements.

ZERØ = 0.0	IDENT = ICNT + 2
SUM = 0.0	MAX = NØ
SUM = SUM + 1.0	SCØRE = 100.
J = 10	L = J2

5.6 Changing Formulas to FORTRAN

To express a mathematical formula in FORTRAN, we must remember how the computer will evaluate the statement. For example, suppose we want to instruct the computer to evaluate the mathematical expression $c(a+b)$. If we write it in FORTRAN as C * A + B, the computer will multiply C by A and then add B to the product. Mathematically this expression would be $c \cdot a + b$. In order to have c multiplied by the sum of a and b, we must use parentheses and write C * (A + B). Since parentheses enclose A + B the computer will first add A and B and then multiply by C.

The following examples show that incorrect values may occur if expressions are not written carefully. Throughout the examples let A = 2.0, B = 3.0, R = 4.0, K = 6, M = 14, J = 2, and N = 5. In case the computer cannot obtain an answer, NV is given for no value.

a. Mathematical formula: $x = a^{-b}$ Computed Value
    Incorrect FORTRAN statement: X = A** − B   NV
    Correct FORTRAN statement: X = A**(−B)   X = .1250

Two arithmetic symbols cannot be written together. In the example we must distinguish between the negative of B (−B) and the operation subtract B, written −B.

b. Mathematical formula: $x = -(a + 2.)$ Computed Value
    Incorrect FORTRAN statement: X = −A + 2.   X = 0.
    Correct FORTRAN statement: X = −(A + 2.)   X = −4.

We cannot eliminate the parentheses from the expression. The problem is to compute the sum of the variable A and the constant 2., and then assign to X the negative of the resulting sum. If we omit the parentheses we obtain the negative of A and then add this to the positive constant 2.

c. Mathematical formula: $y = b^{a+3}$ Computed Value
    Incorrect FORTRAN statement: Y = B**A + 3.0   Y = 12.
    Correct FORTRAN statement: Y = B**(A + 3.0)   Y = 243.

In the incorrect statement, the computer first performs exponentiation because of the hierarchy of operations, that is, it raises the variable B to the power of A and then adds the results. The computation is incorrect because we want to raise B to the power of A + 3.0. By using parentheses we force the computer to perform the operation within parentheses before the exponentiation.

d. Mathematical formula: Computed Value

$$w = r \left(a + \frac{b + 1.}{2. + r} \cdot b \right)$$

Incorrect FORTRAN statement: W = R(A + B + 1. / 2. + R * B)   NV

Correct FORTRAN statement: W = R * (A + ((B + 1.) / (2. + R)) * B)   W = 16.0

At first it seems that the only error in the incorrect statement is the missing * between the R and the left parenthesis. If we write it R * (A + B + 1. / 2. + R * B), the expression would still be incorrect. We find that inside the parentheses the computer follows the intrinsic hierarchy of operations and evaluates the incorrect expression in this way:

1. 1. / 2. = .5
2. R * B = 3. * 4. = 12.0
3. A + B = 2. + 3. = 5.0
4. (result of step 3) + (result of step 1) = 5. + .5 = 5.5
5. (result of step 4) + (result of step 2) = 5.5 + 12. = 17.5
6. R * (result of step 5) = 4. * 17.5 = 70.0

In the correct expression, the steps in the computation are:

1. (B + 1.) = (3. + 1.) = 4.
2. (2. + R) = (2. + 4.) = 6.
3. (result of step 1) / (result of step 2) = 4. / 6.
4. (result of step 3) * B = (4. / 6.) * 3. = 2.0
5. A + (result of step 4) = 2. + 2. = 4.0
6. R * (result of step 5) = 4. * 4. = 16.0

e. Mathematical formula: $\qquad\qquad i = \dfrac{k \cdot m}{j \cdot n}$ $\qquad\qquad$ Computed Value

$\qquad$ Incorrect FORTRAN statement: $\qquad$ I = K * M / J * N $\qquad$ I = 210

$\qquad$ Correct FORTRAN statement: $\qquad$ I = K * M / (J * N) $\qquad$ I = 8

Parentheses are needed in this expression to ensure division by all of the denominator. In the incorrect expression, only the product K * M is divided by J. Then this result is multiplied by N.

f. Mathematical formula: $\qquad\qquad i = \dfrac{k + m}{j}$ $\qquad\qquad$ Computed Value

$\qquad$ Incorrect FORTRAN statement: $\qquad$ I = K + M / J $\qquad$ I = 13

$\qquad$ Correct FORTRAN statement: $\qquad$ I = (K + M) / J $\qquad$ I = 10

Parentheses are needed in this expression to ensure that all of the numerator is divided properly. In the incorrect expression only the value of M is divided by the value of J.

g. Mathematical formula: $\qquad\qquad n = \tfrac{1}{3}(10 + 20)$ $\qquad\qquad$ Computed Value

$\qquad$ Incorrect FORTRAN

$\qquad\quad$ statement: $\qquad\qquad\qquad\qquad$ N = (1 / 3) * (10 + 20) $\qquad$ N = 0

$\qquad$ Correct FORTRAN statement: $\quad$ N = (10 + 20) / 3 $\qquad\qquad$ N = 10

In this example we want to illustrate that it is sometimes necessary to write the expression in a different manner, in order to avoid errors. In the incorrect expression *integer* arithmetic is carried out in (1 / 3). The result is zero because of truncation.

Exercises

1. Write a FORTRAN statement for the given formula.

$\qquad$ a. $\quad y = \dfrac{x}{a + b}$ $\qquad\qquad\qquad\qquad$ d. $\quad t = \dfrac{x \cdot y}{w \cdot z}$

$\qquad$ b. $\quad y = (ax + b)\, x$ $\qquad\qquad\qquad$ e. $\quad r = \dfrac{a / b}{c \cdot d^2}$

$\qquad$ c. $\quad y = \dfrac{a(b + c)}{d}$ $\qquad\qquad\qquad$ f. $\quad w = (a + b) \cdot (c + d)^{n-1}$

2. Given the FORTRAN statement A = X + Z / S + B indicate which of the two following formulas this statement represents.

$\qquad$ a. $\quad a = \dfrac{x + z}{s + b}$ $\qquad\qquad\qquad\qquad$ b. $\quad a = x + \dfrac{z}{s} + b$

5.7 Mixed Mode Expressions

An expression containing *real* and *integer* variables and/or constants is called a mixed mode expression. Mixed mode means that constants and variables in the expression are of different types (*integer* and *real*). For example, the following expression is in mixed mode.

$\qquad$ Z + 2 − MAX / W

Although ANSI FORTRAN does not allow mixed mode expressions (except for allowing the exponent of a *real* quantity to be an *integer*), the FORTRAN compiler for some large computers will allow mixed mode expressions. Throughout this text we will not use mixed mode expressions. However, we feel that you should be aware of their existence and should know how the computer handles them.

Rules for the Evaluation of Mixed Mode Expressions

1. If the expression contains no parentheses and at least one *real* constant or variable, then the values of all integer constants and variables are converted to *real* for evaluation of the expression. The final value computed is a *real* number.

2. If the expression contains a quantity in parentheses, then each quantity is evaluated as a separate entity. If the expression in parentheses contains all *integers* constants and/or variables, then it is evaluated using *integer* arithmetic. If an expression in parentheses contains one *real* constant or variable, the expression is evaluated and a *real* value is obtained. For example,

Expression	Value
3 / 4	0
3.0 / 4	.75
3. * (3 / 4)	0.
3. * (3. / 4)	2.25

Special Terms

1. *arithmetic expression*
2. *arithmetic replacement statement*
3. *constant*
4. *define a variable*
5. *E-notation*
6. *integer constant*
7. *mixed mode*
8. *real constant*
9. *truncation*
10. *variable*

Chapter 6

Writing a Program

6.1 Introduction

In this chapter we present a beginning problem and two problems of moderate difficulty. Study the beginning problem and one of the intermediate ones. The two sample programs labeled "intermediate" present the same new material, but the sample problem in section 6.6 is mathematical in nature and the one discussed in section 6.5 is a data processing problem.

In presenting the sample problems we will follow the problem solving procedure discussed in Chapter 3. First, we give a statement of the problem. Then we discuss a method to solve the problem. Next, we develop the flowchart for the method. Finally, we convert the flowchart into FORTRAN. Each FORTRAN statement is explained as it is used.

In the beginning program, we discuss the FORTRAN statements in an informal manner and in relation to their specific use to the problem. Section 6.3 presents the general form and rules for the use of the FORTRAN statements introduced in this chapter. Appendix A gives a complete reference to all ANSI FORTRAN statements in the text.

6.2 A Beginning Program

Statement of the Problem

Recently the City Council of Longbridge decided to license its entire dog population. The council voted to charge $1 for a neuter dog, $2 for a male, and $3 for a female. Because this process involves over 40,000 animals, the council wants to use the computer to determine how much revenue has been obtained from each type of dog. As each license was granted, a card was punched containing the dog's name, a code for the dog's sex, the owner's name and address, and the license number. The codes for sex are −1 for a neuter, 0 for a male, and 1 for a female.

The format of the cards is:

license number	columns 1–5
owner's name	11–25
owner's address	26–40
dog's name	41–50
dog's sex	51–52

The output should be on three separate lines and in the order shown below.

revenue from neuter dogs
revenue from male dogs
revenue from female dogs

Find a Method

We want this program to compute the revenue from the three different classifications of dogs. The formula for finding revenue is

Revenue = amount per license × number of licenses issued

We know the cost of a license, but we do not know the number of licenses sold, so the program must count the number of male, female, and neuter dogs. We will tally the number of licenses in three different accumulators.

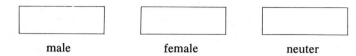

| | male | female | neuter |

After we look at a card and determine the sex of the dog, we will place a mark in the appropriate tally box.

| 1 | | |
| male | female | neuter |

In the program we cannot place a mark in an accumulator, but we can increment an accumulator by one and thereby count the number of dogs. After going through all the cards, we multiply the number of males by 2 and the number of females by 3 to give us the revenue. Since a neuter dog's license costs $1, it is not necessary to multiply the number of neuters by 1.

Flowchart the Method

Let us name the variables we will use in the flowchart and in the program. We will choose the names so that they conform to the rules for forming FOR-TRAN variable names. Even though the data cards contain a lot of information, the only item pertinent to this problem is the sex code. Since the code is an integer value that changes depending on the number punched on the card, let us name it with the FORTRAN variable name ICØDE. We need three

Figure 6.1 Flowchart for Sample Problem

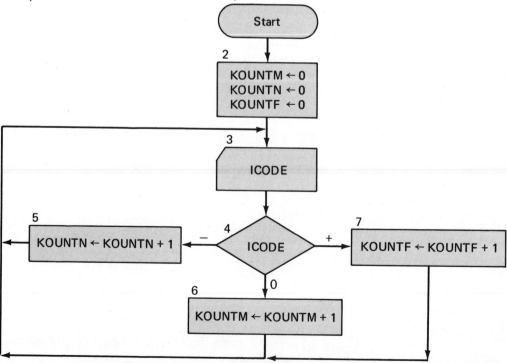

memory locations in which we can count the number of males, females, and neuters. We will call these KØUNTM, KØUNTF, and KØUNTN. Also, we will compute three amounts: MØNYM, MØNYF, and MØNYN. All these variables are *integer,* because their values will be integer numbers.

In box 2 of the flow chart in Figure 6.1, we set the initial value of the accumulators to zero. The next step is to read a value for ICODE. Now we can determine the sex of a dog. Because ICODE has three different values, the decision box 4 of the flowchart shows three possible branches. For example, a negative ICODE means that the dog is neuter, since the code of a neuter dog was −1. Then, KOUNTN is incremented by 1 in box 5. From box 5 the flowchart lines direct us back to box 3. In a similar manner, a positive ICODE will cause the female counter KOUNTF to be incremented in box 7; a zero ICODE will cause the male counter KOUNTM to be incremented in box 6. And from either box 6 or 7, we return to box 3 to read another card.

What happens if there is no other card to read? The flowchart does not show what to do. Therefore, we must include two important items:

1. a check for the end of the data cards
2. steps to follow after all the data has been read

To check for the end of data we need to include a dummy data card. We will place this card at the end of the stack of actual data cards. The dummy data card should have a specific value that we can test for, and one that does not appear in the actual data. Let us use the value of 99. For this problem, we

Figure 6.2   Final Flowchart for Sample Problem

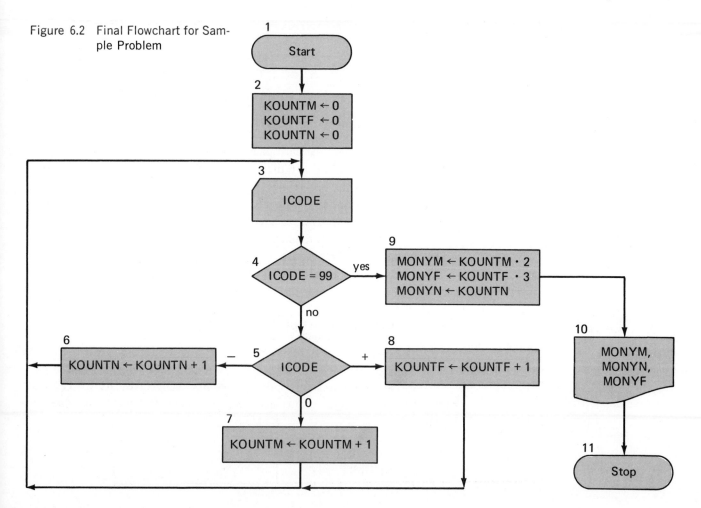

would punch the value in the same columns (51–52) as the sex code values. Each time we read a new card, the next step will be to check if ICODE has the value of 99. When ICODE equals 99, we know that we have reached the end of the data deck. Finally, when all the data has been read, we will compute the amounts—MONYM, MONYF, and MONYN. Our last step will be to write out these values. These additional steps appear in the flowchart in Figure 6.2.

Exercise

Using the following test data cards, construct a trace diagram for the flow-chart in Figure 6.2.

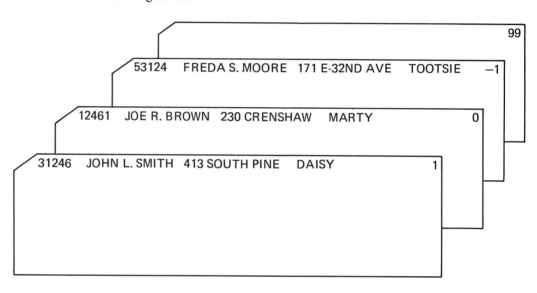

Convert the Flowchart into FORTRAN

Box 1 Usually, the first card of a program is a comment card. The purpose of this card is to identify the program so that other programmers may quickly know what the program is about. Comment cards are not necessary, since they do not state any commands, but they are indeed helpful in following the steps in a program. The comment card requires the letter C punched in column 1. Then, the programmer may write the comment anywhere in columns 2 through 80. In practice, comments are started in column 7, for aesthetic reasons, since the FORTRAN statement begins in that column also. For our program we will have the following comment cards.

```
C       CITY ØF LØNGBRIDGE CØMMUNITY SERVICES
C       DEPARTMENT
C       DØG REVENUE PRØGRAM
```

Box 2 We want to set the three counters KØUNTM, KØUNTF, and KØUNTN to zero. The following three replacement statements initialize the counters.

$$KØUNTM = 0$$
$$KØUNTF = 0$$
$$KØUNTN = 0$$

1

Start

2

KOUNTM ← 0
KOUNTF ← 0
KOUNTN ← 0

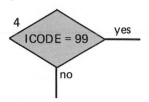

Box 3   Now we wish to read the input numbers punched in columns 51 and 52 of the data cards. Although other information is punched on the cards, it will not be used at this time by the city, and hence it will not be used by the program. The input data values are given a label or name so that the computer may store the value in the labeled memory location. We will use the same variable name of ICODE used in the flowchart. We need two FORTRAN statements to read in the information. The READ statement instructs the computer to read a card; and the FORMAT statement specifies in what columns the number is punched and whether it should be stored as a FORTRAN *real* or *integer* number. The FORTRAN statements for our program are:

```
  3   READ (5,100) ICØDE
100   FØRMAT (50X,I2)
```

Let us discuss the specific items that appear in these two statements. The READ statement is given the number 3 as a **statement label** because the flowchart shows that we will return to it later to read more cards. The word READ is a required word in the instruction to the computer to read a card. The two integers found inside the parentheses, (5,100), have the following meaning: 5 is the "unit number" assigned to the card reader; 100 is the statement label of a FØRMAT statement. (These numbers are discussed further in section 6.3.) The name ICØDE is used to specify the label of the memory location where the value of the ICØDE is stored. The READ statement says "refer" to FØRMAT 100 to find how to read a value for ICØDE. The FØRMAT statement has a statement label 100 because it is the number used in this READ command. Since this program does not use the information punched in the first 50 columns of the data cards, we want to skip them. We use 50X inside the parentheses of the FØRMAT statement to skip 50 columns. If we wanted to skip only 20 columns we would have said 20X. Following the 50X we find the information about the value to be given to ICØDE. Because we want to read the *integer* value in columns 51 and 52, we say I2. The I specifies an *integer* and the 2 means that it is a field two columns long. The parentheses and commas in these two statements are part of the required punctuation when writing these instructions.

Box 4   Now we wish to check if the value of ICØDE is 99. This will be done with a testing instruction called an **arithmetic IF statement.** This statement is able to test an arithmetic expression to see if its value is either negative, zero, or positive. Another way of knowing when ICØDE is equal to 99 is to have

$$ICØDE - 99 = 0$$

Since our arithmetic IF statement can check an expression to see if it is zero, we will use the expression ICØDE − 99 in the statement. Our question in FORTRAN will be

    IF (ICØDE − 99) 5,9,5

In this statement, ICØDE − 99 is considered the arithmetic expression. The numbers 5,9,5 are statement labels of other FORTRAN statements in the program. The program branches to those statements as follows:

1. If ICØDE − 99 is negative, the next statement executed is the statement labeled 5.
2. If ICØDE − 99 is zero, the next statement executed is the statement labeled 9.
3. If ICØDE − 99 is positive, the next statement executed is the statement labeled 5.

In our program both branches, negative and positive, use the same statement label, because here we are only interested in testing for zero. The order of these statement labels is important. The first number given is the label of the statement to go to if the value of arithmetic expression is negative; the second one is the statement to go to if the value of the arithmetic expression is zero; the third is the statement to proceed to if the value of the arithmetic expression is positive.

Box 5 Now we wish to check if the value of ICØDE is negative, zero, or positive, since the sex codes were −1 for a neuter, 0 for a male, and 1 for a female. Again we will use the *arithmetic IF* statement, but here the variable name ICØDE is the arithmetic expression to be tested.

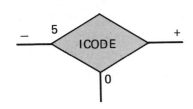

```
5        IF (ICØDE)  6,7,8
```

This statement is labeled 5 because it is referred to by the IF (ICODE − 99) 5,9,5 statement. This IF statement will cause the computer to go to statement 6 if ICØDE is negative; to statement 7 if ICØDE is zero; and to statement 8 if ICØDE is positive.

Box 6 This statement is numbered because the IF (ICØDE) question refers to it.

```
6        KØUNTN = KØUNTN + 1
```

According to the flowchart, after this box we wish to return to the read box. Since the READ statement was numbered 3, we write

```
         GØ TØ 3
```
There is no flowchart symbol which corresponds to the GØ TØ statement. It is represented by the *line* connecting box 6 to box 3.

Box 7 This statement is numbered for the same reason that the statement in box 6 was numbered. Next, we wish to return to the read box.

```
7        KØUNTM = KØUNTM + 1
         GØ TØ 3
```

Box 8 This case is similar to boxes 6 and 7.

```
8        KØUNTF = KØUNTF + 1
         GØ TØ 3
```

Box 9 We come to these commands after we have reached the end of the data deck.

```
9        MØNYM = KØUNTM * 2
         MØNYF = KØUNTF * 3
         MØNYN = KØUNTN
```

Box 10 Now we wish to write the quantities MØNYN, MØNYM, and MØNYF. We must also devise a FØRMAT statement to tell the printer where we want the numbers printed. After consulting the problem statement, we find that we wish to write one number per line. Since all the numbers are integers, each line will have the same FØRMAT. We will leave a 10 space margin and then write the number. How much room shall we leave for the answer? Six digits should be sufficient for this problem. Therefore, our FØRMAT becomes

```
10
MONYN,
MONYM,
MONYF
```

```
110      FØRMAT (10X,I6)
```

Then we wish to use this same FØRMAT in writing 3 separate lines. This is accomplished by having 3 WRITE commands.

```
WRITE (6,110)  MØNYN
WRITE (6,110)  MØNYM
WRITE (6,110)  MØNYF
```

Notice that one FØRMAT is used by all three WRITEs. The 6 in the WRITE statement is the "unit number" assigned to the printer. The FØRMAT statement labeled 110 does not need to follow the WRITE statement. The FØR–MAT statement may be placed anywhere in the program (before the END card). When the computer is ready to read or write, it refers to the FØRMAT statement to learn the form of the input or output.

```
11
Stop
```

Box 11 We must now instruct the computer to stop executing the program. We do this by saying

```
STØP
```

A card which must appear at the end of every FORTRAN program deck is the END card. It signals the compiler that this is the physical end of a complete program unit.

```
END
```
There is no flowchart symbol which corresponds to this FORTRAN statement.

Let us now combine the individual statements into a program listing.

```
C        CITY ØF LØNGBRIDGE CØMMUNITY SERVICES
C        DEPARTMENT
C        DØG REVENUE PRØGRAM
C        INITIALIZE CØUNTERS
         KØUNTM = 0
         KØUNTF = 0
         KØUNTN = 0
C        READ IN ICØDE VALUES
      3  READ (5,100) ICØDE
    100  FØRMAT (50X,I2)
C        CHECK FØR DUMMY DATA CARD
         IF (ICØDE − 99) 5,9,5
C        CHECK FØR SEX CØDE
      5  IF (ICØDE) 6,7,8
C        INCREMENT CØUNTERS
      6  KØUNTN = KØUNTN + 1
         GØ TØ 3
```

```
    7  KØUNTM = KØUNTM + 1
       GØ TØ 3
    8  KØUNTF = KØUNTF + 1
       GØ TØ 3
C      CØMPUTE REVENUE
    9  MØNYM = KØUNTM * 2
       MØNYF = KØUNTF * 3
       MØNYN = KØUNTN
C      WRITE ØUT VALUES ØF REVENUE
  110  FØRMAT (10X,I6)
       WRITE (6,110) MØNYN
       WRITE (6,110) MØNYM
       WRITE (6,110) MØNYF
       STØP
       END
```

The above statements are a FORTRAN source program. To obtain a source deck, we would punch each statement on a separate card. If we also attach the necessary control cards and some test data cards, we could submit the program for compilation and execution on a computer. If we made no card punching errors and we did not violate any rules of the FORTRAN language, then the compiler will translate the program into an object program.

How is the object program executed? First we must remember that comment cards are *not* translated into any machine language instruction and therefore have no meaning when the computer executes the program.

The control section of the computer starts execution with the first statement and proceeds from one statement to another. Sometimes a statement will command the computer to go and execute another portion of the program. If this control proceeds to another location in the program we say that there has been a **transfer of control.**

We will now give a detailed description of what happens during execution if the program uses the same test data as the trace diagram assigned in the exercise on page 52.

```
       KØUNTM = 0
```

This statement will cause the computer to store a zero in the memory location labeled KØUNTM. The statements KØUNTF = 0 and KØUNTN = 0 will cause similar assignments.

```
    3  READ (5,100) ICØDE
  100  FØRMAT (50X,I2)
```

Execution of this statement causes the computer to read the first data card according to the information given in the FØRMAT statement. The value stored in memory location ICØDE will be a 1 (the number found in columns 51–52 of the first data card).

```
       IF (ICØDE − 99) 5,9,5
```

The arithmetic expression is evaluated using the value of 1 for ICØDE. The result is −98. The next statement that the computer executes is the one labeled 5. When this branching occurs, a *transfer of control* takes place.

```
    5  IF (ICØDE) 6,7,8
```

Since ICØDE, in the statement labeled 5, has a value of $+1$, control transfers to the statement labeled 8.

    8   KØUNTF = KØUNTF + 1

The right-hand side of the equal sign is evaluated first. The computer takes the present value stored in KØUNTF (a zero) and adds a 1. The result ($0 + 1 = 1$) will replace the old value of 0 stored in the memory location labeled KØUNTF. This statement does not cause any branching or transfer of control, so the next statement executed is the one that immediately follows it.

        GØ TØ 3

This statement causes a transfer of control to the statement labeled 3, which is the READ statement.

When the computer executes the READ statement again, it will read the second data card. A new value of 0 replaces the old value stored in ICØDE. When the computer evaluates the arithmetic expression ICØDE − 99 of the IF statement, the result is −99. Control again transfers to the statement labeled 5. When the IF statement labeled 5 is executed, ICØDE has a value of 0, and control will transfer to the statement labeled 7.

    7   KØUNTM = KØUNTM + 1

This statement causes the male counter to increase by one (KØUNTM = 1). Following this statement we have

        GØ TØ 3

which causes control to transfer back to the READ statement. The new value of −1 will be stored in ICØDE. After executing the two IF statements, we find that this new value of ICØDE takes the program to the statements

    6   KØUNTN = KØUNTN + 1
        GØ TØ 3

After incrementing the counter for the neuter dogs, control again transfers to the READ statement. The fourth data card is read and the value of 99 is stored in ICØDE. When the computer evaluates the arithmetic expression ICØDE − 99 in the IF statement, the result is a zero. Now, control transfers to the statement labeled 9.

    9   MØNYM = KØUNTM * 2

The value stored in KØUNTM is multiplied by 2 and the result is stored in the memory location labeled MØNYM. Next, values for MØNYF and MØNYN are also computed.

The FØRMAT labeled 110 is not executed because it is a statement used by the WRITE statements. The computer executes the WRITE statements in the same order in which they appear. The first quantity printed will be MØNYN; the second will be MØNYM; and the third, MØNYF. Since we chose only enough sample data to test all branches of the program, the only values printed would be:

```
1
2
3
```

The next instruction found is the STOP statement and the program (execution) stops.

6.3 FORTRAN Statements in Chapter 6

This section gives the general form of the FORTRAN statements discussed in the examples of this chapter. We will use some of the statements and other detailed information given in this section and in section 6.4 in the examples of sections 6.5 and 6.6. Chapter 8 contains information and examples on the READ and WRITE statements.

In Appendix A, the student will find a reference guide to all the ANSI FORTRAN statements presented in this text. Use Appendix A to check on the form, punctuation, and rules of a specific FORTRAN statement.

The statements in the FORTRAN language are classified as executable and non-executable. Executable statements command the computer to perform a task; non-executable statements describe elements in the program. That is, non-executable statements are simply descriptive and help the computer anticipate the form of certain information used in or generated by the program. In the formal description of the FORTRAN statements we will classify them as executable or non-executable.

Arithmetic Replacement Statement—Executable

FORTRAN variable name = FORTRAN arithmetic expression

The arithmetic replacement statement is used to give a value to the variable on the left-hand side of the equal sign. When the computer executes the arithmetic replacement statement, it does two things:

1. evaluates the arithmetic expression
2. stores the value of the expression as the new value of the variable on the left-hand side of the equal sign

The rules for forming arithmetic expressions and for using them in an arithmetic replacement statement are given on pages 40 and 41.

Definition. A string of FORTRAN variable names separated by commas is defined as a **list.** If the list contains only one name, it is not followed by a comma. A list used in a READ statement is called an **input list;** a list used in a WRITE statement is called an **output list.**

Examples

UP, AND, DØWN
SNØØPY, THE, RED, BARØN
NØRTH, SØUTH, EAST, WEST
DEDUCT

READ Statement—Executable

READ (u,n) list

The u specifies the "unit number" assigned to an input device. This unit number will be different from one computer installation to another. Therefore, check with your computer installation for this number. *For all the programs presented in this book we will use the card reader as the input device, and we will assign to it the unit number 5.*

The n is the number of the FØRMAT statement reference. The list is an input list and consists of the names of the items to be read.

Every time the computer executes the READ statement, it reads at least one card. Once the card has been read, the computer cannot read it again. Chapter 8 includes a more detailed discussion of the READ statement.

WRITE Statement—Executable

WRITE (u,n) list

The u specifies the "unit number" assigned to the output device on which data is to be written. This unit number may vary for different installations. Find out this specific unit number for your installation. *For all the programs presented in this book we will use the line printer as the output device and we will assign to it the number 6.*

The n is the number of the FØRMAT statement to which the WRITE statement refers. The list is an output list and consists of the names of the variables whose values are to be written. The WRITE statement may be used to print messages or to label values to make the output more readable to someone not familiar with the program. If we wish to write only text (contained in an H-field in the FØRMAT), then we may omit the list. See Chapter 8 for a more detailed discussion of the WRITE statement.

FØRMAT Statement—Non-executable

n FØRMAT $(s_1, s_2, \ldots, s_k)$

where n is a statement number

$s_1, s_2, \ldots, s_k$ are FØRMAT specifications

A FØRMAT statement is referenced by a READ or WRITE statement. FØRMAT statements are non-executable and may be referenced by more than one READ or WRITE statement. When used with a READ statement, the FØRMAT statement provides information on how the data appears in the fields of a punched card, and how the data will be stored in memory. When used with a WRITE statement, the FØRMAT statement provides information on how the results of a program are to appear on the output page and how they are stored in memory. These details are given in the FØRMAT statement through a set of specifications which are discussed below.

FØRMAT Specifications. Each FØRMAT specification describes the type (*real* or *integer*) and width of information in the data set. The FØRMAT specifications may be separated by a comma (,) or a slash (/). A comma is not used after the last specification. The entire list of FØRMAT specifications must be enclosed in parentheses.

The X, I, F, and H specifications are commonly used by the beginning programmer. The other FØRMAT specifications, A, D, E, G and L, appear later in the text.[1] Appendix A gives a summary of all the specifications.

[1] The A-field is discussed in section 9.4. The D, E, G, and L fields are discussed in sections 13.6, 13.9, 13.9, and 13.8, respectively.

X-field (skip field)
Form: nX

This specification may be used in a FØRMAT statement that is referenced by a READ or a WRITE statement. In an input reference this specification instructs the computer to skip n columns on a data card, where n is a number between 1 and 80. In an output reference this specification instructs the computer to print n blank characters on the output paper. The possible value of n will differ with specific computers.[2]

I-field specification
Form: nIw

where   n   is the number of times the field is to be repeated. If n is one it may be omitted.

       w   is the width of the field (total number of card columns or page spaces). When included, the sign of the number counts as part of the width.

This form is used for the input or output of *integer* constants.

F-field specification
Form: nFw.d

where   n   is the number of times the field is to be repeated. If n is one it may be omitted.

       w   is the width of the field (total number of card columns or page spaces). When inputting numbers, the sign and decimal point, if included, count as part of the width. When outputting numbers, the decimal point will always be printed, and the sign will be printed only for negative numbers. The decimal point and sign count as part of the width.

       d   specifies the number of decimal digits to the right of the decimal point.

This form is used for the input or output of *real* constants without an exponent. (The E-field specification discussed in section 13.9 is used for input and output of *real* constants with exponent.)

H-field specification
Form: nHccc. . .ccc

where   n   is the exact number of characters ccc. . .c to be printed on the output paper.

  ccc. . .c   are letters, numbers, or special characters that immediately follow the H.

Blanks are considered special characters and must be counted when they appear in an H-field specification. The size of n depends upon the computer system.[3] An H-field specification may be continued from one card to another,

---

[2] On the CDC 6000 Series and CYBER 70 the maximum number of characters that may be printed on a line is 136. On the IBM 360/370 the maximum number of characters is 120.
[3] See footnote 2.

but great care must be given so that no unintentional blanks are introduced. For example,

12HBALANCEbØFb$
5HSUM3=

A non-ANSI shorthand version of the H-field specification is the use of primes around the characters to be printed. Various computers use different characters for the prime.[4] Therefore, a programmer wishing to write programs which could easily be run on other machines should use the H-field specification.

Carriage Control Characters

Spacing down the written page is specified to the printer through carriage control characters. The character that the programmer tries to print in column 1 of each line is *always* interpreted as a carriage control character and is *never* printed. The H-field or the X-field may be used to specify carriage control characters. The carriage control characters and their action are given below.

Character	Action
Blank	causes single-spacing before printing
0	causes double-spacing before printing
1	causes skipping to the top of a new page before printing
+	causes suppressing of spacing before printing

For example,

    10   FØRMAT (1H1,10X,5HTØDAY)

Since the first character printed by the FØRMAT is a 1, the printer will start a new page before skipping ten spaces and printing the word TØDAY.

STØP Statement—Executable

This instruction tells the computer to cease execution of the program. It may appear anywhere in the program; and there may be more than one STØP statement in a program.

END Statement—Non-executable

The END statement causes the end of compilation. It is a signal to the compiler that the physical end of a program has been reached. This must be the last statement of a FORTRAN program; hence, there is only one END statement in a program.

[4] On the IBM 360/370, the apostrophe (') is the prime. Therefore, 12HBALANCE-bØFb$ could be written as 'BALANCEbØFb$'. The CDC 6000 Series and CYBER 70 use the asterisk (*) for the prime. Hence, 12HBALANCEbØFb$ could be written *BALANCEbØFb$*.

GØ TØ Statement—Executable

GØ TØ n

where n is a statement label. The computer transfers control to the statement numbered n.

Arithmetic IF Statement—Executable

IF (arithmetic expression) n_1, n_2, n_3

The n_1, n_2, and n_3 are statement labels. First, the computer evaluates the arithmetic expression. If its value is negative, the next statement executed is the statement numbered n_1. If its value is zero, the next statement executed is n_2. If its value is positive, the next one executed is n_3.

Example

```
    IF(ICØDE)  6,7,8
 6  KØUNTN = KØUNTN + 1
    GØ TØ 3
 7  KØUNTM = KØUNTM + 1
    GØ TØ 3
 8  KØUNTF = KØUNTF + 1
    GØ TØ 3
```

Logical IF Statement—Executable

In this chapter we will present a simplified form of the logical IF statement which is generally used by beginning programmers. The complete version is discussed in section 13.8.

The logical IF statement has the general form

IF (relational expression) S

where S is an executable statement.

A **relational expression** consists of two arithmetic expressions separated by a **relational operator.** Both arithmetic expressions must be of the same type (both *integer* or both *real*). The resulting value of the relational expression is either true or false.

The legal FORTRAN relational operators are:

.EQ.	equal to
.NE.	not equal to
.GT.	greater than
.LT.	less than
.GE.	greater than or equal to
.LE.	less than or equal to

For example,

1. A.LT.B
2. N − 1 .GE. J ** 2
3. MIN .GT. 0

The executable statement, S, must *not* be another logical IF statement or a DØ statement. (The DØ statement will be explained in Chapter 10.) The logical IF statement acts in the following manner.

1. If the relational expression is true, S is executed. Then, if S is not a state-

ment that transfers control, the next statement executed is the one immediately below the IF statement.

2. If the relational expression is false, control goes to the next statement below the IF statement, without executing statement S.

For example,

1. IF (A.LT.B) A = W + 1.
   TEMP = A + B
2. IF (R*P .EQ. EPS) GØ TØ 7
   VAL = R * P

6.4 FORTRAN Supplied Functions

Certain calculations such as taking the square root of a number are performed so frequently that programs have been provided in the compiler to perform these calculations. These FORTRAN supplied programs are sometimes called built-in functions. To use these functions in any arithmetic expression we must give the name of the function and the values to be used in the calculations. The values may be any FORTRAN expression, such as a constant, a variable or an arithmetic expression. The general form for referencing these functions is

function name (expression)

The quantity enclosed in parentheses is called the *argument* of the function. For example in the statement

X = SQRT (2.0 + Y)

SQRT is the function name and 2.0 + Y is the argument. If we want to write out the value of SQRT (2.0 + Y), we cannot have this functional reference as an item in the output list. Instead we would say

WRITE (6,100) X

Following is a list of the more commonly used FORTRAN supplied functions. Appendix B presents a complete list. The functions listed below are used with one argument. Because of the way these functions are written it is important to give an argument of the correct type. For example,

X = SQRT (125)   is *not* allowed
X = SQRT (125.0) has the correct type of argument

Name	Type of Argument	Type of Results	Purpose
SQRT	Real	Real	Square root
ABS	Real	Real	Absolute value
IABS	Integer	Integer	Absolute value
FLØAT	Integer	Real	Converts an INTEGER to floating-point form
INT	Real	Integer	Converts a REAL value to INTEGER
SIN	Real (angle in radians)	Real	Trigonometric sine
CØS	Real (angle in radians)	Real	Trigonometric cosine
TAN	Real (angle in radians)	Real	Trigonometric tangent
EXP	Real	Real	$e^{argument}$
ALØG	Real	Real	Natural logarithm
ALØG10	Real	Real	Logarithm to the base 10

6.5 An Intermediate Non-mathematical Program

An introductory course in history at a major university has attracted over 1000 students. By the end of the quarter, each student has acquired points from quizzes, exams, and homework. The instructor would like to have a list of those students who will be eligible for an honor seminar next term. To be eligible for the seminar, the student must have accumulated a certain number of points.

The instructor wants to program the computer so that it will produce the list of eligible students. He punched one card which contains the number of points needed in order to qualify for the seminar. Then he punched for each student one card which contains the student's ID-number and his point total. On the dummy data card, he punched a zero student number.

The format of the cards is:

>Card 1:
>>minimum number of points   columns 1–3
>>needed to be eligible for
>>honor seminar

>Card 2 through last card:
>>student number   columns 1–6
>>student's total points   16–18

The instructor wants the output printed with appropriate headings. He wants the identification number for each eligible student and his point total printed. The printed information should look like the following diagram.

```
             TITLE
STUDENT NO.        POINTS
student no.        points
student no.        points
     .                .
     .                .
     .                .
```

Find a Method

The problem is to print a list of students eligible for the honor seminar. We can do this by processing one student's card at a time. After reading a student's data card, we can determine whether or not he has enough points. If he does, then we print his ID-number and point total. If he does not have enough points, then we do not print anything. After processing one student, we will go on to process another student until we have checked all the students.

Flowchart the Method

One of the first things we should do before drawing the flowchart is decide what items we will need from the data and how we will name them. Three quantities come from the cards: the number of points needed to be eligible for the honor seminar, a student's ID-number, and his point total. We will name the items:

Figure 6.3 Flowchart for Intermediate Non-mathematical Program

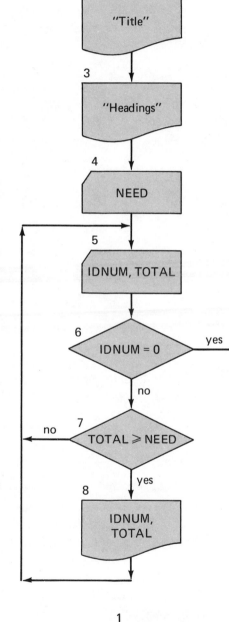

NEED—number of points needed
IDNUM—ID-number
TØTAL—point total

The heading or title of the output page should be printed only once, so this is done at the beginning of the program. This title could be something like "ELIGIBLE STUDENTS FØR SEMINAR." We will include headings to identify the student number and the student's point total. The headings could be

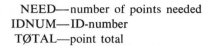

The flowchart in Figure 6.3 includes two decision boxes. The first one asks if the student number just read is zero. If it is, we have come to the dummy card which signals the end of the data deck and we stop. If it is not zero, we proceed to the next decision box to see if the student's total number of points is greater than or equal to the number needed. An eligible student's ID-number and point total are printed; an ineligible one's are not. The next step in the flowchart is to read another student's card.

Convert the Flowchart to FORTRAN

Box 1 The first cards will be comment cards to summarize what the program does and what variable names are used.

```
C       THIS PRØGRAM DETERMINES THE STUDENTS
C       ELIGIBLE FØR THE HØNØR SEMINAR
C
C       NEED—MINIMUM NUMBER ØF PØINTS A STUDENT
C       MUST HAVE
C       IDNUM—STUDENT ID–NUMBER
C       TØTAL—TØTAL PØINTS ACCUMULATED
```

Box 2 To print a title we use the H-field specification in the FØRMAT statement. The FORTRAN command to print on the output page is WRITE. If there are no values to be printed, then no list of variable names is present. The statement for our program is

WRITE (6,100)

The number 100 refers to the FØRMAT statement which is

100   FØRMAT   (1H1,46X,29HELIGIBLEbSTUDENTSbFØRbSEMINAR)

Since the FØRMAT begins with a 1H1, the printer will go to a new page before writing anything. The 46X will cause the printer to skip 46 spaces on the line before writing the title.

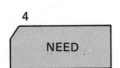

3
"Headings"

Box 3   We need another FØRMAT statement to print the headings. The necessary instructions are

WRITE (6,200)
200   FØRMAT (1H0,48X,11HSTUDENTbNØ.,22X,6HPØINTS)

The first printed character, a zero, causes double spacing before printing. Then the printer skips 48 spaces before writing the heading "STUDENT NØ." and skips 22 spaces before writing "PØINTS."

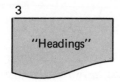

4
NEED

Box 4   The first data card contains the value for NEED. The FORTRAN statement to read this value from the card is

READ (5,300) NEED

The number 300 refers to the FØRMAT statement for the READ instruction. The FØRMAT statement is

300   FØRMAT (I3)

Because the name NEED is an *integer* variable name, the I-field specification is used in the FØRMAT. The I3 says that NEED is a 3-digit *integer*.

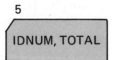

5
IDNUM, TOTAL

Box 5   This box says to read one student's information using the variable names IDNUM and TØTAL. Again we will use a READ statement and a corresponding FØRMAT statement. The READ statement is labeled 5 because later we will refer to this statement.

5   READ (5,400) IDNUM, TØTAL
400   FØRMAT (I6,9X,F3.0)

The FØRMAT statement says that the value for IDNUM is in columns 1–6 and that it is an *integer*. Then, the FØRMAT says to skip 9 spaces (columns 7–15) and find a *real* number in columns 16–18. The F3.0 must be used for reading in the value of TØTAL because TØTAL is a *real* variable and the F-field specification is used for input and output of *real* values. The "3" part of the F3.0 says that the value of TØTAL occupies 3 columns of the card. The ".0" part of the F3.0 FØRMAT specification says that there will be no decimal places.

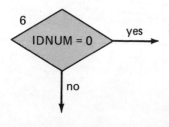

6
IDNUM = 0
yes
no

Box 6   To have the computer check if IDNUM is zero, we will use a **logical IF statement.**

IF (IDNUM .EQ. 0) STØP

This IF statement asks the question: is IDNUM equal to zero? The answer to this question is either yes or no. (You may also say that the answer is either true or false.) If the answer is yes, then the computer executes the STØP. If the answer is no, the computer does not execute the STØP, but goes on to the statement following the IF statement.

The expression "IDNUM .EQ. 0" is a **relational expression,** and the ".EQ." is a **relational operator** which means equal to.

Box 7 We now have the computer make another decision. Again we will use the logical IF statement.

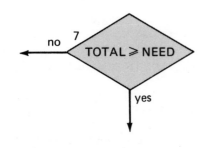

IF (TØTAL .GE. FLØAT(NEED)) WRITE (6,500) IDNUM, TØTAL

This statement tells the computer that if the value of TØTAL is greater than or equal to the value of NEED, then the computer should write the values of IDNUM and TØTAL. If the value of TØTAL is less than the value of NEED, the computer will not write anything. After processing the IF statement, the computer will proceed to the statement following the IF. This next statement should be

GØ TØ 5

so that we will return to read another student's card.

The relational expression inside the parentheses of the IF statement may *not* be of mixed mode. Therefore, we used the FLØAT function to make the value of NEED a *real* one, so that it could be compared with the value of TØTAL, which was already a *real* value. The IF statement could have been written as

IF (INT(TØTAL) .GE. NEED) WRITE (6,500) IDNUM, TOTAL

The INT function converts the value of TØTAL to an *integer,* so that it may be compared to the *integer* value of NEED. The INT and FLØAT functions are examples of FORTRAN supplied functions.

Box 8 Writing has been included as part of the preceding IF statement. However, we do need to put in a FØRMAT statement labeled 500 which the WRITE statement will use.

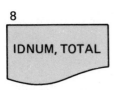

500   FØRMAT (1Hb,48X,I6,27X,F4.0)

The different parts of the FØRMAT statement tell the printer how and where to write the values of IDNUM and TØTAL. We print a blank as the first character on the line so that the printer will single space. This first blank is the carriage control character. The 48X in the FØRMAT says to skip 48 spaces. The I6 specification says that the value of IDNUM will be printed in the next 6 spaces and that IDNUM is an *integer.* Next, the printer will skip 27 more spaces (because of the 27X in the FØRMAT) and write the value of TØTAL. The F4.0 specification says that 4 spaces are allowed for printing the value of a real variable. A decimal point will occupy 1 of the 4 spaces. Therefore, 3 spaces are left for printing the 3-digit value of TØTAL with no digits following the decimal point. The FØRMAT could also have been written

500   FØRMAT (49X,I6,27X,F4.0)

where 1Hb and 48X have been combined into 49X.

Box 9   We have already included the STØP command as part of the IF statement for box 6. Therefore, if we have no more statements in the program, we must include an END statement to denote the program's physical end.

END

The complete program is:

```
C        THIS PRØGRAM DETERMINES THE STUDENTS
C        ELIGIBLE FØR THE HØNØR SEMINAR
C
C        NEED—MINIMUM NUMBER ØF PØINTS A STUDENT
C        MUST HAVE
C        IDNUM—STUDENT ID–NUMBER
C        TØTAL—TØTAL PØINTS ACCUMULATED
         WRITE (6,100)
  100    FØRMAT(1H1,46X,29HELIGIBLEbSTUDENTSbFØRbSEMINAR)
         WRITE (6,200)
  200    FØRMAT (1H0,48X,11HSTUDENTbNØ.,22X,6HPØINTS)
         READ (5,300) NEED
  300    FØRMAT (I3)
    5    READ (5,400) IDNUM, TØTAL
  400    FØRMAT (I6,9X,F3.0)
         IF (IDNUM .EQ. 0) STØP
         IF (TØTAL.GE.FLØAT(NEED))WRITE (6,500) IDNUM, TØTAL
         GØ TØ 5
  500    FØRMAT (1Hb,48X,I6,27X,F4.0)
         END
```

6.6 An Intermediate Mathematical Program

Statement of the Problem

Find the real roots of a quadratic equation with general form $ax^2 + bx + c = 0$. The value of the coefficients are punched on a card such that

Columns	1–10	contain the value for	a
	11–20	contain the value for	b
	21–30	contain the value for	c

Find a Method

Consulting the algebra book, we find that by asking several questions about the coefficients or the discriminant (discriminant $= b^2 - 4ac$) we can obtain the real roots, if they exist. When $a \neq 0$, the following possibilities exist.

1. If $b^2 - 4ac$ is less than zero, there are no real roots.
2. If $b^2 - 4ac$ is equal to zero, the roots (x_1 and x_2) are equal and $x_1 = x_2 = -b/2a$.
3. If $b^2 - 4ac$ is greater than zero, the roots (x_1 and x_2) are real and distinct.

$$x_1 = \frac{-b + \sqrt{b^2 - 4ac}}{2a} \quad \text{and} \quad x_2 = \frac{-b - \sqrt{b^2 - 4ac}}{2a}$$

When $a = 0$, the quadratic equation becomes $bx + c = 0$, and the only root is $x = -\frac{c}{b}$. If $a = 0$ and $b = 0$, then we have no roots to find.

Flowchart the Method

We want to write a general flowchart that reads in the value of the coefficients a, b, and c. The flowchart should ask the appropriate questions that would lead to the computation of the real roots or output appropriate messages if there are no real roots.

The messages that we would like our program to give us are:

1. "There Are No Real Roots" when the value of $b^2 - 4ac$ is less than zero.
2. "This Is the Degenerate Case" when both $a = 0$ and $b = 0$.
3. When real roots exist, print the values of a, b, and c, and the values of the roots found after the title "The Real Roots Are."

The flowchart for our problem appears in Figure 6.4.

Again we have labeled the boxes in the flowchart with a number, so that in writing the FORTRAN program from our flowchart we can use the box numbers as a reference.

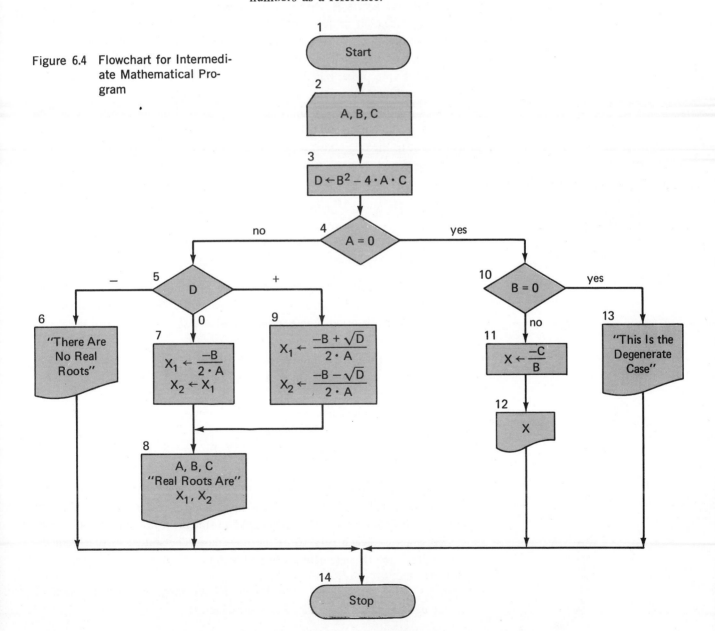

Figure 6.4 Flowchart for Intermediate Mathematical Program

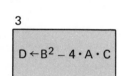

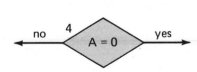

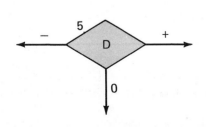

Convert the Flowchart to FORTRAN

Box 1   We will start the program with some identifying comments.

```
C        THIS PRØGRAM WILL FIND THE REAL
C        RØØTS ØF THE EQUATIØN
C        A * X**2. + B * X + C = 0
```

Box 2   The values that we wish to read are the coefficients, and as variable names we can use A, B, and C. Our input statement is

```
READ  (5,100)  A,B,C
```

The number 100 refers to the FØRMAT statement that we will use with the READ instruction. We write the FØRMAT statement next.

```
100   FØRMAT  (3F10.5)
```

Because the letters A, B, and C represent real variable names, we use the F-field specification in the FØRMAT. The specification F10.5 means a field of 10 columns, 5 of which are after the decimal point. This could be depicted as x x x x . x x x x x where each x represents one digit. Note that the decimal point takes up a place, but there are still 5 decimal positions. Because of the manner in which the values are punched, we want to repeat the same field specification three times. In the FØRMAT statement above, the number 3 in front of F10.5 means repeat the field three times. A FØRMAT statement equivalent to the one above is:

```
100   FØRMAT  (F10.5,F10.5,F10.5)
```

Box 3   Here we want to compute the discriminant of any given quadratic equation.

$$D = B * B - 4.0 * A * C$$

Note that the value of B was not squared by using exponentiation, but by multiplying B by itself. This is done for efficiency. In the computer, multiplication is a faster operation than exponentiation.

Box 4   Here we will use the *logical IF statement* where the result of the expression in question is either true or false. To ask if A is equal to 0.0 the expression part is written as A .EQ. 0.0. The symbol .EQ. means "equal to" and it is the **relational operator.** The expression A .EQ. 0.0 is the **relational expression.** The FORTRAN statement is:

```
IF  (A .EQ. 0.0)  GØ TØ 10
```

When the relational expression A .EQ. 0.0 is true, control will go to the statement labeled 10; if A .EQ. 0.0 is false, control will go to the statement immediately following the IF statement. The statement labeled 10 will be discussed when we reach Box 10 of the flowchart. The statement that immediately follows the IF statement corresponds to box 5.

Box 5   Here we will use an arithmetic IF statement to check the value of D, the discriminant. The FØRTRAN statement is

IF (D) 6,7,9

Box 6 The flowchart tells us that when the discriminant is negative, we want to print a message. The FORTRAN feature that allows us to do this is the H-field specification given in the FØRMAT statement.

The FORTRAN command to have something printed on the output page is WRITE. If there are no values to be printed, then no list of variable names is present. The statement for our program is

6 WRITE (6,200)

The number 200 refers to the FØRMAT statement which is

200 FØRMAT (1H1,10X,23HTHEREbAREbNØbREALbRØØTS)

The first character is not printed but is used for carriage control. Since the 1H1 specification says write a 1 as the first character, the printer will start a new page. The 10X will cause the printer to skip 10 spaces on the line, and then the printer will write the characters in the H-field specification.

The flowchart indicates that after printing the above message, we are to go to box 14 to stop the program. Our next FORTRAN instruction is

GØ TØ 14

Box 7 Here we compute the expressions indicated by the flowchart. We have two statements.

$$X1 = -B / (2. * A)$$
$$X2 = X1$$

Box 8 The flowchart indicates that we are to print

1. the values of A, B, and C
2. the message "Real roots are"
3. the values of X_1 and X_2.

It would be more meaningful to print "A=" and next to it the value stored under the variable name A. Similarly, for B and C. The following WRITE and FØRMAT statements accomplish step 1.

8 WRITE (6,300) A,B,C
300 FØRMAT (1H1,10X,4HAb=b,F10.5,5X,4HBb=b,F10.5,5X,
    4HCb=b,F10.5)

For printing out the values of X1 and X2 with the appropriate titles we have

WRITE (6,400) X1,X2
400 FØRMAT (1H0,10X,14HREALbRØØTSbARE,3X,7HRØØT1b=,
    F8.3,3X,7HRØØT2b=,F8.3)

In the FØRMAT labeled 400 note the following:

1. 1H0 at the beginning of the FØRMAT causes double spacing of the printer's paper.
2. The title RØØT1 is completely arbitrary, ANS1 or VALUE1 would have been just as good. The computer does not know that RØØT1 and X1 are related in any way.

6

"There Are
No Real
Roots"

7

$$X_1 \leftarrow \frac{-B}{2 \cdot A}$$
$$X_2 \leftarrow X_1$$

8

A, B, C
"Real Roots Are"
X_1, X_2

3. The way we indicate how we want the value stored in X1 printed is through the use of the F8.3 field specification; similarly, for X2.
4. FØRMAT 400 is continued onto a second card, because it is too long to be punched on one card. We placed a period in column 6 to show that the line beginning with F8.3 is a continuation of the FØRMAT statement. (Similarly the period is used in FØRMAT 300 to continue it onto a second card.)

Since we are finished, we have a transfer of control to our stop. Again, we have the statement

GØ TØ 14

Box 9 If the value of the discriminant is positive, control of the program goes to statement 9 directly. The flowchart indicates that the roots may be found by using the quadratic formula, which involves finding the square root of D ($\sqrt{D}$). At this point we wonder if we will have to write in our program a "square root finder process." Because finding square roots is very common in mathematical problems, such a process has been added as a FORTRAN supplied function. The FORTRAN expression for finding the square root of D would be SQRT(D).

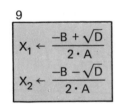

The FORTRAN statements for box 9 of the flowchart are

9   X1 = (−B + SQRT(D)) / (2. * A)
    X2 = (−B − SQRT(D)) / (2. * A)

And, control goes to box 8 for printing out the values, with the statement

GØ TØ 8

Box 10 If the value of *a* is zero, then the quadratic equation really becomes $bx + c = 0$. To find out if B is equal to zero or not we will again use the logical IF statement.

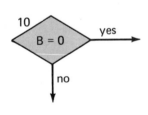

IF (B .EQ. 0.0) GØ TØ 13

The logical IF statement will transfer control to the statement labeled 13 if the relational expression is true; if false, control goes to the statement immediately following the IF statement (in our example, it will be the statement corresponding to box 11).

Box 11 We are to compute only one root according to the flowchart. The FORTAN statement is

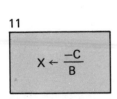

X = −C / B

It is not necessary to label this statement 11, because no other statement in the program refers to it. For example, there is no statement which says GØ TØ 11.

Box 12 Here we want to print the value of X just found by the preceding statement. With appropriate labeling given by the FØRMAT statement, we can write the required FORTRAN statement

WRITE (6,500) X
500   FØRMAT (1H1,10X,18HØNEbREALbRØØTbXb=b,F8.3)

And, the transfer of control given by

GØ TØ 14

Box 13 Another WRITE command, with its FØRMAT, will print the desired message. The FORTRAN statements are

13 WRITE (6,600)
600 FØRMAT (1H1,10X,27HTHISbISbTHEbDEGENERATEbCASE)

Box 14 The next two statements are the STØP and END statements. As stated in our previous example, all FORTRAN programs must include these statements.

14 STØP
    END

The complete program is:

```
C        THIS PRØGRAM WILL FIND THE REAL
C        RØØTS ØF THE EQUATIØN
C        A * X**2. + B * X + C = 0
C
C        READ IN CØEFFICIENTS
C
         READ (5,100) A,B,C
100      FØRMAT (3F10.5)
C
C        CØMPUTE DISCRIMINANT
         D = B * B - 4.0 * A * C
         IF (A .EQ. 0.0) GØ TØ 10
         IF (D) 6,7,9
C        NØ REAL RØØTS
6        WRITE (6,200)
200      FØRMAT (1H1,10X,23HTHEREbAREbNØbREALbRØØTS)
         GØ TØ 14
C
C        CØMPUTE EQUAL REAL RØØTS
C
7        X1 = -B/(2. * A)
         X2 = X1
8        WRITE (6,300) A,B,C
300      FØRMAT   (1H1,10X,4HAb=b,F10.5,5X,4HBb=b,F10.5,5X,
        .    4HCb=b,F10.5)
         WRITE (6,400) X1,X2
400      FØRMAT    (1H0,10X,14HREALbRØØTSbARE,3X,7HRØØT1b=,
        .    F8.3,3X,7HRØØT2b=,F8.3)
         GØ TØ 14
C
C        CØMPUTE DISTINCT REAL RØØTS
C
9        X1 = (-B + SQRT(D))/(2. * A)
         X2 = (-B - SQRT(D))/(2. * A)
         GØ TØ 8
C
C        CØMPUTE RØØT OF B * X + C = 0
C
10       IF (B .EQ. 0.0) GØ TØ 13
         X = -C / B
         WRITE (6,500) X
```

```
        500   FØRMAT (1H1,10X,18HØNEbREALbRØØTbXb=b,F8.3)
              GØ TØ 14
         13   WRITE (6,600)
        600   FØRMAT (1H1,10X,27HTHISbISbTHEbDEGENERATEbCASE)
         14   STØP
              END
```

Exercises

1. Compute the current balance for one person's checking account. The first card of the data deck contains:

account number	columns	1–6
current balance		11–18 (The number has two decimal digits and is written in the form xxxxx.xx)

   All the rest of the data cards are in the following form:

account number	columns	1–6
transaction amount		11–18 (The number has two decimal digits and is written in the form xxxxx.xx)
code		21

   The code is either "1" or "0." A "1" means that the transaction is a deposit; a "0" is a check.

   The problem is to compute this account's current balance. Your output should take the following form and should start on a new page.

   > ACCOUNT account number
   > PREVIOUS BALANCE = xxxxx.xx
   > CURRENT BALANCE = xxxxx.xx

2. Read a number "n" from columns 1–5 of a card. Compute the finite sum

   $$1 + \frac{1}{2} + \frac{1}{3} + \ldots + \frac{1}{n} = \sum_{i=1}^{n} \frac{1}{i}$$

   Print the value of "n" and the value of the sum at the top of a new page. Label these values with an appropriate message.

3. Find all the prime numbers between 1 and 1000. A number p is prime if p is not equal to 1 and the only divisors of p are 1 and p.

   One suggested method to use is that of trial and error. To find if a number p is prime, find its square root. If the number is a perfect square, then it is not prime. Otherwise, truncate the square root so that it is a whole number. Then divide p by 2 and see if there is a remainder. If there is a remainder, divide p by 3 and see if there is a remainder. If there is a remainder, divide p by 4 and check for a remainder. Continue dividing p by 4, 5, and so on, until p is divided by its square root. If all of the numbers divided into p produce a remainder, then p is a prime. If one of the numbers divides evenly into p, then p is not a prime.

   Print out all the prime numbers between 1 and 1000. Start the list on a new page and title it appropriately.

4. Ultra Private School has started a new semester and the President is getting ready to make his report to the Trustees. He wants to tell them:
   1. the total enrollment for the previous semester, the percentage of boys enrolled, and the percentage of girls enrolled
   2. the enrollment of the current semester, the percentage of boys enrolled, and the percentage of girls enrolled
   3. whether enrollment has increased, decreased, or remained the same

   The summary for the President must be tabulated from registration for this quarter. The card deck obtained from the Registrar is arranged in this order:

   card 1:
       columns   1–5   total enrollment last semester
                      6–10 number of boys enrolled
                     11–15 number of girls enrolled
   card 2 through next to last data card:
       column   22 sex (1 means male; 2 means female)
                       There is one card included for each person enrolled this semester.
   last data card:
       column   22 contains the number 0. This signals the end of the data deck.

   Use the data and prepare a report for the President. The output should start at the top of a new page and should look like the following table.

   ULTRA PRIVATE SCHOOL PRESIDENT'S REPORT

   FALL SEMESTER ENROLLMENT: 368
   60% BOYS
   40% GIRLS
   SPRING SEMESTER ENROLLMENT: 398
   55% BOYS
   45% GIRLS
   THE ENROLLMENT HAS INCREASED BY 30

5. Study the following program and tell *precisely* what each FORTRAN statement does.

```
      READ (5,1) K
 1    FØRMAT (I5)
      ITØTAL = 1
      J = 2
 2    ITØTAL = ITØTAL + J**J
      J = J + 1
      IF (J−K) 2,2,3
 3    WRITE (6,4) ITØTAL
 4    FØRMAT (1H1,10X,7HITØTAL=,I10)
      STØP
      END
```

6. A student wants to find the largest of an arbitrary amount of numbers. He has written a flowchart and FORTRAN program for the problem, but the flowchart has an error in logic which makes the program incorrect. First

correct the error in the flowchart, and then correct the program. The variable names used in the flowchart are

N—total amount of numbers in the problem
A—the actual numbers for which the program is to find the largest
BIG—the largest number found from the numbers that have been processed; BIG should contain the value of the number we are looking for.

The flowchart is:

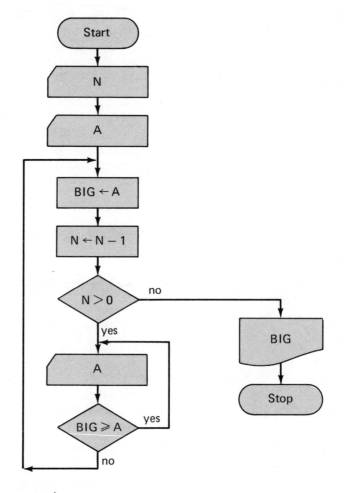

The program is:

```
        READ (5,1) N
        READ (5,2) A
   20   BIG = A
        N = N − 1
        IF (N) 5, 10, 5
    5   READ (5,2) A
        IF (BIG − A) 20, 5, 5
   10   WRITE (6,3) BIG
    1   FØRMAT (I3)
    2   FØRMAT (F5.2)
    3   FØRMAT (1H1,10X,F6.2)
        STØP
        END
```

7. French and American research scientists carried out a project using the

joint facilities of a French laboratory and an American laboratory. The work involved recording the temperatures of organisms. The French recorded their findings in degrees Centigrade. A programmer at the American laboratory must write a program that will convert the Centigrade temperatures to their Fahrenheit equivalents. The following formula changes a Centigrade temperature to a Fahrenheit temperature.

$$F = \frac{9C + 160}{5}$$

Each Centigrade temperature is punched in columns 1–5 of a data card with two decimal places in the number.

The output should give the original recording in Centigrade followed by its equivalent in Fahrenheit as follows:

xx.xx CENTIGRADE EQUIVALENT TO xx.xx FAHRENHEIT

8. A procedure to find the cube root of a positive number A is given by the sequence defined by

$$x_{n+1} = \frac{1}{3}\left(2x_n + \frac{A}{x_n^2}\right)$$

The sequence should start with $x_1 = 1.0$. Find the cube root of the number A with 6 decimal places of accuracy. A is punched in columns 1–10 with 4 decimal places.

The following title should be centered on the output page and the values should be written below the title.

A   CUBE RØØT ØF A

Special Terms

1. *accumulator*
2. *argument*
3. *built-in functions*
4. *carriage control*
5. *executable*
6. *F-field*
7. *H-field*
8. *I-field*
9. *input list*
10. *list*
11. *non-executable*
12. *output list*
13. *relational expressions*
14. *relational operators*
15. *transfer of control*
16. *unit number*
17. *X-field*

Chapter 7

Finding and Correcting Errors

7.1 Debugging Programs

A programmer often unintentionally introduces errors into his program. By carefully checking the most common sources of errors, he can eliminate many of these errors or "bugs" as they are called. In this chapter, we will give a guide to those errors most commonly encountered. Some errors may be found before a program is submitted for a run; we will call these **pre-run errors.** Other errors do not become evident until after a program has been run at least once; we will call these **post-run errors.** Boxes 1–9 of the following flowchart describe the errors which may be found during the pre-run procedure. Section 7.2 discusses in detail these pre-run errors. Boxes 10–32 of the flowchart describe the error finding process during post-run. Section 7.3 discusses how to eliminate the post-run errors.

7.2 Pre-run Errors

Check the Flowchart

After writing the flowchart a programmer should select some sample data and go through the steps in the flowchart using a trace, as we illustrated in section 1.3. The ability to select a representative sample of data develops with practice, but the data should test as many of the different branches of the flowchart as possible.

Insert Print Statements

As a precautionary measure, we must insert statements throughout the program to write out values of different variables as they are computed. If the program works, these print statements are unnecessary and can be removed for the next run. But, if the program does not produce the desired results, these print statements may help us find out what is wrong, because we can compare the printout to our hand calculations (trace).

One common source of error is that the data is read with the wrong FØR-MAT. If the data is read incorrectly, the rest of the program cannot be expected to produce the correct answers. Therefore, we should print out the input. Consider several examples.

Example 1

Data cards are punched:

test score 1	in columns 1–3
test score 2	in columns 6–8

```
      READ (5,100) TEST1,TEST2
100   FØRMAT (F3.0,3X,F3.0)

      WRITE (6,110) TEST1,TEST2
110   FØRMAT (10X,F4.0,10X,F4.0)
```

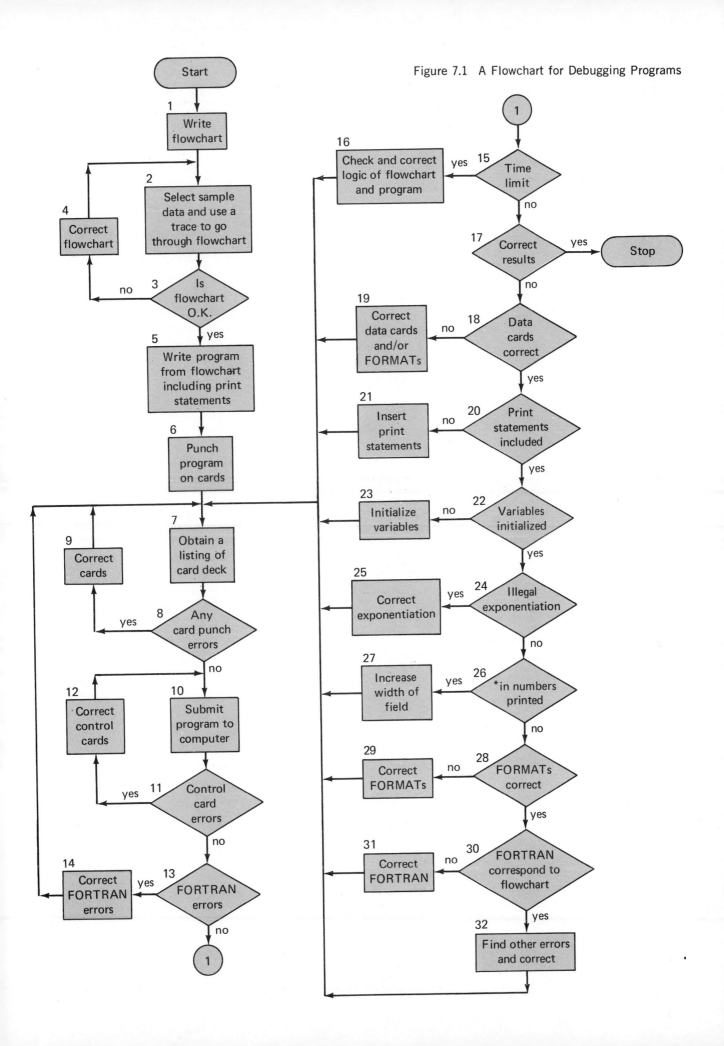

Figure 7.1 A Flowchart for Debugging Programs

```
100bbb78b
```

FØRMAT 100 says that the first number will be in columns 1–3 and the second will be in columns 7–9. The WRITE statement will print out

>   100.   780.

Since the blanks on the card were interpreted as zeros, TEST2 = 780 instead of 78.

The *correct* FØRMAT is

> 100   FØRMAT (F3.0,2X,F3.0)

Example 2

Data cards contain:

>   social security number   columns   1–9
>   GRE verbal score   columns 11–13

```
      READ (5,100) SØCSEC,GRE
100   FØRMAT (F9.0,1X,I3)

      WRITE (6,110) SØCSEC,GRE
110   FØRMAT (10X,F10.0,10X,I3)
```

```
123456789b619
```

The data will be printed as

>   123456789.   619

and there is no apparent error. However, GRE is a *real* variable and it was read with an *integer* (I3) format specification. This means that GRE is stored in the computer as an integer and not as a real number. On some computers, whenever GRE is used in computation, either the results will be incorrect or an error message will be printed. Other computers will not compile these statements correctly. The format for a *real* number should be F; for an *integer* it should be I.

The correct FØRMAT is

> 100   FØRMAT (F9.0,1X,F3.0)

Example 3

The following program has its intermediate results printed.

```
        SUM = 0.0
  10    CØUNT = CØUNT + 1.0
  20    READ (5,100) X
 100    FØRMAT (F5.2)
        IF (X .EQ. 0.) GØ TØ 30
        WRITE (6,110) X
 110    FØRMAT (10X,F7.2)
        SUM = SUM + X
        GØ TØ 10
  30    WRITE (6,120) SUM,CØUNT
 120    FØRMAT (10X,4HSUM=,F10.2,10X,6HCØUNT=,F5.0)
        AVG = SUM / COUNT
        WRITE (6,130) AVG
 130    FØRMAT (10X,4HAVG=,F10.2)
        STØP
        END
```

Exercise

The program above contains errors which will prevent it from working correctly. What changes will correct the program?

Card Punching Errors

After a programmer writes a program and punches it on cards, the cards may contain card punch errors. We could check each card by hand, but it is easier to obtain a printed listing of the card deck and proofread his listing. A machine such as the IBM 407 Accounting Machine may be used for this purpose.

Some errors to look for while proofreading the listing of the card deck are:

1. misspelled words
2. typing a 0 instead of an Ø and vice versa
3. typing in the wrong columns. Remember that the FORTRAN statement must be between columns 7 and 72. The listing will let you see if all the statements begin in the same column. However, it is not easy to tell if you have typed a statement past column 72, because the listing shows what is punched on the whole card. Check the card deck to see if any long statements go past column 72.
4. omitting a C on a comment card
5. omitting a continuation punch
6. forgetting to remove mispunched cards from deck
7. cards out of sequence
8. omitting statement labels

Exercise

Identify as many card punching errors as you can in the program listing below and on the following page.

```
1 2    5 6 7
             THIS PRØGRAM CØNTAINS MANY ERRØRS
  C          IT IS SUPPØSED TØ READ A NUMBER X, SQUARE
                IT, AND CUBE IT.
       10    READ (5,100) X
      100    FØRMAT (F5.0)
             IF (X .EQ. 0) GØ TØ 30
```

```
        |SQUARE = X * X
        |CUBE = SQUARE * X
        |WRITE (6,110) X, SQUARE, CUBE
    100 |FØRMAT (10X,F10.0,10X,F10.0,10X,F10.0)
    110 |FØRMAT (10X,F10.0,10X,F10.0,10X,F10.0)
        |GØ TØ 10
      3 |STØP
        |END
```

7.3 Post-run Errors

Control Card Errors

After you have run the program on the computer, you will receive some printed output. If there were any errors in the control cards, the computer will not have been able to do everything you requested (compile and execute the program). Check with your instructor for the appropriate control cards to use at your computer center. Examine the cards carefully to make sure that the punctuation is correct. It is possible that an omitted comma will cause a control card error.

FORTRAN Errors

A message such as "004 FORTRAN ERRORS" on the printout indicates that the compiler found 4 FORTRAN errors in the program. Additional details about the errors appear with the listing of the program. Hopefully all FORTRAN errors would have been detected when the program was listed initially. However, the ability to detect these errors usually improves with experience. The following list gives a few common errors to watch out for:

1. unbalanced parentheses
2. incorrect punctuation (syntax)
3. forgetting the END card
4. invalid FORTRAN name
5. omitting the multiplication sign
6. having two statements with the same number
7. forgetting to number a statement which is referenced
8. errors in format specifications
9. errors with the input or output

Different FORTRAN compilers give different error messages for the same FORTRAN error. Sometimes the message does not point out the specific error, but indicates a mistake in the FORTRAN statement. To figure out what is incorrect, the programmer should refer to the text to check the rules and form of the statement. Let us repeat, the ability to correct FORTRAN errors improves with experience. Some compilers list all error messages on one page separate from the program; others print the message beneath the statement in which the error occurred. We will not state the error messages of a specific compiler. We will, however, give an example in which each line of the program has been numbered so that the error message may refer to it.

Example

LINE NO.		FORTRAN STATEMENT
0001	10	READ (5,100) A,B,C,I,J
0002		IF (I .EQ. −9999) GØ TØ 40
0003	10	SUMREALS = A + B + C
0004		I − J = K
0005		IF (K) 20, 20, 30
0006		WRITE (6,110) K
0007	20	K = −K
0008	30	M = 2K
0009		WRITE (6,120) SUMREALS,M
0010		STØP
0011	100	FØRMAT (3F10.0,2I5
0012	110	FØRMAT (10X,I5)
0013	120	FØRMAT (10X,F10.0,10X,I10)
0014	C	END

LINE NO.	ERROR MESSAGE
0002	REFERRING TØ UNDEFINED STATEMENT LABEL
0003	DUPLICATE STATEMENT LABEL
0003	NAME GREATER THAN 6 CHARACTERS
0004	UNRECØGNIZABLE STATEMENT
0006	NØ PATH TØ THIS STATEMENT
0008	INVALID VARIABLE
0009	NAME GREATER THAN 6 CHARACTERS
0011	UNBALANCED PARENTHESES
0015	END ØF PRØGRAM DECK ENCØUNTERED: NØ END CARD

We shall now discuss what caused the errors and how to correct them.

Line 0002   Undefined statement label means that the label referred to in line 0002 does not appear in the program. Is there a statement numbered 40? No there is not. In order to correct this error, we must know what the programmer intended. If he wanted to stop the program when I equals −9999, then we would label the STØP statement (line 0010) number 40.

Line 0003   Duplicate statement label says that there are two statements with the same number. In this program there are two statements numbered 10. This could be corrected by erasing the 10 in line 0001. The way this error is corrected depends upon the logic of the program.

Line 0003   Name greater than 6 characters means that one of the names is not a valid FORTRAN name. SUMREALS is 8 characters long, but could be shortened to SUMRLS.

Line 0004   Unrecognizable statement means that there is something wrong with the form of the statement. Is this the way an arithmetic replacement statement is written? No, it isn't, because there must be *one* variable on the left-hand side of the equals sign. Perhaps the programmer intended this statement to be K = I − J.

Line 0006   No path means that there is no way for the computer to get to this statement. The preceding IF statement (line 0005) says to go either to statement 30 or to statement 20 and skip over line 0006. The WRITE statement is not numbered, so control cannot transfer to it from some other part of the program.

Line 0008   Invalid variable says that some variable in line 0008 does not follow the rules for valid FORTRAN names. M is valid but 2K is not. Probably the multiplication sign was omitted and 2K should have been written 2 * K.

Line 0009   Refer to line 0003.

Line 0011   Unbalanced parentheses means that the number of right parentheses counted was not equal to the number of left parentheses. In this line there is no right parentheses at the end of the FORMAT statement.

Line 0015   There is no END card. Line 0014 is a comment card containing the word END; it is not an END card. Line 0014 is ignored by the compiler because it is a comment.

Mixed Mode Errors

The term mixed mode applies to FORTRAN arithmetic and relational expressions that contain *real* variables and/or constants and *integer* variables and/or constants. Two examples of statements containing mixed mode expressions are:

    VAL = IN * PAY − DEC / N
    IF (A .EQ. 0) GØ TØ 5

We must correct these statements because a mixed mode expression is not allowed in ANSI FORTRAN. To correct the first statement we could use the INT or FLOAT function and write:

    VAL = FLØAT(IN) * PAY − DEC / FLØAT(N)

or

    VAL = IN * INT(PAY) − INT(DEC) / N

To correct the IF statement we need only place a decimal point after the zero.

    IF (A .EQ. 0.) GØ TØ 5

Even though some computers are able to handle mixed mode expressions, it is best to avoid them to save computer time. In order to evaluate a mixed mode expression, the computer must convert all *integer* values to their *real* equivalent before performing any operations.

Time Limit

If you receive a "time limit" message on your computer output, this means that the program ran the total length of time allowed and did not finish. A never-ending loop probably caused this error. Check the logic of the program carefully.

Execution Errors

After the first run of a program, a programmer may find that his program did not execute as expected. Sometimes the compiler diagnostics are a help in finding errors, but experience and insight are also required in order to debug a program. There are as many possible errors as there are programmers, but we will try to discuss those errors which are most frequently encountered by beginning programmers.

A. In the eagerness of submitting the first run, sometimes data cards are not included in the deck. Check all data cards carefully, but preferably have the program print out all input data. This will assure you that your data is being read correctly.

B. If the program does not print out any results, you might not have included the necessary write statements in the program.

C. The computer cannot correctly execute a statement if one of the variables has not been defined previously. This occurs very often when a programmer forgets to give a variable its initial value or forgets to read in a needed value.

D. At all times we must be aware of errors that may be introduced when using *integer* arithmetic. For example, if we want to find the average of the numbers 2 and 3, we might write the following FORTRAN statements

```
I = 2
K = 3
ISUM = I + K          or  IAVG = (I + K) / 2
IAVG = ISUM / 2
```

What is the value stored in IAVG? The value stored in IAVG is 2; but it is incorrect because the average of the given numbers is $(2 + 3)/2 = 2.5$.

E. Exponentiating incorrectly will cause error messages during execution. *Real* constants or variable names may be raised to *real* or *integer* exponents, but *integer* constants or variable names may be raised only to *integer* exponents. The computer does not permit you to raise a negative expression to a real power. The expression A**B is evaluated using the logarithmic formula $e^{B \log_e A}$ and it is impossible to take the logarithm of a negative number. The computer does permit you to raise a negative expression to an *integer* power, because the expression A**I is done by multiplication. A diagnostic will also be given when zero is raised to the zero power.

F. Sometimes results will not "look" correct because there is something wrong with the output FØRMAT statement. For instance, trying to print the value of a *real* variable with an I-field specification or an *integer* variable with an F-field specification would cause incorrect output. The way different compilers will print their numbers varies. Therefore, we suggest that whenever a program does not print the correct results, check the FØRMATs.

Another possibility for error in a FØRMAT specification is that the field width specified is not large enough to print the value. For example, a 4-digit integer cannot be printed under an I2 FØRMAT specification. Neither can a number such as −37.6 be printed using an F4.1 specification. (There is no place saved for the minus sign.) Again, different compilers will handle this situation in different ways.[1] It is sound programming practice to use wide fields and always to allow for digits to the right of the decimal point.

G. Sometimes statements in a program may cause the computer to calculate either an "infinite" value or an "undefined" value. For example, an infinite value would be computed if a number were divided by zero. An undefined value would result from trying to compute the square root of a negative number or trying to take the logarithm of zero—two operations which are not mathematically possible.

The way computers handle infinite or undefined values varies. Some computers may stop immediately when one of these values is computed and will print out a message to this effect:

INFINITE VALUE CALCULATED
UNDEFINED VALUE CALCULATED BY SQRT FUNCTIØN

Other computers will not stop when infinite or undefined values are calculated, but will continue execution. Then, when the program starts to print out these values the output will contain special symbols to denote an infinite value and an undefined value. For example, INF may represent an infinite value and UND may represent an undefined value. Check at your computer installation to find out exactly how the computer handles infinite and undefined values.

H. A program could be incorrect when the FORTRAN statements do not correspond to the flowchart. A correct flowchart is the first step, but it is useless if the FORTRAN statements do not carry out the same procedure.

I. Sometimes a program does not have FORTRAN syntax (punctuation) errors or any of the typical execution errors mentioned above, and does not give correct results. The programmer should go back to the flowchart and try to find any errors in logic and correct them. It is easier to correct a FORTRAN program once the flowchart has been revised, rather than trying to correct the FORTRAN statements.

Special Terms

1. *debugging*
2. *FORTRAN errors*
3. *post-run errors*
4. *pre-run errors*
5. *syntax*
6. *time limit*

---

[1] The IBM 360/370 will fill the entire field with asterisks if the field width is too small to accommodate the number. The CDC 6000 series and CYBER 70 computers will print as much of the number as possible, and will place an asterisk in the left-most position of the field.

Chapter 8

More on Input and Output of Simple Variables

8.1 Introduction

The action of the READ and WRITE statements at execution time depends upon their respective FØRMAT statements. Many combinations of the input/output list and FØRMAT specifications will provide a variety of results. The purpose of this chapter is to state more detailed rules for input and output and show how they may be applied in specific examples. The READ statement is covered in section 8.2 and the WRITE statement in section 8.3. Only the X-, F-, I-, and H-field specifications are used in the examples in this chapter. Refer to section 9.4 for examples of the A-field and to Chapter 13 for examples of D, E, G, and L specifications.

8.2 READ Statements Using Simple Variables

Field Repetition

If two or more FØRMAT specifications are repeated successively, it is not necessary to list them in the FØRMAT. An integer constant preceding a specification indicates the number of times the specification is to be repeated. The following are equivalent statements.

```
100    FØRMAT  (F5.1,F5.1,6X,I4,I4,I4)
100    FØRMAT  (2F5.1,6X,3I4)
```

Example

Given the following READ statement and its FØRMAT statement

```
       READ  (5,100)  A,B,C,I,J
100    FØRMAT  (2F5.1,1X,F4.1,2I4)
```

and the data card

Figure 8.1

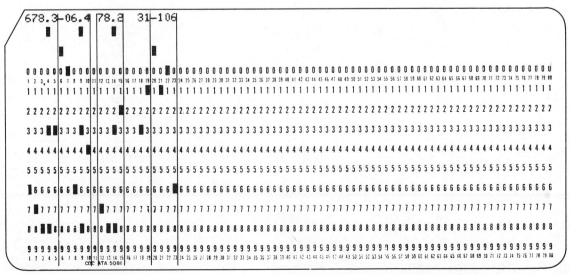

the values read from the card are assigned to the variables as follows:

$$
\begin{array}{ll}
A = 678.3 & \text{read from columns } 1–5 \\
B = -6.4 & \text{read from columns } 6–10 \\
C = 78.2 & \text{read from columns } 12–15 \\
I = 31 & \text{read from columns } 16–19 \\
J = -106 & \text{read from columns } 20–23
\end{array}
$$

Group Repetition

A group of specifications may appear consecutively in a FØRMAT. To indicate repetition of the group of specifications, enclose the group in parentheses and precede it with an integer constant that indicates the number of times the group is to be repeated. The following are equivalent statements.

```
100    FØRMAT  (2X,F4.1,I3,I3,2X,F4.1,I3,I3)
100    FØRMAT  (2(2X,F4.1,2I3))
```

Example

Given the following READ statement and its FØRMAT statement

```
       READ (5,100)  NUM,X1,LIM,X2,MAX,X3
100    FØRMAT  (3(I5,F10.3))
```

Figure 8.2

and the data card

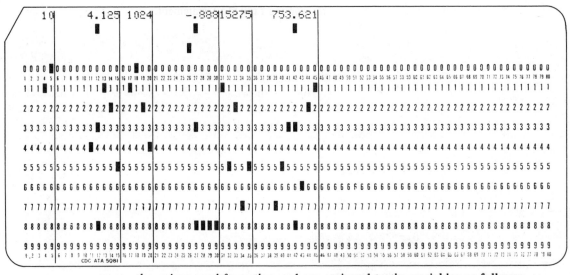

the values read from the card are assigned to the variables as follows:

$$
\begin{array}{ll}
NUM = 10 & \text{read from columns } 1–5 \\
X1 = 4.125 & \text{read from columns } 6–15 \\
LIM = 1024 & \text{read from columns } 16–20 \\
X2 = -.888 & \text{read from columns } 21–30 \\
MAX = 15275 & \text{read from columns } 31–35 \\
X3 = 753.621 & \text{read from columns } 36–45
\end{array}
$$

Relationship of Input List Size and FØRMAT Statement

We will look at several examples in which the number of variable names in the input list is not equal to the number of field specifications in the FØR-

MAT. (The X-field specification is not counted because values are not read in by this specification.)

Example A

The number of variables in the input list is *less than* the number of specifications in the FØRMAT statement.

When all the variables in the input list have received a value, the remaining field specifications are ignored. For example,

```
      READ (5,100)  A
100   FØRMAT (3F10.0)
```

According to the FØRMAT labeled 100, *three* real numbers could be read from the card. But the READ statement says to read just *one* variable, and therefore A is read from columns 1–10. The rest of the FØRMAT is not used.

This rule could be used when more than one READ statement refers to the same FØRMAT. We could have the following statements in a program.

```
      READ (5,100) A
      READ (5,100) X,Y,Z
100   FØRMAT (3F8.2)
```

Example B

The number of variables in the input list is *greater than* the number of specifications in the FØRMAT statement.

At execution time when the computer encounters the last right parenthesis of the FØRMAT statement, the computer searches the FØRMAT statement from right to left until it finds the next right parenthesis. The left parenthesis which matches this right parenthesis marks the beginning of that portion of the FØR-MAT which will be repeated until the entire input list is read. Any group repetition number preceding the left parenthesis will be used. If there is no right parenthesis found when the FØRMAT is searched, then the entire FØRMAT will be repeated. The last right parenthesis of the FØRMAT indicates the end of a unit record of input. Whenever this last right parenthesis is encountered, a new card is read. For example,

```
      READ (5,130) A,B,C
130   FØRMAT (F10.0)
```

In this case there are *three* numbers to be read and the FØRMAT specifies that the number is to be found in columns 1–10. The computer will read 3 numbers, but from 3 separate cards. A will be read from columns 1–10 of the first card; B will be read from columns 1–10 of the next card; and C will come from columns 1–10 of the third card.

```
      READ (5,140) IA,IB,IC,ID,IE
140   FØRMAT (5X,2(I5,2X))
```

The values will be read from the cards as follows:

Card 1:   IA will be read from columns 6–10
          IB will be read from columns 13–17
Card 2:   IC will be read from columns 1–5

ID will be read from columns 8–12

Card 3:   IE will be read from columns 1–5

When the FØRMAT is repeated, only the 2(I5,2X) part of the FØRMAT is used.

```
      READ (5,150) K,P,Q,R,S
150   FØRMAT (I5,(F10.0,2(F5.0,10X)))
```

The values will be read from the cards as follows because the (F10.0,2(F5.0, 10X)) part of the FØRMAT is repeated.

Card 1:   K will be read from columns 1–5

P will be read from columns 6–15

Q will be read from columns 16–20

R will be read from columns 31–35

Card 2:   S will be read from columns 1–10

Multiple Records

A slash (/) may be used in a FØRMAT specification to indicate the end of an input record (that is, a data card).

Example A

```
      READ (5,100) A,B,C
100   FØRMAT (F10.0/F10.0/F10.0)
```

will accomplish the same purpose as

```
      READ (5,110) A,B,C
110   FØRMAT (F10.0)
```

The slash in the FØRMAT labeled 100 signals the end of a data card; it indicates that no more numbers are to be read from that card. Instead, the next number will be read from the next data card. The right parenthesis in the FØRMAT statement labeled 110 behaves the same as the slash in FØRMAT 100.

Example B

```
      READ (5,100) N,A,B,C
100   FØRMAT (I3/(F10.0))
```

The value of N is read from columns 1–3 of the first card. The slash indicates that no more values are to be read from the first card. Therefore, the value of A is read from columns 1–10 of the second card. The last right parenthesis is encountered, indicating the end of this record. Since there are more numbers to be read in, the F10.0 specification is repeated until B and C have been read in, each from a different data card. Altogether four data cards are read.

Example C

```
      READ (5,100) N,A,B,C,D
100   FØRMAT (I3/2(F10.0),F12.5)
```

Because the F10.0 specification enclosed in parentheses has a repetition factor of two, the values will be read from cards as follows:

Card 1: N will be read from columns 1–3
Card 2: A will be read from columns 1–10
         B will be read from columns 11–20
         C will be read from columns 21–32
Card 3: D will be read from columns 1–10

Example D

The first left parenthesis of a FØRMAT statement indicates the beginning of an input record. If the left parenthesis is immediately followed by a slash, a card will be skipped. Two consecutive slashes placed after a FØRMAT specification will also cause the computer to skip a card. In general, if not at the beginning of the FØRMAT, n consecutive slashes will cause $n - 1$ cards to be skipped.

```
      READ (5,100) A,B,ID
100   FØRMAT (/2F10.5//I3)
```

The FØRMAT above will cause the following cards to be processed.

Card 1: will be skipped
Card 2: value of A is read from columns 1–10
         value of B is read from columns 11–20
Card 3: will be skipped
Card 4: value of ID is read from columns 1–3

More on Input of Real Values

Example A

When a *real* value is punched on the card *without a decimal point* remember that:

1. Values should be right-adjusted in the field.
2. Blanks are interpreted as zeros.
3. The number of decimal places assigned to the value in storage is specified by the value of d in the Fw.d specification.

Figure 8.3

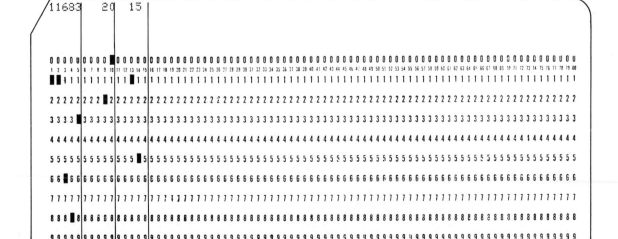

The following example will clarify these points:

```
      READ (5,100) X,Y,Z
100   FØRMAT (F5.2,2F5.0)
```

The FØRMAT specification F5.2 specifies that X is to have two decimal places. Therefore, the last two digits of the number 11683 are assumed to be the decimal digits and X = 116.83. The value for Y is 20 because it is right-adjusted in the field. The decimal point is assumed to be after the fifth character. The value for Z is 150 because blanks are interpreted as zeros and Z is not right-adjusted. A person who has lots of numbers to punch on a single card may eliminate punching the decimal points and in this way put more numbers on each card.

Example B

When a *real* constant is punched *with a decimal point* on the card, the number of decimal places indicated by the specification is ignored. The value stored will be exactly the number punched on the card.

```
      READ (5,100) Y
100   FØRMAT (F8.2)
```

Figure 8.4

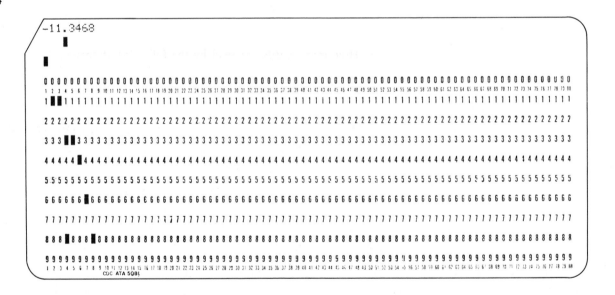

In this example, Y is supposed to contain only 2 decimal digits, but the number punched on the card has 4. The computer will ignore the 2 in the F8.2 specification and will read Y from the first 8 columns of the card (as usual) and will keep the four decimal places. Therefore, Y = −11.3468. This feature could be a convenience in punching real values, because when the decimal point is punched, it is not necessary to right-adjust the number in the field. With the statements

```
      READ (5,100) Z
100   FØRMAT (F10.0)
```

any of the following data cards could be used to assign the value of 3.1415 to Z.

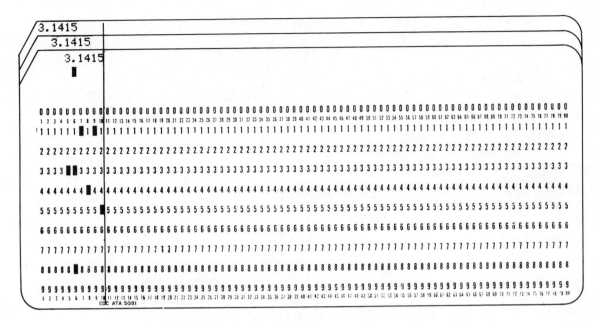

Figure 8.5

Exercises

1. The statement FØRMAT (3F12.4,2F12.5) specifies a total of _____ numbers per card.

2. The statement FØRMAT (12F6.2) specifies a total of _____ card columns.

3. How many cards are read by the following statements?

```
      READ  (5,100)  A,B,C,D,E
100   FØRMAT  (2F12.4)
```

4. Write a simpler FØRMAT that will accomplish the same as the given FØRMAT.

```
      READ  (5,10)  A,B,C,D,E,F,G,H,P,Q,R,S,T,V,W
10    FØRMAT  (3F25.8/4F20.8/4F20.8/4F20.8)
```

5. Write the appropriate input statements to read the following data card.

11.23	bbbbb1024	
W	K	

6. What are the values read for A, B, C, D, and N?

```
      READ  (5,20)  A,B,C,D,N
20    FØRMAT  (F7.2,F10.3,2F5.0,I1)
```

0123456789012345678901234567890b0123456789

7. The statements

> READ (5,30) A,B
> 30 FØRMAT (6F12.4)

will read through column _____ on the card.

8.3 WRITE Statements Using Simple Variables

Field Repetition

If two or more FØRMAT specifications are repeated successively, it is not necessary to list them. An integer constant preceding a specification indicates the number of times the specification is to be repeated. The following are equivalent statements:

> 100 FØRMAT (1H0,I3,I3,10X,F6.2,F6.2)
> 100 FØRMAT (1H0,2I3,10X,2F6.2)

Example

Suppose that in storage the variables have the following values:

$$KØUNT = 23$$
$$MAX = -100$$
$$VAL = 125.50$$
$$SUM1 = 47.88$$
$$SUM2 = -13.25$$

With the following WRITE statement and its FØRMAT statement:

> WRITE (6,200) KØUNT,MAX,VAL,SUM1,SUM2
> 200 FØRMAT (1H0,2I5,10X,3F10.2)

the following material is printed on the output page:

bbb23b−100bbbbbbbbbbbbbbb125.50bbbbb47.88bbbb−13.25

| I5 | I5 | 10X | F10.2 | F10.2 | F10.2 |

Group Repetition

A group of specifications may appear consecutively in a FØRMAT. To indicate repetition of the group of specifications, enclose the group in parentheses and precede it with an integer constant that indicates the number of times the group is to be repeated. The following statements are equivalent.

> 100 FØRMAT (10X,I3,2X,F10.2,I3,2X,F10.2,I3,2X,F10.2)
> 100 FØRMAT (10X,3(I3,2X,F10.2))

Example

Suppose that in storage the listed variables have the following values:

$$X = 1999.991$$
$$Y = -75.025$$

With the following WRITE statement and its FØRMAT statement:

```
      WRITE (6,200) X,Y
200   FØRMAT (1Hb,2(10X,F12.3))
```

the printout would look like this:

bbbbbbbbbbbbbb1999.991bbbbbbbbbbbbbb−75.025

    10X   F12.3   10X   F12.3

Relationship of Output List Size and Format Statement

We will look at several examples in which the number of variable names in the output list is not equal to the number of field specifications in the FØRMAT statement. (The X- and H-field specifications are not counted because values are not printed by these specifications.)

Example A

The number of variables in the output list is *less than* the number of specifications in the FØRMAT.

When all the variables in the output list have been printed, the remaining field specifications are ignored.

```
      WRITE (6,100) A
100   FØRMAT (1H0,3F10.2)
```

According to the FØRMAT labeled 100, *three* numbers could be printed on the output page. Only the value of A will be printed, because the WRITE statement says to write just the value of A.

Example B

The number of variables in the output list is *greater than* the number of specifications in the FØRMAT statement.

At execution time when the computer encounters the last right parenthesis of the FØRMAT statement the computer searches the FØRMAT statement from right to left until it finds the next right parenthesis. The left parenthesis which matches this right parenthesis marks the beginning of the portion of the FØRMAT which will be repeated until the entire output list is written. Any group repetition number preceding the left parenthesis will be used. If there is no right parenthesis found when the FØRMAT is searched, then the entire FØRMAT will be repeated. The last right parenthesis indicates the end of a unit record of output. Whenever this last right parenthesis is encountered a new line is printed. The following example and examples *b* and *c* in "Multiple Records" of section 8.3 (see below) illustrate the repetition of a FØRMAT specification.

```
        WRITE  (6,100)  X,Y,Z,Q
100   FØRMAT  (1Hb,10X,F12.3)
```

The WRITE statement says to write 4 numbers, but the FØRMAT statement has only one output specification, F12.3. In this case the entire FØRMAT is used until all numbers are printed. Each will be written on a separate line, as shown in the following diagram where an X represents a digit.

```
                    XXXXXXXX.XXX

                    XXXXXXXX.XXX

                    XXXXXXXX.XXX

                    XXXXXXXX.XXX
```

Multiple Records

A slash (/) may be used in a FØRMAT specification to indicate the end of a unit record of output (that is, a printed line).

Example A

```
        WRITE  (6,200)
200   FØRMAT    (1H1,62X,13HSTØCKbSUMMARY/1H0,50X,5HSTØCK,
        26X,5HPRICE)
```

With this FØRMAT specification, the computer will write two lines: one at the top of a page, and the next double-spaced below it. *Each new line must have its own carriage control.*

We can also write the above example as

```
        WRITE  (6,200)
200   FØRMAT  (1H1,62X,13HSTØCKbSUMMARY)
        WRITE  (6,205)
205   FØRMAT  (1H0,50X,5HSTØCK,26X,5HPRICE)
```

When we wish to print only Hollerith characters as in the above examples, we do not have a list in the WRITE statement.

Example B

```
        WRITE  (6,200)  N,A,B,C
200   FØRMAT  (1H1,2X,I3/(5X,F10.2))
```

With this FØRMAT the first line will be at the top of a page. Then, two spaces are skipped and the value for N is printed. The slash indicates the end of that line. On the new line 4 spaces are skipped (here we are using a blank for carriage control) and then the value for A is printed. Since there are more items in the output list, the (5X,F10.2) specification in the FØRMAT is repeated. In the following diagram of the output each x represents a digit. The carriage control characters are included in the diagram, but would *not* appear on the printed page.

↓ carriage control

```
value of N →   1  bbxxx
value of A →   b  bbbbxxxxxxx.xx
value of B →   b  bbbbxxxxxxx.xx
value of C →   b  bbbbxxxxxxx.xx
```

Example C

```
      WRITE  (6,100)  X,Y,Z,SUM
100   FØRMAT  ((10X,F10.2)///4X,6HSUMb=b,F10.2)
```

Because there is no 3 preceding the (10X,F10.2) in FØRMAT 100, the computer will write the value of X; then it will write the value of Y following the word SUM; next, it will write Z's value; and it will write the value of SUM after the word SUM. The output page will look as follows:

```
line 1     bbbbbbbbbbxxxxxxx.xx
line 2
line 3
line 4     bbbSUMb=byyyyyyy.yy
line 5     bbbbbbbbbbzzzzzzz.zz
line 6
line 7
line 8     bbbSUMb=bsssssss.ss
```

The x represents the value of the variable X. Similarly, y represents the value of Y, z the value of Z, and s the value of SUM.

Example D

The first left parenthesis of a FØRMAT statement indicates the beginning of a record. If the left parenthesis is immediately followed by a slash, a line will be skipped. Two consecutive slashes placed after a FØRMAT specification instruct the computer to skip a line. In general, if not at the beginning of the FØRMAT, n consecutive slashes will cause the printer to skip $n - 1$ lines.

```
      WRITE  (6,200)  I,K,ANS
200   FØRMAT  (/5X,2I10///10X,F6.1)
```

instructs the computer to print out the values in the following manner:

```
line 1     will be skipped
line 2     values for I and K will be printed
line 3     will be skipped
line 4     will be skipped
line 5     value for ANS will be printed
```

More on Output of Real Values

The number of decimal places printed for a real value depends on the value of d given in Fw.d specification. We will consider several examples in which X = 3.14159 is in storage.

Example A

```
      WRITE  (6,200)  X
200   FØRMAT  (1H1,F10.5)
```

The output page will be

> bbb3.14159
>
> F10.5

Example B

```
      WRITE  (6,210)  X
210   FØRMAT  (1H1,F10.4)
```

The output page will be

> bbbb3.1416
>
> F10.4

Since we ask for only 4 decimal places, the computer will look at the fifth decimal and will round off the number. The following example will further illustrate machine round off.

```
      WRITE  (6,220)  X
220   FØRMAT  (1H1,F10.2)
```

The output page will be

> bbbbbb3.14
>
> F10.2

Example C

```
      WRITE  (6,230)  X
230   FØRMAT  (1H1,F10.0)
```

The output page will be

> bbbbbbbb3.
>
> F10.0

When no decimal places are specified ($d = 0$), then only the whole part of the number followed by a decimal point is printed. Machine round off will still take place, as the following example shows.

In storage Y = 4.8

```
        WRITE (6,240) Y
240  FØRMAT (1H1,F10.0)
```

The output page will be

bbbbbbbb5.

F10.0

Exercises

1. In storage A = −10.5, B = 45.3, K = 358. Show the output produced by the following statements. Use a "b" to indicate a blank space.

```
        WRITE (6,20) A,B,K
20  FØRMAT (1H0,2F5.1,I9)
```

2. Write output statements to print the value stored in ITEMP and the following sentence at the top of a new page. Allow 3 places for printing ITEMP.

THE HIGH FOR TODAY IS (the value for ITEMP should be printed here) DEGREES

3. Write statements for printing the values of A, B, C, and D on two separate lines. Allow a maximum of 10 spaces for each number with 3 decimal places. The printout does *not* need to start a new page. The spacing on the lines should be as follows:

first line: skip 10 spaces, print the value of A, skip 10 spaces, print the value of B.

second line: skip 10 spaces, print the value of C, skip 10 spaces, print the value of D.

4. Write statements to print the values of I, J, and K, allowing 8 places for printing each variable. They should be printed on the indicated lines. The printout does not need to start on a new page.

first line: value for I
third line: value for J
fifth line: value for K

5. Write statements for printing the values of N, A, B, C, and D. Allow a maximum of 11 spaces for each number with 2 decimal places. Allow 10 spaces for printing the value of N. The statements should accomplish the following:

1. Go to the top of a new page, skip 20 spaces, and print the value of N.
2. Skip 5 lines.
3. Double space, skip 10 spaces, and print the value of A.

4. Double space, skip 10 spaces, and print the value of B.
5. Double space, skip 10 spaces, and print the value of C.
6. Double space, skip 10 spaces, and print the value of D.

Special Terms

1. *field repetition*
2. *FØRMAT specification*
3. *group repetition*
4. *input record*
5. *machine round off*
6. *output record*
7. *right-adjusted*

Chapter 9

Single Subscripted Variables

9.1 Introduction

In our previous programs we have

1. read a set of data values
2. performed the required computations for the problem with the values just read
3. repeated steps 1 and 2 if there were more data; otherwise, we have printed the result.

Not all problems can be arranged to follow the above pattern. Sometimes, because of the nature of the problem, we must read in all the data before the computer can carry out any computations. In other problems which have large amounts of data, we must handle the data efficiently. We will study two similar problems in this section. The first one finds the largest of three numbers; the second one finds the largest of a group of 18 numbers. We will use **simple variables** (variables which are not subscripted) to solve the first problem, and introduce subscripted variables in the solution to the second problem. Even though the first problem would be easier to solve by hand than by computer, we have chosen it as an introduction to the general solution of finding the largest number in a group.

Example 1

The TV weather girl wants to find the highest temperature of the day. She gets a report with the high temperature from 3 different weather stations. Our job is to write a program that will find the highest (largest) of the three temperatures. The printout should consist of the weather station number and the temperature. All the temperatures are different. The weather girl will punch the data as follows:

card 1:	columns 1–3	temperature from station 1
card 2:	columns 1–3	temperature from station 2
card 3:	columns 1–3	temperature from station 3

In writing the flowchart, we label ST1, the temperature from weather station 1, and ST2 and ST3 the temperature from stations 2 and 3, respectively. After reading just the first temperature we cannot tell if it is the highest, so we will read all 3 temperatures and then tell the computer how to find the largest. In the complete flowchart that follows, carefully study the decision boxes. Go through the flowchart with some sample values in order to understand the logic fully.

The FORTRAN program for the flowchart is:

```
C       STATIØN WXYZ–TV WEATHER REPØRT
C       THIS PRØGRAM FINDS THE HIGHEST TEMPERATURE
C       REPØRTED BY 3 WEATHER STATIØNS
C
C       READ THREE TEMPERATURE VALUES
        READ (5,100) ST1,ST2,ST3
100     FØRMAT  (F3.0)
C
```

```
         IF  (ST1 .GT. ST2)  GØ TØ 10
         IF  (ST2 .GT. ST3)   GØ TØ 40
         GØ TØ 20
     10  IF  (ST1 .GT. ST3) GØ TØ 30
C
     20  WRITE  (6,400) ST3
         GØ TØ 50
     30  WRITE  (6,200) ST1
         GØ TØ 50
     40  WRITE  (6,300) ST2
    200  FØRMAT  (1H0,60X,13HSTATIØNbNØ.b1,5X,F4.0)
    300  FØRMAT  (1H0,60X,13HSTATIØNbNØ.b2,5X,F4.0)
    400  FØRMAT  (1H0,60X,13HSTATIØNbNØ.b3,5X,F4.0)
     50  STØP
         END
```

Figure 9.1 Flowchart for Finding the Highest of Three Temperatures

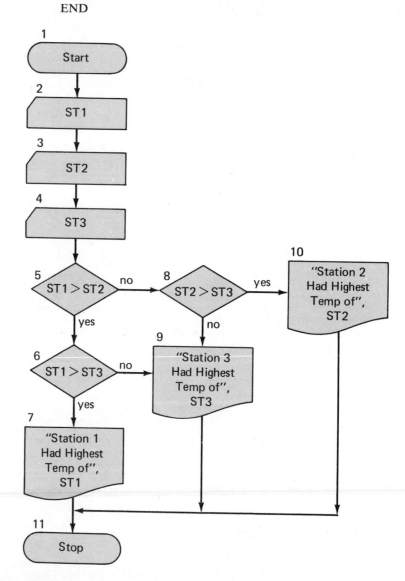

Example 2

The TV weather girl wishes to expand the program in the previous example. She now has temperatures from 18 different weather stations throughout the state, and wants to know the highest of these. The printout should say "THE HIGHEST TEMPERATURE IS" with the answer following it. She will punch the data as follows, with one card for each station.

Weather station number   columns   1–5
Temperature   columns   11–13

First, we try to expand the flowchart in Figure 9.1 so that we can find the highest of the 18 temperatures. One main difficulty stands out: *how many decision boxes will we need in order to find the highest temperature?* It would be difficult to imagine the number of decisions needed to enlarge upon the method used in Figure 9.1. Therefore, let us find a different procedure to use in our flowchart.

Instead of naming the temperatures T1, T2, T3, T4, and so on, let us picture the temperatures as a collection of numbers all with the same name T. How do we tell these numbers apart? We use a subscript to point to specific numbers in the collection. Mathematically, the name of the first temperature would be written as t_1 or T_1. The subscript is the small number written below the name. But in FORTRAN, the first temperature would be written T(1); the subscript is enclosed in parentheses. The mathematical notation compared to FORTRAN notation for the temperatures follows.

Table 9.1

Mathematical Notation	FORTRAN Notation
t_1	T(1)
t_2	T(2)
t_3	T(3)
.	.
.	.
.	.
t_{18}	T(18)

In FORTRAN the collection of values which has the same name and uses a subscript to refer to separate items in the group is called an **array**. A **subscript** is written in parentheses following the name of the array. In FORTRAN the variable name given to an array is called a **subscripted variable**. An **array element** is one item from an array. Variables in ANSI FORTRAN may have one, two, or three subscripts. For example, T(1) is a single subscripted variable; X(1,3) is a double subscripted variable; Z(2,4,8) is a triple subscripted variable. An array which has only one subscript is called a **one-dimensional array**; an array with two subscripts is a **two-dimensional array**; an array with three subscripts is a **three-dimensional array**. We will discuss two- and three-dimensional arrays in Chapter 11.

For our problem, T is the name of the array. Elements in the array are called T(1), T(2), . . . , T(18). To the computer, T(1) is the first item in the array, T(2) is the second item, and so on. The name T(1) is not the same as T1; the first name is a subscripted variable and the second one is a simple variable.

Now that we have named the variables, let us develop a method which will find the highest temperature. Let us compare each temperature to some value called HIGH. At the end of the process, we want HIGH to contain the highest of all the temperatures. Initially, we can let HIGH take on the value of T(1). Then, we can compare T(2) with HIGH. If T(2) is greater than HIGH, we want to replace the value of HIGH with the value of T(2). Otherwise, HIGH will still be the larger of the first two temperatures. Then, compare T(3) and HIGH. If T(3) is larger, change the value of HIGH. Otherwise, go on and compare T(4) with HIGH. We can continue this process until we have compared the 18th temperature to HIGH. At the end, HIGH contains the largest temperature.

The flowchart in Figure 9.2 illustrates the above process.

This flowchart seems to be no better than what we were trying to avoid. However, a pattern does appear in our flowchart. The subscript is the only thing that changes from one box to another. Let us substitute an *integer* variable for the numerical subscript. We can initialize this variable name at 2, increase it by 1, and repeat the process until the value of the subscript has exceeded 18. Our final flowchart, in Figure 9.3, incorporates this technique, using a loop to determine the highest temperature. Also, we will print out the array T after the program has read it in to find out if the program read in the temperatures correctly.

Now that the flowchart is complete, choose some sample numbers and trace through the flowchart. We will not include the trace here, but will proceed to convert the flowchart into FORTRAN.

First of all we must tell the compiler that T is a subscripted variable and that 18 storage locations should be reserved for the array. This is done in a DIMENSIØN statement.

DIMENSIØN T(18)

It tells the compiler that there will be variables named T(1), T(2), T(3), and so on through T(18). Pictorially, in the computer's memory we would have

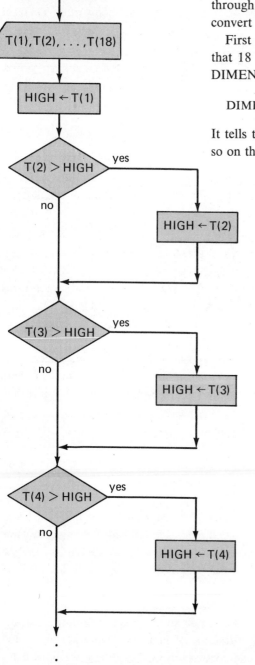

Figure 9.2 Process for Finding Highest Temperature in the Array

T(1)

T(2)

T(3)

.   .

.   .

.   .

T(18)

Section 9.2 gives detailed information about the DIMENSIØN statement.

Now that the computer knows that T is an array, we may proceed with box 2 of the flowchart in Figure 9.3 and write the following instructions to read in the array.

```
READ  (5,10)  T(1)
READ  (5,10)  T(2)
READ  (5,10)  T(3)
              .
              .
              .
READ  (5,10)  T(17)
READ  (5,10)  T(18)
10    FØRMAT  (10X,F3.0)
```

Of course we would really include 18 separate READ statements. We cannot write . . . and expect the computer to know that we intend to have all 18 cards read. Instead of having the 18 separate READ statements, we could have just one which would be punched on two cards. We are using the period to indicate the continuation of the first card. We have included extra spaces after the period to emphasize that this is a continued statement.

```
READ  (5,10)  T(1),T(2),T(3),T(4),T(5),T(6),T(7),T(8),T(9),
      T(10),T(11),T(12),T(13),T(14),T(15),T(16),T(17),T(18)
```

By now, you must be thinking that all this is ridiculous. Subscripted variables seem to have no advantages except that the procedure for finding the highest temperature has been shortened.

Let us examine the set of 18 READ statements and see if we can notice any similarities. The only thing that changes in the above statements is the number that refers to the different temperatures. Instead of using a specific number, let us use an INTEGER variable name, like K, and let it assume values from 1 to 18. That is, we initialize K at 1, then we read $T(K)$, which would really be $T(1)$; then we increment K by 1 so that K equals 2 and then we read $T(K)$, which would be $T(2)$; and so on, for all values of K less than or equal to 18. The following flowchart segment describes this looping process.

Figure 9.3 Final Flowchart for Finding the Highest Temperature

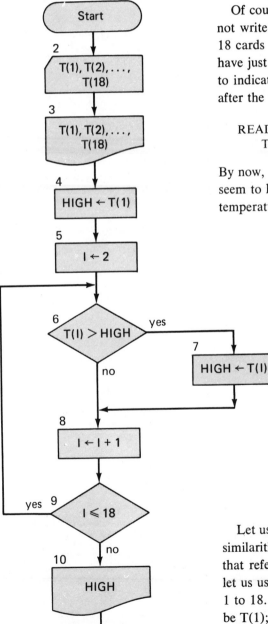

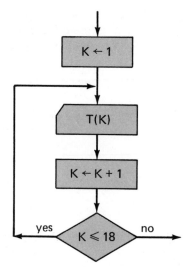

The FORTRAN statements equivalent to the flowchart would be

```
     K = 1
  1  READ (5,10) T(K)
     K = K + 1
     IF (K .LE. 18) GØ TØ 1
           .
           .
           .
```

Our program can use the method of input described above. However, we will show another way that is somewhat simpler, but applicable only in certain cases.

For a program in which the size of the array that we want to read is exactly the size dimensioned, the following form of the READ statement will read all values automatically. In our example, because T has been dimensioned at 18, the following READ statement will read all 18 values. The first value is still stored in T(1), the second in T(2), the third in T(3), and so on.

```
     READ (5,10) T
```

Since we punched the numbers one per card, the FØRMAT statement would be

```
  10 FØRMAT (10X,F3.0)
```

We can do the output of the array in a similar manner. The complete FORTRAN program is:

```
C        STATIØN WXYZ–TV WEATHER REPØRT
C        THIS PRØGRAM FINDS THE HIGHEST
C        TEMPERATURE FRØM 18 WEATHER STATIØNS
C        STØRAGE ALLØCATIØN
         DIMENSIØN T(18)
C
C        INPUT ØF ALL ITEMS IN THE T ARRAY
         READ (5,10) T
  10     FØRMAT (10X,F3.0)
C        CHECK INPUT VALUES
         WRITE (6,20) T
  20     FØRMAT (1H1,5X,10HINPUTbDATA///(5X,F4.0))
C        INITIALIZE HIGH
```

```
          HIGH = T(1)
C
C      CHECK T ARRAY VALUES WITH VALUE
C      STØRED IN HIGH
C      INITIALIZE INDEX I
          I = 2
   30  IF (T(I) .GT. HIGH) HIGH = T(I)
C      INCREMENT AND CHECK INDEX I VALUE
          I = I + 1
          IF (I .LE.18) GØ TØ 30
C      WHEN ALL T ARRAY VALUES HAVE BEEN
C      CØMPARED, HIGH CØNTAINS THE HIGHEST
C      TEMPERATURE
C
C      WRITE ØUT VALUE STØRED IN HIGH
C
          WRITE (6,40) HIGH
   40  FØRMAT (1H1,40X,27HTHEbHIGHESTbTEMPERATUREbISb,
          F4.0)
          STØP
          END
```

9.2 DIMENSIØN Statement

The DIMENSIØN statement tells the compiler how many storage locations to reserve for each array.

The DIMENSIØN statement is a **specification statement,** a non-executable statement which gives information to the compiler about the variables in the program.

The general form of the DIMENSIØN statement is

DIMENSIØN $a_1(n_1), a_2(n_2), \ldots, a_k(n_k)$

where a is the name of an array

         n is an unsigned integer constant

The expression $a(n)$ is called an **array declarator** because it tells the number of storage locations to be reserved for the array a. The *dimension* or size of the array a is the number n. For example,

DIMENSIØN A(3),IX(4)

This statement reserves a total of 7 locations for the two arrays A and IX. We may picture memory as:

A(1)

A(2)

A(3)

IX(1)

IX(2)

IX(3)

IX(4)

Rules for the Use of the DIMENSIØN Statement

1. A program may contain more than one DIMENSIØN statement.
2. Each subscripted variable must appear in one and only one DIMENSIØN statement.
3. The DIMENSIØN statement(s) must precede the first executable statement of the program.
4. Control cannot be transferred to a DIMENSIØN statement.
5. Array declarators must be separated by commas.
6. Array names must be followed by parentheses enclosing the unsigned integer constant that gives the maximum size of the subscript.
7. During execution the value of a subscript must not exceed the size of the array.
8. In a program the value of a subscript may be less than or equal to the n specified in the DIMENSIØN statement, but it cannot be less than or equal to zero.

Subscript Expressions

In our previous example, we used either an integer constant or an integer variable for the subscript. Other expressions are allowed for the subscript of an array. In the complete list of expressions which follow, the constants must be *integer* constants and the variables *integer* variables.

Allowable Subscript Expressions	Examples
constant	35
variable	K
variable + constant	$I + 2$
variable − constant	$J - 5$
constant * variable	$2 * M$
constant * variable + constant	$2 * N + 1$
constant * variable − constant	$2 * N - 1$

For example, $I + J$ is *not* a valid subscript expression.

The value of a subscript expression must be greater than zero and may not exceed the dimension of the array.

Possible Sources of Program Errors for Subscript Expressions

1. negative or zero subscript
2. subscript which exceeds the dimension of the array
3. when an array is dimensioned for a maximum of n elements and a particular set of data uses only m of these ($m < n$), an error occurs when the value of a subscript inadvertently assumes a value between m and n

If an array B is dimensioned by the following statement

DIMENSIØN B(100)

then the subscript for B must always be an integer between 1 and 100. Because computers and compilers vary, it is hard to predict what type of error message the computer would print if a program tries to use a subscript which is not between 1 and the size of the array. We suggest that you insert many WRITE statements in a program which may have a subscript error, so that the computer will print out the values of the subscripts at different points of the program. This way, you may be able to spot the error.

Example A

The value of the subscript was never defined and therefore caused an error.

```
DIMENSIØN   X(10)
Y = X(I)
        .
        .
        .
```

Example B

The value of the subscript was zero.

```
DIMENSIØN  NUM(30)
I = 1
IF (NUM(I) .GT. NUM(I–1)) GØ TØ 10
        .
        .
        .
```

Example C

The value of the subscript started out at 1, but was changed during execution so that it exceeded the dimension of the array.

```
        DIMENSIØN  MØ(150)
        J = 1
10      MØ(J) = 0
        J = J + 1
        IF (J .LE. 200) GØ TØ 10
```

9.3 Type Statement

A *type* statement in a program declares what kind of value a variable will have. Normally the variable MØNEY is an *integer* value because it begins with the letter M. However, a programmer may wish to use the name MØNEY for a dollars and cents quantity, a *real* value. To make MØNEY a *real* variable, use the following *type* statement.

```
REAL MØNEY
```

Similarly, if we want always to use CØUNT as an integer value, the following *type* statement would declare CØUNT an *integer* variable, even though it begins with the letter C.

```
INTEGER CØUNT
```

FORTRAN programs may also use LØGICAL, CØMPLEX, and DØUBLE PRECISIØN variables which are declared in *type* statements. We will discuss these variables in Chapter 13, and we will consider the REAL and IN–TEGER *type* statements in this section.

The general forms of these statements are:

```
REAL list
INTEGER list
```

where   list   consists of variable names, array names, array declarators, and/
or programmer supplied function names (discussed in Chapter
12).

Rules for the Use of *Type* Statements

1. All items in the list are separated by commas. If there is only one item, no comma is necessary.
2. A *type* statement is non-executable and is a specification statement.
3. A *type* statement must precede all executable statements in the program.

Suppose we have an array named SCØRE which we wish to declare *integer* and an array LENGTH which we wish to make *real*. SCØRE is an array of 300 items and LENGTH, 125 items. We can make an entire array *real* or *integer* in one of two ways.

```
Method 1:    DIMENSIØN SCØRE(300), LENGTH(125)
             INTEGER SCØRE
             REAL LENGTH
Method 2:    INTEGER SCØRE(300)
             REAL LENGTH(125)
```

In Method 2, the *type* statements accomplish two purposes: they change the *type* of the array, and they dimension the array. An array cannot be dimensioned twice. For example,

```
DIMENSIØN  TEMP(30)
INTEGER  TEMP(30)
```
                              is *not* allowed

The DIMENSIØN TEMP(30) should be omitted.
   Including statements such as

```
REAL  X,Y
INTEGER  MØNEY,ITEM,JNØ
```

is not necessary, but it is not wrong. Sometimes a programmer who wants to emphasize that X and Y are names where real numbers are stored will include such a statement. On the other hand,

```
REAL Z̸(200)
```

serves the purpose of dimensioning Z̸.

9.4 More on One-dimensional Arrays

In this section we will discuss two problems where it is advantageous to use subscripted variables. We will flowchart the solution to each problem and then write the program in FORTRAN. We will also introduce a new FØRMAT specification, the A-field, which we will use to read and write a person's name.

Problem 1

We have a deck of cards containing the following information:

student's name	columns 1–20
test score 1	31–33
test score 2	34–36
test score 3	37–39
test score 4	40–42
test score 5	43–45
test score 6	46–48
test score 7	49–51
test score 8	52–54
test score 9	55–57
test score 10	58–60

The dummy data card in the deck has test score 1 equal to −99.

We want to print a list of students' names and their average test scores, as in the following diagram.

Name	Average
John Little	82.3
Mary Stevens	68.7
Bill Bones	86.5

The average will be printed with one decimal place. The output will have a title and will start on a new page.

Let us now decide what variable names to use in the flowchart and in the program. We could name the first score A, the second one B, the third C, and so on. We name the last two scores P and Q instead of I and J to prevent mixed modes. The average (AVG) could be computed by saying

$$AVG = (A+B+C+D+E+F+G+H+P+Q)/10.0$$

This method does not seem very complicated, but it could become involved if there were 20 or 25 test scores instead of just 10. We would rather develop a more general method—one which would average 10 scores, but could easily be changed to average a different amount. The problem in section 3.2 found the average by reading a number, adding it to the sum, reading another number, adding it, and continuing this process until all numbers were read. The main difference between this problem and that one is the form of the data. In this problem one card contains all the numbers; in the previous one, each number was on a separate card. The number read was named VALUE. After it was added to SUM, a new card was read. This number replaced the previous number stored in VALUE. Since the 10 scores that we want to average in this problem are on one card, all of them must be read at one time. This means that each number must have a different name. Let us call the entire group of scores, SCØRE, and differentiate the items with a subscript. Therefore, the names of the test scores will be SCØRE(1), SCØRE(2), SCØRE(3), SCØRE(4), SCØRE(5), SCØRE(6), SCØRE(7), SCØRE(8), SCØRE(9), and

SCØRE(10). Using the method in section 3.2, our procedure becomes the one shown in the flowchart in Figure 9.4.

Figure 9.4 Initial Method for Summing Scores and Computing Average

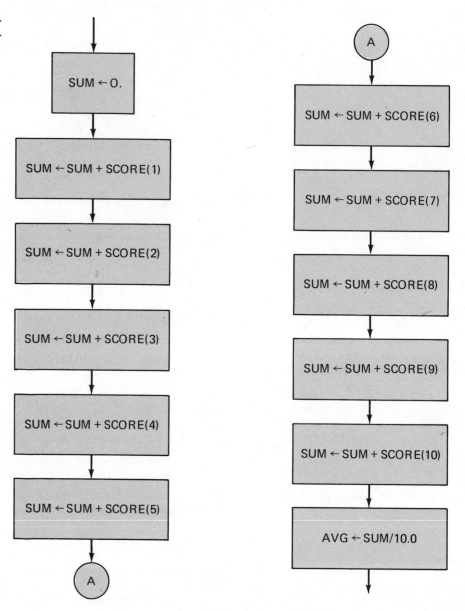

The use of subscripts does not seem to have improved our method; instead, it has gotten longer. Perhaps we can find some way to shorten these steps. Are there any similarities in any of the flowchart commands? Most of them are identical, except for the subscript. The subscript starts at 1, changes by 1 from step to step, and has a maximum value of 10. We know that a subscript does not have to be a number; it may be a variable name, as long as it is an integer. This means that we could have written

$$\text{SUM} \leftarrow \text{SUM} + \text{SCORE(I)}$$

What does I equal? At the moment it doesn't have any value, but we do want it to be 1 initially.

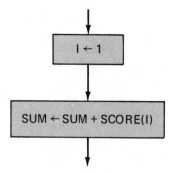

These commands are identical to the single command

$$SUM \leftarrow SUM + SCORE(1)$$

However, we can increase I by one and loop back to add on the next number.

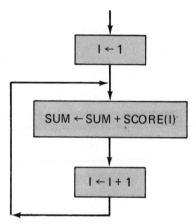

This new procedure will allow us to accomplish many of the things which were in our flowchart of the original procedure, but the new procedure condenses the original one. But is there a way to stop adding? No, there isn't. The above example is a **never-ending loop.** We want to quit after we have added SCØRE(10) to SUM. In other words, if I is larger than 10, we want to leave the loop. This exit is shown in the following flowchart segment which we will incorporate in our final flowchart.

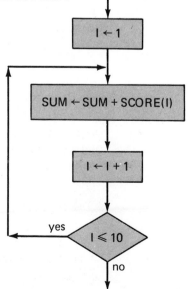

We could have checked the value of I before adding one, as in the following diagram:

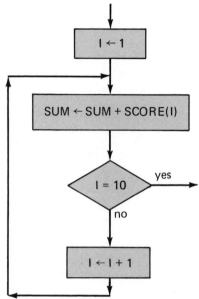

We will now write the flowchart for the entire problem. Note in Figure 9.5 that the flowchart contains two loops—one inside the other. The inside loop sums the 10 scores and the outer loop computes the average for many students. Also note that both loops have a way of terminating so that the computer will not loop forever.

The flowchart in Figure 9.5 initializes SUM at zero after a card has been read. What would happen if box 5 (where SUM is zeroed) had been placed outside the biggest loop in the flowchart, say between box 1 and box 2? To see what affect, if any, this change would have, let us imagine that the first person's card has just been read, the scores have been totaled and SUM = 783. Then box 10 computes AVG = 78.3. After printing the student's name and average, the flowchart takes us to box 3 to read another card. Let us assume that SCØRE(1) on this card is 90. Therefore, after setting I to 1, we add SCØRE(1) to SUM and obtain a new value of SUM. This means that we would have SUM = 783 + 90 = 873, after adding just one score to the sum. The second student's average will *not* be computed correctly unless the SUM is zeroed after a new student's card is read.

In our problem we want to read and then print students' names. This means that our data cards will contain alphabetic characters, and we cannot use either the F-field or I-field specification in the FØRMAT. Those specifications are strictly used with numerical values. In order to write a name punched on a card, we must first read the name and store it in memory. Then we can instruct the computer to write the name that is in memory.

The maximum number of characters which can be stored in one memory location varies from one computer to another.[1] In this book we will write programs which store only 4 characters in one memory location. Then our programs may be run on a computer which can store 4 characters per memory location or on one which can store 10 characters per memory location.

The student's name in this problem is 20 characters long. Thus, we need to divide the name into five parts so that we may store it in the computer.

---

[1] On the IBM 360 and IBM 370 computers, the maximum is 4; on the CDC 6000 Series and CDC CYBER 70 computers the maximum is 10.

Figure 9.5 Final Flowchart for Averaging Ten Scores

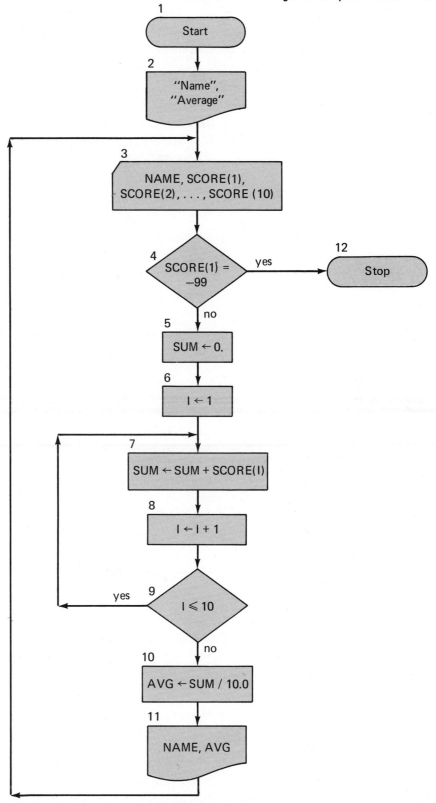

These five parts will be the first 4 characters, the second 4 characters, the third 4 characters, the fourth 4 characters, and the last 4 characters. We could use the variables NAMEA, NAMEB, NAMEC, NAMED, NAMEE to represent the five parts of the name or we could use subscripts and call them NAME(1), NAME(2), NAME(3), NAME(4), and NAME(5). The FØRMAT specification used for reading characters is the A-field.

For the problem we have just flowcharted, the FØRMAT for the input cards would be

300 FØRMAT (5A4,10X,10I3)

For example, suppose the computer reads the following data card using the FØRMAT above.

JACQUELINEbSHØEMAKERbbbbbbbbbb70

If the characters of the name are stored in locations NAME(1), NAME(2), NAME(3), NAME(4), and NAME(5), then memory contains

NAME(1)	JACQ
NAME(2)	UELI
NAME(3)	NEbS
NAME(4)	HØEM
NAME(5)	AKER

The general form of the A-field specification is

nAw

where n is the number of times the field is to be repeated. If n is 1, it may be omitted.

   w is the width of the field (number of characters stored in one memory location). The maximum size of w will vary with different computers.

Exercises

1. What should be changed in the flowchart of Figure 9.5 so that 100 scores could be averaged?

2. Write the FORTRAN program for the flowchart in Figure 9.5.

Problem 2

A city is divided into 20 districts. We wish to find the number of students in each district and the total number of students in the city. We are given one card for each student in the city. The dummy data card has a district number of 99. The format of these cards is:

name	columns	1–20
sex		21
district number		23–24
address		26–40

The printout should be a list of district numbers and the number of students in that district. The total number of students in the city should also be printed.

Let us now choose the names to use in solving the problem. From the data cards we need only one item—the district number, which we name NDIST. We will calculate 20 district totals: DIST(1), DIST(2), . . . ,DIST(20); and a city total: CITY. This means that DIST(1) will contain the number of students in district 1; DIST(2) will be the number of students in district 2; and so on. We begin the solution with a rough flowchart in Figure 9.6.

Figure 9.6 Rough Flowchart for Finding District and City Totals

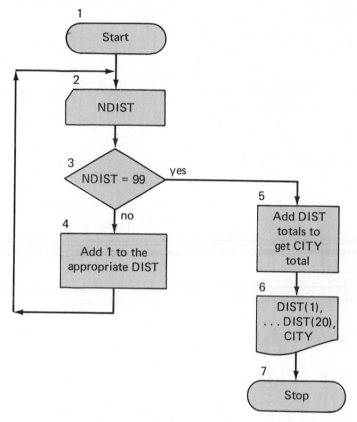

What is meant by "appropriate DIST" in the flowchart? If the student whose card is read lives in district 1, then 1 should be added to DIST(1). If he lives in district 3, 1 should be added to DIST(3), and so on. The district number is called NDIST. Therefore, if a child lives in district NDIST, 1 should be added to DIST(NDIST).

After all the cards have been read, we compute CITY in a manner similar to the one used in Figure 9.5, where numbers were added before computing an average.

Is there anything else which we did not include in the flowchart? We have not initialized the 20 DIST counters or the CITY counter. We have added these changes to the detailed flowchart in Figure 9.7 which contains three separate loops. The first loop initializes to zero the 20 district counters. The second loop counts the number of students in each district. The third loop computes the total number of students in the city.

The names we chose are *real* names, yet in this problem all numbers computed are *integers*. Rather than changing the names to ones like IDIST or ICITY, we will insert a *type* statement to make the variables DIST and CITY *integers*.

We would like to print out something like the following:

DISTRICT	NO. OF STUDENTS
1	350
2	675
3	408
4	1012
.	.
.	.
.	.

Figure 9.7 Detailed Flowchart for Finding District and City Totals

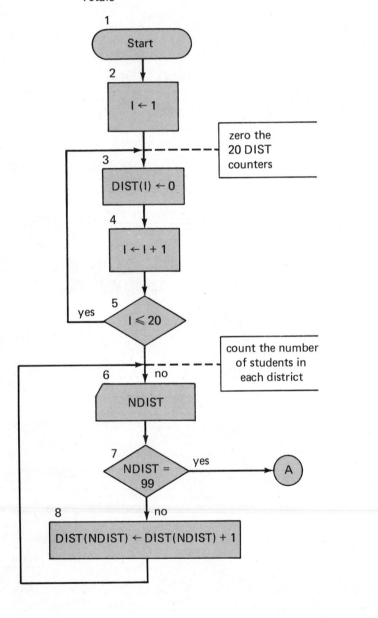

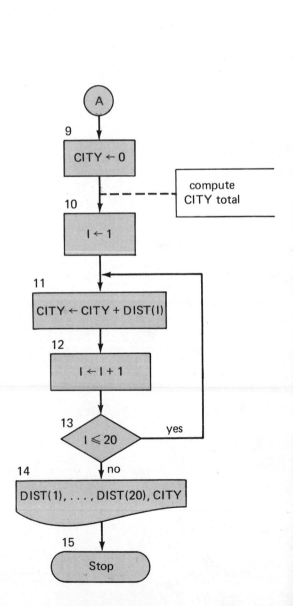

Our flowchart box 14 in Figure 9.7 does not show in detail the necessary steps for our printout. The following flowchart segment depicts an easy way to print the headings, the district number and the number of students in that district. We will use this method in our program.

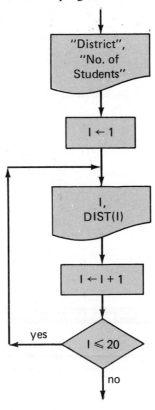

Here is the complete program.

```
C        THIS PRØGRAM CØMPUTES THE TØTAL NUMBER ØF
C        STUDENTS IN EACH DISTRICT AND THE TØTAL
C        NUMBER ØF STUDENTS IN THE CITY.
C
         DIMENSIØN DIST(20)
         INTEGER CITY,DIST
         I = 1
C        ZERØ THE 20 DISTRICT CØUNTERS
    10   DIST(I) = 0
         I = I + 1
         IF (I .LE. 20) GØ TØ 10
C        CØMPUTE THE DISTRICT TØTALS
    20   READ (5,100) NDIST
   100   FØRMAT (22X,I2)
         IF (NDIST .EQ. 99) GØ TØ 40
    30   DIST(NDIST) = DIST(NDIST) + 1
         GØ TØ 20
    40   CITY = 0
         I = 1
C        CØMPUTE THE CITY TØTAL
    50   CITY = CITY + DIST(I)
         I = I + 1
         IF (I. LE. 20) GØ TØ 50
         WRITE (6,110)
         I = 1
    60   WRITE (6,120) I,DIST(I)
```

```
                    I = I + 1
                    IF (I .LE. 20) GØ TØ 60
                    WRITE (6,130) CITY
      110   FØRMAT  (1H1,20X,8HDISTRICT,10X,15HNØ.bØFbSTUDENTS)
      120   FØRMAT  (1H0,22X,I3,20X,I6)
      130   FØRMAT  (1H0,20X,13HCITYbTØTALb=b,I6)
                    STØP
                    END
```

9.5 Input and Output of One-dimensional Arrays

There are three cases to consider when reading and writing arrays.

1. The exact number of items in the array is known before the program is written.
2. The exact number of items in the array must be counted by the program.
3. The exact number of items is variable and it is read in as part of the data.

Case 1

If the exact number of items in the array is known, the array can be dimensioned at that number. If we wish to input or output the array, we use just the name of the array in the READ or WRITE statement and all elements in the array are read or printed. For example,

```
            DIMENSIØN A(100)
            READ (5,10) A
      10    FØRMAT (F10.3)
            WRITE (6,20) A
      20    FØRMAT (1H0,10F12.3)
```

The READ statement reads one number from each of 100 cards. The WRITE statement prints 10 numbers per line. The order in which the variables are referenced is A(1), A(2), A(3), . . . , A(100).

Case 2

Even though the exact size of the array is not known, it must be dimensioned at some maximum amount. Not all the storage locations reserved have to be used. As each item of the array is read we can keep count of the number of items. If this number exceeds the dimension of the array, we can print an error message and stop the program.

Example

We wish to read a set of no more than 50 numbers into the array IQ. The dummy data card contains a zero. The flowchart containing a loop which reads in the array appears in Figure 9.8. The flowchart follows the FORTRAN statements of the procedure.

```
            DIMENSIØN IQ(50)
            I = 1
      10    READ (5,100) IQ(I)
            IF (IQ(I) .EQ. 0) GØ TØ 40
      20    IF (I .EQ. 50) GØ TØ 30
            I = I + 1
```

```
     GØ TØ 10
30   WRITE (6,110)
110  FØRMAT (1H1,22HDATAbEXCEEDSbDIMENSIØN)
     STØP
100  FØRMAT (I3)
40   N = I − 1
```

Figure 9.8 Flowchart for Reading an Array

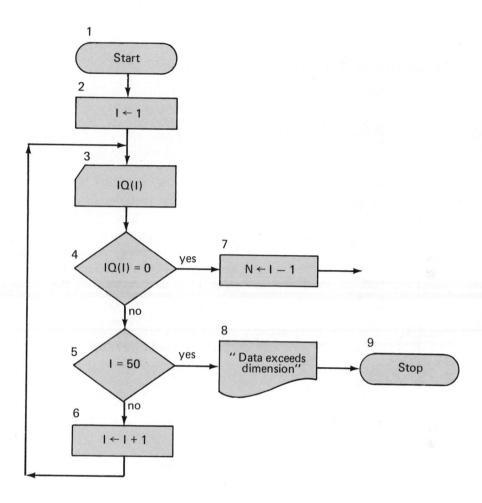

If there are 20 data cards not including the dummy data card, not all of the array IQ is used. The dummy data card will be read into IQ(21) and the final value of I is 21. In statement 40 we compute N as the number of data cards, and N equals 20.

If there had been exactly 50 data cards not including the dummy data card, then this program would print the message that "DATA EXCEEDS DIMEN-SION" and would stop. What must we change so that the program would read a maximum of 51 cards (50 data cards plus 1 dummy data card)?

Case 3

As in case 2, the dimension of the array is large enough to accommodate different amounts of data. The first card in the data deck will contain the exact number of items in the array. The array will be read using an **implied loop** in the READ statement. This technique allows us to use the same program with different sets of data.

Figure 9.9 Procedure for Reading an Array Containing a Variable Number of Elements

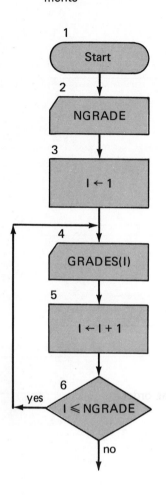

Example

We want to read many grades into an array called GRADES. The number of items in the array is named NGRADE. Therefore, we want to read in GRADES(1), GRADES(2), GRADES(3), and so on. The last grade read will be placed in location GRADES (NGRADE). The flowchart for this loop appears in Figure 9.9.

One way that we can convert this flowchart into FORTRAN is to use an implied loop in the list of the READ statement. Boxes 3–6 of the flowchart are incorporated into the implied loop in the READ statement.

```
      DIMENSIØN GRADES(35)
      READ (5,100) NGRADE
100   FØRMAT (I2)
      READ (5,110) (GRADES(I), I=1,NGRADE,1)
110   FØRMAT (5F5.0)
```

The implied loop automatically sets I to 1. After GRADE(I) is read, I is incremented by 1 and the value of I is compared to the value of NGRADE. If I is less than or equal to NGRADE, another grade is read, I is incremented and tested again to see if it has exceeded the value of NGRADE. The loop of reading, incrementing, and testing continues until I is greater than NGRADE. Note that FØRMAT 110 specifies that five numbers are to be read from each card. We assume that there will be no more than 35 grades; therefore, the dimension of the array GRADES is 35.

The two READ statements above may be combined into one statement using a different FØRMAT.

```
      DIMENSIØN GRADES(35)
      READ (5,120) NGRADE, (GRADES(I), I=1,NGRADE,1)
120   FØRMAT (I2/(5F5.0))
```

Implied Loop

The implied loop has two general forms.

$$(\text{list}, i = m_1, m_2, m_3)$$
$$(\text{list}, i = m_1, m_2)$$

where   list   is an input list or an output list

        i is a simple *integer* variable and is the index of the loop

       m_1 is the initial value of the index; it may be a positive *integer* constant or a non-subscripted *integer* variable.

       m_2 is the upper bound of the value of the index. It may be a positive *integer* constant or a non-subscripted *integer* variable.

       m_3 is the increment to the index. It may be a positive *integer* constant or a non-subscripted *integer* variable.

Rules for the Use of the Implied Loop

1. It may be used only in the list of READ or WRITE statements.
2. If m_3 is omitted, it is assumed to be 1.

Example

```
        DIMENSIØN  X(75),Y(75)
        READ  (5,100)  N,  (X(I),  I=1,N),  (Y(I),  I=1,N)
100     FØRMAT(I2/(F10.4))
        WRITE  (6,110)  (X(I),  Y(I),  I=1,N)
110     FØRMAT  (20X,F12.4,20X,F12.4)
```

In this example, N specifies the number of items in the X array and in the Y array. The items will be *read* in the following order and the value of each number is taken from a separate card.

$$
\begin{array}{c}
N \\
X(1) \\
X(2) \\
\cdot \\
\cdot \\
\cdot \\[4pt]
X(N) \\
Y(1) \\
Y(2) \\
\cdot \\
\cdot \\
\cdot \\[4pt]
Y(N)
\end{array}
$$

The variables will be *printed* in the following order.

$$
\begin{array}{c}
X(1) \\
Y(1) \\
X(2) \\
Y(2) \\
X(3) \\
Y(3) \\
\cdot \\
\cdot \\
\cdot \\[4pt]
X(N) \\
Y(N)
\end{array}
$$

Because of the FØRMAT, two numbers will be printed on one line. The X's will be printed in one column and the Y's will be printed in another.

X(1)	Y(1)
X(2)	Y(2)
.	.
.	.
.	.
X(N)	Y(N)

Example

```
        DIMENSIØN  X(75),Y(75)
        READ  (5,100)  NX,NY,(X(I), I = 1, NX),  (Y(I), I = 1, NY)
100     FØRMAT  (2I2/(F10.4))
```

The variable NX gives the number of items in the X array and NY gives the number of items in the Y array.

Exercises

1. Give an input statement to read the information on the data card.

SUNSHINE STATE UNIVERSITY

2. Write a statement which will save space for a variable Y which is to be subscripted to a maximum of 500.

3. List in order the variables which would be read with the following statements.

```
DIMENSIØN  X(2),Y(2)
READ  (5,10)  X,Y
```

4. Which variables will the following statement print?

```
WRITE  (6,200)  (KAT(I),I=6,10)
```

5. Write FORTRAN statements for the following flowchart segment. Use one statement to represent each box. Do not use an implied loop.

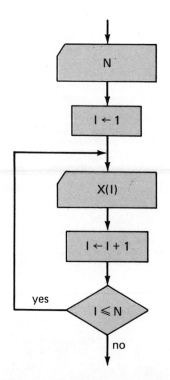

6. Write statements which will print the array A in a column. Single space the output. Allow a maximum of 10 places for printing a value in A and print no decimal places. Dimension the array A at 100.

7. Write statements which will read the values of the array MAX. Let the value of N represent the number of elements in the array. Assume N is less than or equal to 75 and has already been read in. Each card contains 8 numbers, 10 digits long. You do not need to dimension the array.

8. Write statements which will print every third element of array JAX. This means write the values of JAX(3), JAX(6), JAX(9), etc. Write the numbers in a row across the paper, 6 numbers to each row. Allow 10 digits for each number and 10 spaces between each number. Double space the output. Dimension the array JAX at 35.

9. Replace these two statements by one which accomplishes the same purpose.

   DIMENSIØN   TEMP(75)
   INTEGER TEMP

10. What variables will be read by the following statement?

    READ (5,100) (X(I),I=1,11,3)

11. Explain in one sentence what the following statements accomplish.

```
        DIMENSIØN I(1000)
        K = 1
   10   I(K) = K
        K = K + 1
        IF  (K .LE. 1000) GØ TØ 10
```

12. Given the following statements

```
        DIMENSIØN  NAME(2),SCØRE(5)
        READ  (5,100) NAME, SCØRE
   100  FØRMAT  (2A4,F2.0,4F3.0)
```

    name the variables in the order that they will be read. How many variables will be read from one data card?

13. A data card contains the following numbers in the given columns.

Columns		
	1–10	10.3
	11–20	−4.7
	21–30	3.4
	31–40	1.5
	41–50	−1.8
	51–60	41

    Give the values assigned by the following statements to each variable.

```
        READ  (5,10)  (X, A(I), I=1,3)
   10   FØRMAT  (8F10.1)
```

Program Assignments

Supply an appropriate dummy data card when writing the following programs.

1. The results of the SIT test have been recorded on punched cards. The information on each card is:

social security number	columns	1–9
last name		10–19
first name		23–32
SIT composite score		43–45
other SIT data		46–56
sex		60

It is your job as consultant to the SIT test bureau to list the names and SIT composite scores in the order they are read. Then start a new page and list the SIT scores and names in descending order (from highest score to lowest score).

2. Professor Lazy Goof has just given a 50 question multiple-choice test. He wants a program written which will read the first card, containing the correct answers, and then read each student's answer card and grade the test. Each question counts two points. Use subscripted items to store the correct answers and the student's answers.

The format of the data card is:

> card 1:
>   columns 1–50 correct answers (The answer to question 1 is in column 1; the answer to question 2 is in column 2, etc.)
> card 2 through end of data deck:
>   columns 1–50 student's answers to test
>   61–80 student's name

For the output, print the student's name and his test grade.

3. Happy Jack's Discount House has computerized its billing system. Currently they are stocking only 50 sale items at a new low, low price.

The data deck contains three groups of information:

a. The first group of cards in the data deck contains the item numbers of the 50 items. These numbers are punched 16 per card and each number is 5 digits long. This means that the first item's number is in columns 1–5 of the first card; the second item's number is in columns 6–10 of the first card; etc. Altogether there are 4 cards containing the item numbers.

b. The second group of cards in the data deck contains the current discount prices of the items. They are punched 16 per card in the form XX.XX

c. The third group of cards are order cards with the following format:

order number	columns	1–6
item ordered		7–11
quantity ordered		12–15

The problem is to process the order cards. On one page print the item numbers and current discount prices. Then on a new page, print for each order:

1. the order number
2. the item ordered
3. the quantity ordered
4. price per item
5. total price of the order. (If the quantity ordered is greater than 100, an additional 10% discount is given.)

What should the program do if the item of an order card is incorrect?

4. Problem: Evaluate a polynomial $a_1x^n + a_2x^{n-1} + \cdots + a_nx + a_{n+1}$ for the following values of x: -10, -9, -8, ..., 0, 1, 2, 3, ..., 9, 10. The maximum degree of the polynomial is 10. Use a one-dimensional array to store $a_1, a_2, \ldots, a_{n+1}$ (the coefficients of the polynomial).

The input of the program consists of:

n	(the degree of the polynomial)	columns 1–2
a's	(coefficients of the polynomial)	1–5 of the succeeding cards

The output should be: (1) the coefficients of the polynomial, and (2) the values of x and the corresponding values of the polynomial.

5. The final exam scores of a course have been recorded on cards. Write a program which will determine the following information:

1. the highest grade
2. the lowest grade
3. the mean (average grade)
4. the median (middle grade)

The median grade can be found by placing the scores in an array. Then order the scores from high to low (or low to high) and find the score which is in the middle of the list. This is the median score. For example, if there are 5 scores: 98, 82, 63, 50, 36, then the third score of 63 is the median. If there were 6 scores: 98, 80, 66, 64, 50, 36, then the median is not the third score, but is an average of the third and fourth scores $\left(\dfrac{66+64}{2} = 65\right)$.

Since there is no "middle" score in a list of 6, an average is taken to determine the median. Write the program so that it will find the median whether there is an even or an odd number of scores.

For the input, each card contains:

student number	columns 1–5
score	11–13

Output: On the first page list student numbers and scores. Then on a new page print the high, low, mean, and median grades. Make the output neat and label the numbers printed.

Special Terms

1. *A-field*
2. *array*

3. *array declarator*
4. *array element*
5. *dimension of array*
6. *double-subscripted variable*
7. *implied loop*
8. *never-ending loop*
9. *one-dimensional array*
10. *simple variable*
11. *single-subscripted variable*
12. *specification statement*
13. *subscript*
14. *subscripted variable*
15. *three-dimensional array*
16. *two-dimensional array*
17. *triple-subscripted variable*

Chapter 10

Loops and the DØ Statement

10.1 Introduction

In many of our programs we used a loop when we wanted to repeat a group of instructions. One important part of a loop is a way to tell when to end it; otherwise, the loop would be a never-ending one. One way of controlling the loop so that it is executed only a certain number of times is to use an index. We start the index at some value, go through the instructions in the loop, add a value to (increment) the index, and test the index to see if it has exceeded its final value. If it has, then we exit from the loop. If it has not, then we repeat the instructions in the loop, add a value to the index and test it again. In flowchart form we could express this loop in the following manner.

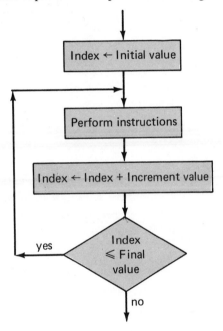

Because we find loops controlled by an index in so many programs, the FORTRAN language has developed a statement—the DØ statement—which simplifies the counting involved in the use of an index.

10.2 The DØ Statement

Suppose we wanted to add ten values of an array X(1), X(2), . . . , X(10). Figure 10.1 on page 130 shows the flowchart segment to do this task.

To control the loop we used three boxes; namely

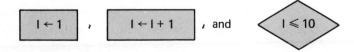

We would always need these three flowchart boxes to set up the loop counting process, because we use them for initializing, incrementing, and testing an index parameter. If we study the list of flowchart symbols given in Chapter 1 we

Figure 10.1 Flowchart Segment for Adding Ten Values of an Array

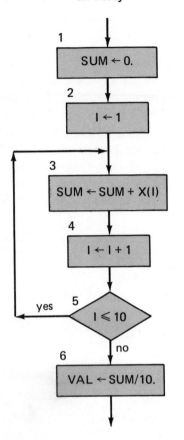

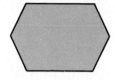

find that the preparation symbol may be used for setting up steps in the flowchart which are not part of the problem's computations. Let us define the loop process using the preparation box. We will let the preparation box control the index. First, the computer initializes the index. Then, the computer performs the steps inside the loop before it increments the index. If the index is less than or equal to its maximum value, the computer performs the steps again. If the index is greater than its maximum value, the looping stops.

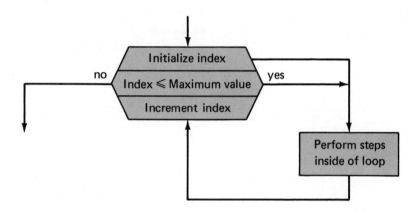

Now let us rewrite the flowchart segment in Figure 10.1 for the addition of our ten items, using the preparation symbol to replace boxes 2, 4, and 5. Both the flowchart segment in Figure 10.1 and the following segment in Figure 10.2 accomplish the same task. The latter uses the preparation box, the former does not.

Figure 10.2 Loop Controlled by Preparation Symbol

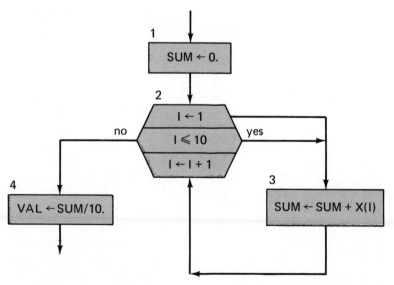

The FORTRAN language has a statement that parallels the loop controlled by the preparation box. The DØ statement will automatically initialize, increment and test the index parameter. Before giving a formal definition of the DØ statement, let us study how we would use it in our example. In the DØ statement

$$\text{DØ} \quad 3 \quad I = 1,10,1$$

the index parameter I is given; the 1 that immediately follows I is the initial value of I; the 10 is the maximum value that I can assume; the 1 that follows the 10 is the increment to I. The FORTRAN program segment using a DØ statement for the flowchart in Figure 10.2 is:

```
      SUM = 0.
      DØ 3 I =1,10,1
        SUM = SUM + X(I)
    3 CØNTINUE
      VAL = SUM / 10.
```

The DØ statement, during execution, produces the following action.

1. The index is initialized $(I = 1)$.
2. The statement or statements following the DØ statement through the statement labeled 3 are said to be within the **range** of the loop. The statements within the range are executed next.

```
        SUM = SUM + X(I)
    3 CØNTINUE
```

The statements within the range of the loop (except for the last one) are indented to emphasize that they are in the loop. Indenting the statements is not necessary, but it facilitates recognizing the range of the loop.

3. After the last statement in the range of the loop

```
    3 CØNTINUE
```

is executed, the DØ statement automatically increments the index $(I \leftarrow I + 1)$ and tests the index against the maximum value $(I \leq 10)$. If I is less than or equal to 10, the loop statements are repeated. When I is greater than 10, the execution proceeds with the instruction immediately after the last statement in the loop.

```
      VAL = SUM / 10.
```

The DØ statement may be one of the following forms:

```
DØ  n     i = m_1, m_2, m_3
DØ  n     i = m_1, m_2
```

where n is a statement label of the last statement in the loop.

i is the index parameter. It is an unsigned nonsubscripted *integer* variable name.

m_1 is the initial value of the index. It is a positive *integer* constant or a nonsubscripted *integer* variable name.

m_2 is the upper bound of the index. It is a positive *integer* constant or a nonsubscripted *integer* variable name.

m_3 is an increment on the index. If m_3 is omitted, as in the second form of the DØ statement, then m_3 is assumed to be one. m_3 is a positive *integer* constant or a nonsubscripted *integer* variable name.

All the statements from the DØ statement through the last statement in the range form what is called a **DØ loop**. The **range of a DØ loop** consists of the statements from the first statement following the DØ statement through the statement labeled n.

Rules for the Use of DØ Statements

1. The last statement labeled *n* must be executable. It *cannot* be another DØ statement, an IF statement, a GØ TØ statement or a STØP. Often a CØNTINUE statement is used as the last statement in a DØ loop.
2. The variables i, m_1, m_2, m_3 cannot be redefined within the range of a DØ loop. In particular, they may not appear on the left-hand side of an equal sign.
3. No comma appears between the statement label and the index of the DØ statement.
4. Upon completion of the DØ statement, execution proceeds with the first executable statement following the last statement in the range of the loop.
5. The value of m_1 must be less than or equal to the value of m_2.
6. The value of the index parameter is no longer defined upon completion of a DØ loop. If control is transferred outside the DØ loop before completion, then the index retains its current value.

CØNTINUE Statement

The CØNTINUE statement is executable, but the computer performs no operation when it executes this statement. The following two sets of statements will produce the same results in a program.

```
SUM = 0.                          SUM = 0.
CØNTINUE                          K = K + 1
K = K + 1                         SUM = A + B
CØNTINUE
SUM = A + B
```

The CØNTINUE statements have no affect on the execution of the other statements. Each CØNTINUE statement tells the computer to keep on executing the statements in sequence.

When the CØNTINUE statement is the last one in a DØ loop, it tells the computer to continue executing the loop. This means that when the computer reaches the CØNTINUE statement it increments the index and tests its value. If the value of the index is less than or equal to the maximum, the computer executes the statements in the loop another time. If the value is greater than the maximum set, the computer has completed the DØ loop and continues executing the statements following the CØNTINUE statement.

The CØNTINUE statement does not have to be used as the last statement in a DØ loop. Our previous example of adding the ten values of the array X may be written as follows:

```
      SUM = 0.
      DØ  3  I = 1,10,1
    3 SUM = SUM + X(I)
      VAL = SUM / 10.
```

We may omit the CØNTINUE statement because the arithmetic replacement statement is executable. Since the last executable statement in a DØ loop cannot be another DØ statement, an IF statement, a GØ TØ statement, or a STØP statement, a CØNTINUE statement is often used. Let us now look at an example in which we *need* to use a CØNTINUE statement.

Suppose we want to read entries into an array. We do not know how many entries there are, but there is a dummy data card with a 99 punched in the appropriate columns. The array is dimensioned at 50, so we do not want to read more than 50 entries into the array. The name of our array is TABLE. The flowchart segment of our problem is

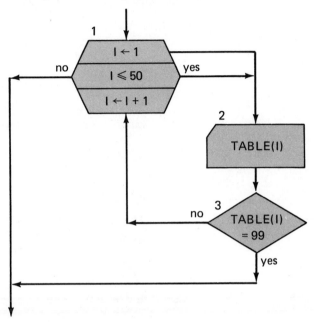

The flowchart indicates the following steps:

1. The index I is initialized.
2. A value of TABLE(I) is read.
3. Check for dummy data value (TABLE(I) = 99).
4. If TABLE(I) does not equal 99, increment and test the index I and repeat the loop.
5. If we have encountered the dummy data card, then we are to leave the loop.

In trying to convert the flowchart into FORTRAN, we start with

```
30   DØ 10 I = 1,50
        READ (5,100) TABLE(I)
        IF (TABLE(I) .EQ. 99.) (leave loop)
        GØ TØ (increment I)
```

In order to increment I, can we transfer to statement labeled 30? No! Going back to statement 30 will initialize I all over again. The index is incremented only when the statement labeled 10 is reached. Where is statement 10? So far there is no statement labeled 10. Here we can use a CØNTINUE statement, to indicate the last statement in the DØ loop. When the CØNTINUE statement is encountered, the index given in the DØ statement is automatically incremented and tested. To leave the loop, all we need is a transfer of control to a statement outside the range of the loop. The complete instructions are:

```
30   DØ 10 I = 1,50
        READ (5,100) TABLE(I)
        IF (TABLE(I) .EQ. 99.) GØ TØ 20
10   CØNTINUE
20   (next instruction in program)
```

Comments on DØ Statements

1. The following statements are *not* allowed.

    a. DØ 3 I = 1, N(K)

    The maximum value of the index cannot be a subscripted variable, but we can achieve our purpose with the following statements.

    ```
    J = N(K)
    DØ 3 I = 1, J
    ```

    b. DØ 3 I = 1, N + 2

    The maximum value of the index must be an *integer* constant or an *integer* variable, but not an expression such as N + 2. Instead we may write

    ```
    K = N + 2
    DØ 3 I = 1, K
    ```

    c. DØ 3 N(I) = 1, 10

    The index of a DØ loop must be a nonsubscripted *integer* variable. Instead we write

    ```
    DØ 3 K = 1, 10
    ```

    d. DØ 7 A = 2, 8

    The index of a DØ loop must be an *integer* variable. We can change this to

    ```
    DØ 7 KA = 2, 8
    ```

2. If the value of m_1 equals the value of m_2, the statements in the range of the DØ loop are executed once.

3. The statement DØ 3 NN = 1,10,2 will cause the index parameter NN to assume the values of 1, 3, 5, 7, 9. After the loop has been executed with NN = 9, NN will be incremented (NN = 11). Since NN now equals 11, and 11 is greater than 10, the loop is terminated.

4. We may use the index parameter as a value to compute some other value, or we may print the index parameter as a value. In the following example, we compute the sum of the even numbers between 1 and 100.

    ```
      ISUM = 0
      DØ 5 IEVEN = 2,100,2
        ISUM = ISUM + IEVEN
    5 CØNTINUE
    ```

    In the following example, we write the value of an array and label each element.

    ```
      DØ 5 K = 1, 100
          WRITE (6,100) K, PRICE(K)
    5 CØNTINUE
    100 FØRMAT (1H0, 5X, 6HPRICE(, I3, 4H)b=b, F7.2)
    ```

5. The index parameter may be used as a subscript within the range of a loop. Consider the following example in which each entry in a table is incremented by 1, and each new value is printed.

```
          DØ  7  IN = 1,LAST
              TABLE(IN) = TABLE(IN) + 1.
              WRITE  (6,100)  TABLE(IN)
     7    CØNTINUE
   100    FØRMAT  (10X,F10.3)
```

Rules for Transfer of Control in DØ Loops

1. Transfer of control is not permitted into the range of any DØ loop from outside its range.

```
          GØ  TØ  30                                  not allowed
              .
              .
              .
          DØ  20  I = 1,15
              SUM  (I) = X(I) + 1.0
     30       WRITE  (6,100)  SUM  (I)
     20   CØNTINUE
```

2. Transfer of control from inside the range of a DØ loop to another statement inside the range of the same loop is permissible.

```
          DØ  40  K = 1,10
              IF  (K .EQ. I)  GØ  TØ  30          allowed
              M(K) = N(J)
              GØ  TØ  40
     30       M(K) = NM
     40   CØNTINUE
```

3. Transfer of control from inside the range of a DØ loop to outside its range is permitted.

```
          DØ  10  I = 1,50
              READ  (5,1000)  X(I)
              IF  (X(I) .EQ. 0.0)  GØ  TØ  20      allowed
     10   CØNTINUE
     20 SUM = 0.0
```

4. Transfer of control from a statement *outside the range* of a DØ loop to the DØ statement is permitted. This action initializes the specific DØ loop.

```
          READ  (5,1000)  DATA
          IF  (DATA)  99,99,10                      allowed
     10   DØ  20  N = 1,30
              CØUNT  (N) = 0.0
     20   CØNTINUE
              .
              .
              .
     99   STØP
```

Example Using the DØ Statement

Our problem will be Problem 1 of section 9.4. We want to show how that problem may be written using a DØ statement. First we will redesign the flowchart of Figure 9.5 using the preparation symbol to indicate the looping process. The new flowchart appears in Figure 10.3.

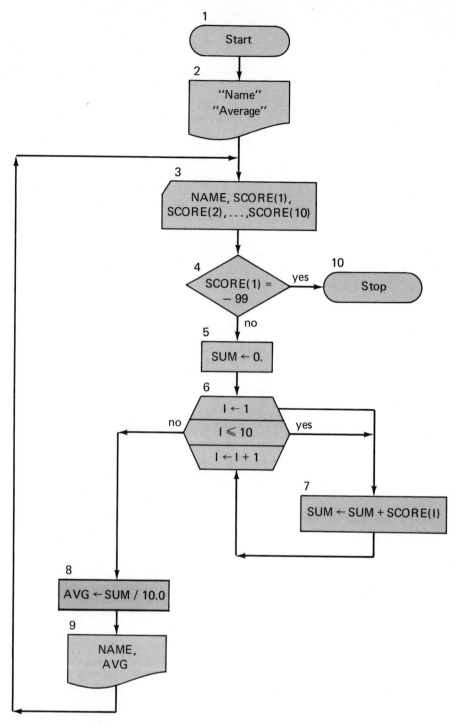

Figure 10.3 Flowchart Using the Preparation Box for Averaging Scores

The corresponding FORTRAN program is:

```
C        PRØBLEM 1 ØF SECTIØN 9.4 USING DØ STATEMENT
         INTEGER NAME (5)
         REAL SCØRE (10)
         WRITE (6,100)
C        READ IN STUDENTS NAME AND 10 SCØRES
   10    READ (5,110) NAME, SCØRE
         IF(SCØRE (1) .EQ. −99.) GØ TØ 30
         SUM = 0.0
C        THE DØ LØØP WILL ADD 10 SCØRES
         DØ 20 I = 1,10
             SUM = SUM + SCØRE (I)
   20    CØNTINUE
```

```
         AVG = SUM / 10.0
         WRITE  (6,120)  NAME, AVG
         GØ TØ  10
  30     STØP
 100     FØRMAT  (1H1,27X,4HNAME,19X,7HAVERAGE//)
 110     FØRMAT  (5A4,10X,10F3.0)
 120     FØRMAT  (21X,5A4,11X,F5.1)
         END
```

Exercises

1. Identify where a preparation box could be used in this flowchart segment. Construct a new flowchart which uses the preparation box to control the loop.

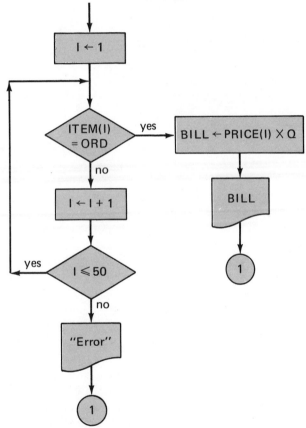

2. Convert the following flowchart segment into FORTRAN. Assume that the subscripted variables have been dimensioned.

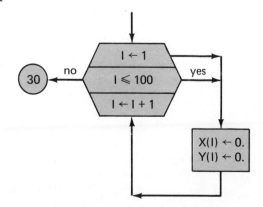

3. Convert the following flowchart into FORTRAN. Assume that the subscripted variables have been dimensioned. What is this flowchart doing?

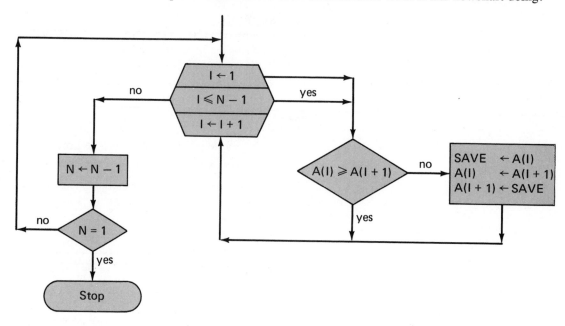

4. Go through this program segment "playing computer." What are the final values of A(1), A(2), A(3), . . . , A(10)?

```
    DØ 10 I = 1,  10
       A(I) = I
10  CØNTINUE
```

5. Go through this program segment "playing computer." What will be printed finally? Assume P is an *integer* and has the value 35.

```
     NP = P − 1
     DØ 20 J =2, NP
        IF (P − P / J * J .EQ. 0) GØ TØ 30
20   CØNTINUE
     WRITE (6,100)
100  FØRMAT (10X, 5HPRIME)
     STØP
30   WRITE (6,110)
110  FØRMAT (10X, 9HNØTbPRIME)
     STØP
```

6. Convert the following flowchart segment into FORTRAN. Assume the variables have been dimensioned.

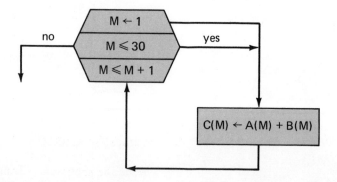

7. Do a trace of the following program segment. Assume N has the value 4.

```
        NFACT = 1
        DØ 10 I = 2, N
            NFACT = NFACT * I
   10   CØNTINUE
```

8. What does the following program segment compute?

```
        INTEGER EVEN (10)
        DØ 10 I =1,10
            EVEN (I) = 2 * I
   10   CØNTINUE
```

9. What is the following program segment doing? Assume array A has been read in.

```
        DIMENSIØN A(100), B(100)
        N = 100
        DØ 3 I = 1,N
            K = N + 1 - I
            B(I) = A(K)
    3   CØNTINUE
```

10. If B(1) = 1.0, B(2) = .5, B(3) = .25, B(4) = 0.0, B(5) = 1.0, what is the value stored in LØC after the following program segment has been executed?

```
        DIMENSIØN B(5)
              .
              .
              .
        DØ 10 I = 1, 5
            IF( B(I) .EQ. 0.0) GØ TØ 20
   10   CØNTINUE
        LØC = 0
        GØ TØ 25
   20   LØC = I
   25   (next statement in program)
```

11. Study the following program and tell *precisely* what each FORTRAN statement does.

```
        READ (5,1) K
    1   FØRMAT (I5)
        ITØTAL = 1
        DØ 3 J = 2, K
            ITØTAL = ITØTAL + J**J
    3   CØNTINUE
        WRITE (6,4) ITØTAL
    4   FØRMAT (1H1, 10X, 6HITØTAL, I10)
        STØP
        END
```

Program Assignments

Write the program assignments for Chapter 9 using DØ statements.

10.3 Nested DØ Loops

When a DØ loop is contained inside another DØ loop, the interior loop is said to be **nested.** A DØ loop may contain a set of nested loops. When loops are nested, the range of a nested DØ loop must be contained inside the range of the outer DØ loop. Following are two examples of nested loops showing both the FORTRAN statements and a diagram illustrating the nesting.

Example

```
        DØ  3  I = 1,50,2
        TERM (I) = 0
            DØ  5  J = 1,5
            TERM (I) = TERM (I) + X (J)
5           CØNTINUE
3       CØNTINUE
```

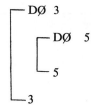

Example

```
        DØ  50  K =  1,MAX
                .
                .
                .
        DØ  10  L1 = 1,10
                .
                .
                .
10          CØNTINUE
        DØ  20  L2 = 1,25,3
                .
                .
                .
20          CØNTINUE
                .
                .
                .
50          CØNTINUE
```

Rules for the Use of Nested DØ Loops

1. Any nested DØ loop may *not* have the same index variable as that of an outer DØ loop in the same nest.

```
      DØ  10  I = 1,N
      DØ  20  I= 1,15,3                    not allowed
            SUM  (I) = 0.0
  10  CØNTINUE
  20  CØNTINUE
```

2. The same index variable name may be used in sequential DØ loops which are not nested.

```
      DØ  3  I = 1,10,2
            X(I) = A(I)
  3   CØNTINUE
      DØ  5  I = 2,10,2                     allowed
            Y(I) = A(I)
  5   CØNTINUE
```

3. Any inner DØ loop may *not* redefine the parameters of the outer loop.

```
      DØ  3  I = N,M
      DØ  5  N = 10,20                      not allowed
            SUM = X + Y
  5   CØNTINUE
  3   CØNTINUE
```

4. Nested DØ loops may end at the same instruction.

```
      DØ  7  I = 1,5
            A(I) = X * W(I)
            DØ  7  J = 5,100,5
                  B(I) = X(J) + 1.
  7   CØNTINUE
```

Diagram of nesting

```
 ┌─DØ  7
 │
 │  ┌─DØ  7
 │  │
 │  │
 └──┴─7
```

Example Using Nested DØ Loop

A teacher has given two tests and wants to find the average grade on each test. The teacher has 25 students and the data is punched as follows:

Card 1: 25 scores from test 1
Card 2: 25 scores from test 2

These two cards provide all the information needed to solve the problem; therefore, the program does not require a dummy data card.

Let us outline what we want the program to do.

1. Read the 25 scores for test 1 and store them in a one-dimensional array called SCØRE.

2. Add the scores for test 1.
3. Find the average grade for test 1.
4. Repeat steps 1, 2, and 3 for the scores on test 2.
5. Print the average grade for test 1 and test 2.

Since we want to repeat steps 1 through 3 two times, we can have an index I that takes the values 1 and 2 in the loop. To add the 25 scores we may have another index, J, that takes values 1 through 25. The index J is used to reference each score in the SCØRE array. As the computer finds the averages, we will store them in AVG(1) and AVG(2), respectively.

Figure 10.4 shows the flowchart for this problem, and the FORTRAN program follows the flowchart.

Figure 10.4 Flowchart Using Nested Loops

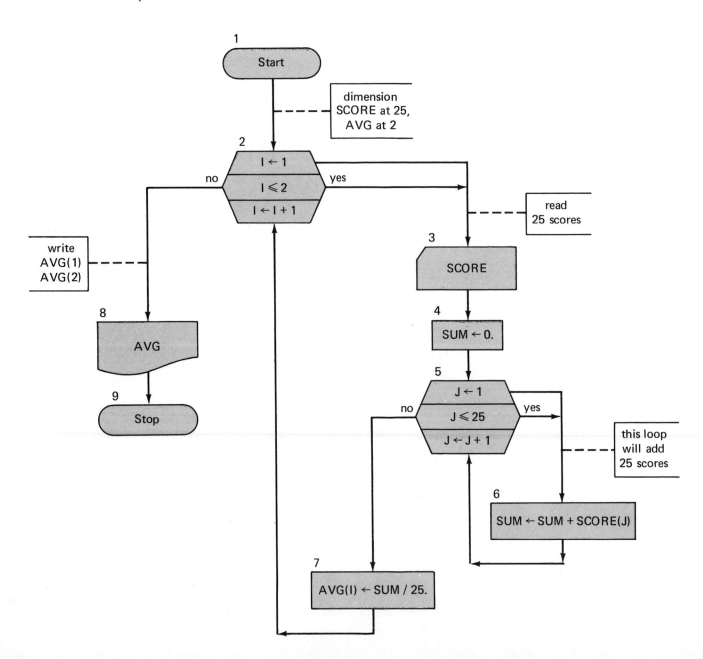

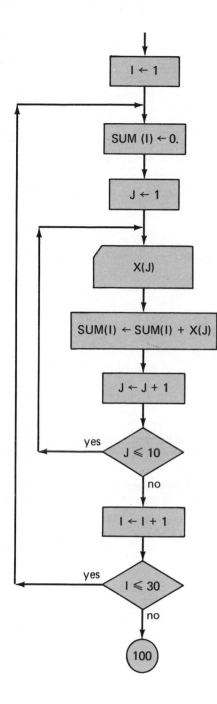

```
C        FIND AVERAGE GRADE ØN TWØ TESTS
         DIMENSIØN SCØRE(25), AVG(2)
         DØ 5 I = 1,2
C        READ IN 25 SCØRES
         READ (5,100) SCØRE
  100    FØRMAT (25F3.0)
         SUM = 0.
C        THIS NESTED LØØP WILL ADD 25 SCØRES
         DØ 3 J = 1,25
              SUM = SUM + SCØRE (J)
    3    CØNTINUE
C        CØMPUTE AVERAGE
         AVG (I) = SUM / 25.
    5    CØNTINUE
         WRITE (6,200) (AVG(I), I=1,2)
  200    FØRMAT (1H1,10X,7HAVG1b=b,F4.0,10X,7HAVG2b=b,F4.0)
         STØP
         END
```

Note that in the program, the index parameter J of the nested loop must be different than the index parameter I of the outside loop. When a loop is terminated, the same index may be used in subsequent loops. This is why we may use the index I again in the WRITE statement.

Exercises

1. Rewrite the flowchart segment to the left using preparation boxes to control the loops.

2. Convert the following flowchart segment into FORTRAN. Assume that the subscripted variables have been dimensioned. What is this flowchart doing? See exercise 3.

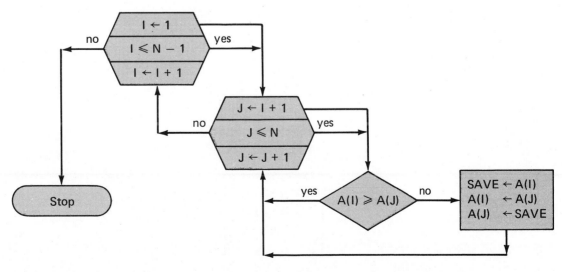

3. To understand how the flowchart segment in exercise 2 works, use the following values to construct a trace diagram.

$$N = 5$$
$$A(1) = 3.0$$
$$A(2) = 5.0$$
$$A(3) = 2.0$$
$$A(4) = 4.0$$
$$A(5) = 7.0$$

Program Assignments

Refer to program assignments 1, 4, and 5 in Chapter 9. Additional programs which use nested loops are given at the end of section 11.2.

Special Terms

1. *DØ loop*
2. *inner loop*
3. *nested DØ loops*
4. *outer loop*
5. *preparation box*
6. *range of a DØ loop*

Chapter 11

Two- and Three-Dimensional Arrays

11.1 Variables with Two Subscripts

A **two-dimensional array** is one in which two subscripts are used to refer to an entry in the array. As an example of a two-dimensional array consider the following table, called TABLE.

	Col. 1	Col. 2	Col. 3
Row 1	A	B	C
Row 2	D	E	F

We refer to a specific element by giving its row and column position. For example, since B is in row 1 and column 2, using subscripts we could say that the item in $TABLE_{1,2}$ is B. If we say that B is in column 2 and row 1, then using subscripts $TABLE_{2,1}$ could refer to B. To avoid ambiguity between $TABLE_{1,2}$ and $TABLE_{2,1}$ we should decide whether the first subscript indicates the row or the column. We will use the row number as the first subscript and the column number as the second subscript. Therefore, $TABLE_{1,2}$ is entry B, and $TABLE_{2,1}$ is entry D.

In FORTRAN, a double subscripted variable is one with two subscripts. The subscripts are enclosed in parentheses and separated by a comma; for example, TABLE (1,2).

Storage locations must be reserved for two-dimensional arrays through a DIMENSIØN or a TYPE statement. The general form of the array declarator would be

    array name (maximum number of rows, maximum number of columns)

or

    array name (maximum number of columns, maximum number of rows)

In a problem we must decide from the beginning whether the first subscript will be the number of columns or rows and dimension the array accordingly. To reserve locations for our TABLE we would say

    DIMENSIØN TABLE (2,3)

The actual number of storage locations reserved are $2 \times 3 = 6$. Specifically, they are labeled

TABLE (1,1)   [ ]

TABLE (2,1)   [ ]

TABLE (1,2)   [ ]

TABLE (2,2)   [ ]

TABLE (1,3)   [ ]

TABLE (2,3)   [ ]

Let us now study an example in which double subscripts are used to store information. We will use the same data presented in Problem 2 of section 9.4. Its format was

name	columns	1–20
sex		21
district number		23–24
address		26–40

The problem now is to count the number of boys and girls in each district of the city. The sex which is punched in column 21 of the data card is an integer. A code of 1 means that the student is a boy; a code of 2 means that the student is a girl.

We wish to print the totals in the form of a table.

DISTRICT	BØYS	GIRLS
1	200	150
2	400	275
3	200	208
.	.	.
.	.	.
.	.	.
20	75	95

Let us now choose the names we want to use in solving the problem. Since there are 20 districts, we must compute 40 totals in all. We could name the counters DIST(1) . . . DIST(40) or TØTAL(1) . . . TØTAL(40), but perhaps we should attach two subscripts to the array name DIST. One of the subscripts will represent the district number and the other subscript will represent the sex of the students. Looking at just the variable DIST(1,2) we cannot tell if this is the name representing the total number of girls in district 1 or the total number of boys in district 2. We should decide before proceeding what each subscript will represent. Let us use the first subscript to signify the district number and the second subscript the sex. In general, we may say

DIST (district number, sex)

Thus, the value stored in DIST(1,2) will be the total number of girls in district 1. To count the number of students by district and sex, each time a data card is read we increment the appropriate counter by one. If the student is a male (sex = 1) who lives in district 1, we add 1 to DIST(1,1). If the boy lives in district 2, we add 1 to DIST(2,1). If we use the variable name NDIST to represent the district number read from a card, then, in general, to increment the male counters we compute

DIST (NDIST, 1) + 1

Similarly, to count a girl living in district NDIST we compute

DIST (NDIST, 2) + 1

Since we must determine whether the student is a boy or a girl, we should also read the sex code. Let us store the value under the variable name of SEX. Since

SEX = 1 means the student is a boy and SEX = 2 means the student is a girl, then to increment any counter we write

    DIST (NDIST, SEX) + 1

If we wish to use the variable SEX as a subscript, then we must type it *integer*.

We should also include in our program a check to see if SEX is either a 1 or a 2 and to see if NDIST is between 1 and 20. If one of these items was punched incorrectly on the card, what should we do then? We could ignore the card and read another one. Or we could print an error message such as "INCORRECT SEX" or "INCORRECT DIST" and the name which appeared on the card. In case there is some incorrect data, we could correct those cards after the program has been run, and rerun it with the new data deck. Figure 11.1 shows our flowchart solution to the problem.

Before writing the program corresponding to the flowchart, let us discuss the method for zeroing the 40 counters—DIST(1,1), DIST(1,2), DIST(2,1), DIST(2,2), and so on. The flowchart says that there will be two DØ loops used, one nested inside another. Let us go through the flowchart step by step and see what it says to do.

1. (Box 2) Set I to 1
2. (Box 3) Set J to 1
3. (Box 4) Set DIST(I,J) to 0
        Since I = 1 and J = 1, DIST(1,1) = 0.
4. (Box 3) Add 1 to J. So now J = 2. Is J less than or equal to 2? Yes.
    (Box 4) So we repeat the statement DIST(I,J) = 0. But this time I = 1 and J = 2, so DIST(1,2) = 0.
5. (Box 3) Add 1 to J. This makes J = 3. Is 3 less than or equal to 2? No, so we leave the inner loop.
6. (Box 2) Add 1 to I. (I = 2). Is I less than or equal to 20?
    (Box 3) Yes, so we reset J to 1.
7. (Box 4) Set DIST(I,J) to 0. What are the current values for I and J? I = 2 and J = 1 so DIST(2,1) = 0.
8. (Box 3) Add 1 to J. (J = 2)
    (Box 4) Since J is less than or equal to 2, DIST(2,2) = 0.
9. (Box 3) Add 1 to J. (J = 3) and we leave the inner loop.

Continuation of this process will initialize all 40 DISTs to zero. If you are not satisfied that this method will work continue to go through it by hand, converting the above step by step process into a trace diagram.

Since DIST is an array, we must dimension it with either a DIMENSIØN or an INTEGER type statement.

    INTEGER DIST(20,2)

The largest value of the first subscript is 20 and the largest value of the second subscript is 2. Altogether there are 40 items ($20 \times 2 = 40$) reserved for the array DIST.

In the flowchart we are asking several complicated questions, such as is SEX a 1 or a 2? Is NDIST a number between 1 and 20? Using FORTRAN relational expressions, we would write these questions as:

    Is SEX .EQ. 1 or SEX .EQ. 2 ?
    Is NDIST .GE. 1 and NDIST .LE. 20 ?

Figure 11.1 Flowchart for Counting Number of Boys and Girls in each School District

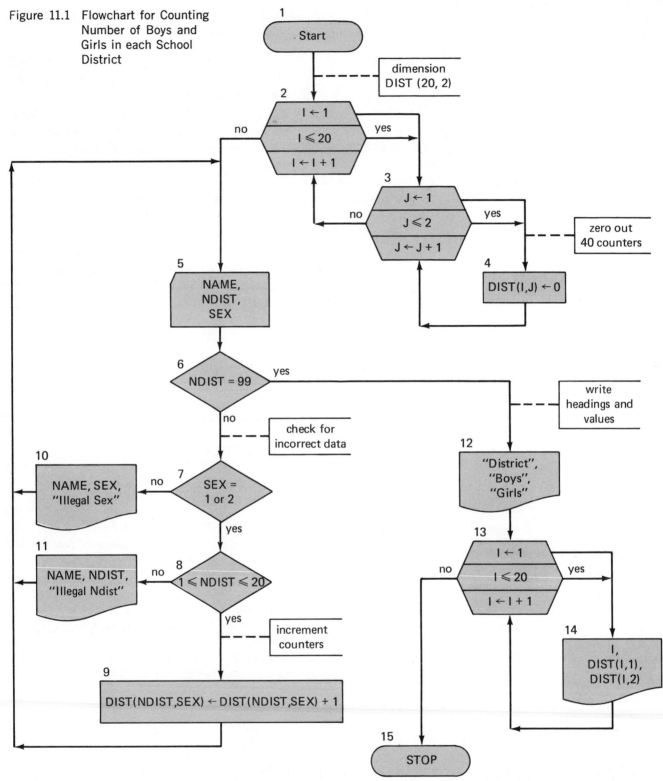

The answer expected would be either true or false. The logical IF statement that we have previously used contained only one relational expression. The FORTRAN language has the logical operators .ØR. and .AND. to connect two relational expressions. When two relational expressions are connected with a logical operator, then the complete expression is called a logical expression. (See section 13.8 for more detailed information on logical variables and expressions.) Using a logical IF statement, we write our questions as:

```
IF (SEX .EQ. 1 .ØR. SEX .EQ. 2)
IF (NDIST .GE. 1 .AND. NDIST .LE. 20)
```

The first IF statement will be true if either relational expression is true. The second IF statement will be true only if both relational expressions are true. We will use these IF statements in our program.

The output (flowchart boxes 13 and 14) will be printed using a DØ loop. The variables printed will be I, the district number; DIST(I,1), the number of boys in each district; and DIST(I,2), the number of girls in each district.

```
        DØ 70 I = 1,20
            WRITE (6,1040) I, DIST(I,1), DIST(I,2)
70   CØNTINUE
```

The complete FORTRAN program for our problem is:

```
C       PRØGRAM TØ CØUNT NUMBER ØF BØYS AND GIRLS
C       IN EACH DISTRICT
C
        INTEGER DIST(20,2), SEX, NAME(5)
        DØ 20 I = 1,20
            DØ 10 J = 1,2
                DIST(I,J) = 0
10          CØNTINUE
20      CØNTINUE
30      READ (5,1010) NAME, SEX, NDIST
        IF (NDIST .EQ. 99) GØ TØ 60
        IF ( SEX .EQ. 1 .ØR. SEX .EQ. 2 ) GØ TØ 40
        WRITE (6,1020) NAME, SEX
        GØ TØ 30
40      IF (NDIST .GE. 1 .AND. NDIST .LE. 20 ) GØ TØ 50
        WRITE (6,1030) NAME, NDIST
        GØ TØ 30
50      DIST(NDIST, SEX) = DIST(NDIST, SEX) + 1
        GØ TØ 30
60      WRITE (6,1000)
        DØ 70 I = 1,20
            WRITE (6,1040) I, DIST(I,1),DIST(I,2)
70      CØNTINUE
        STØP
1000    FØRMAT (1H1,10X,8HDISTRICT,10X,4HBØYS,9X,5HGIRLS////)
1010    FØRMAT (5A4,I1,1X,I2)
1020    FØRMAT (10X,5A4,2X,I3,13HbbILLEGALbSEX)
1030    FØRMAT (10X,5A4,2X,I3,15HbbILLEGALbNDIST)
1040    FØRMAT (14X,I2,12X,I5,9X,I5)
        END
```

11.2 Input and Output of Two-dimensional Arrays

For the input and output of two-dimensional arrays, there are cases similar to the input and output of one-dimensional arrays.

1. We know the exact dimensions of an array before the program is written.
2. One of the dimensions of the array is known before the program is written; the other dimension must be counted by the program.
3. The exact dimensions are variable and are read as part of the data.

We will study each case and give examples.

Case 1

If we know the exact dimensions of the array, we may dimension the array at those amounts. If we wish to input or output all the items in the array, we may use just the array name in the READ or WRITE statement and the computer will read or print all elements in the array.

Example

```
      DIMENSIØN  A(3,3),  B(2,3)
      READ  (5,10)  A,  B
  10  FØRMAT  (F5.3)
```

The computer will read the elements in the arrays in the following order in which the first subscript changes more rapidly than the second one. The order of the variables would be the same if we had used a WRITE statement instead of the READ statement.

$$
\left.
\begin{array}{l}
A(1,1) \\
A(2,1) \\
A(3,1) \\
A(1,2) \\
A(2,2) \\
A(3,2) \\
A(1,3) \\
A(2,3) \\
A(3,3)
\end{array}
\right\} \text{A array}
$$

$$
\left.
\begin{array}{l}
B(1,1) \\
B(2,1) \\
B(1,2) \\
B(2,2) \\
B(1,3) \\
B(2,3)
\end{array}
\right\} \text{B array}
$$

Case 2

If we know only one dimension of the array, we must estimate the other dimension at some maximum amount. We do not need to use all of the storage locations reserved for the array. In the following example, one of the dimensions of TEST is 3; the other dimension is estimated at 50.

Example

The exact number of data cards is not known, but is less than 50. An index named I is used to control the number of cards read. A dummy data card is used to signal the end of the deck. Each data card contains three values—TEST(1,I), TEST(2,I), TEST(3,I). An implied loop will be used in the READ statement to vary the first subscript of TEST.

```
       INTEGER  TEST  (3,50)
       I = 1
  10   READ  (5,100)  (TEST(J,I),  J = 1,3)
 100   FØRMAT  (3I5)
       IF  (TEST(1,I)  .EQ.  99999)  GØ  TØ  30
  20   I = I + 1
```

```
        GØ TØ 10
    30  N = I − 1
```

Case 3

The exact dimensions of the array are variable and are read as part of the data. Even though not all of the locations may be used in the program, we must reserve a certain number of storage locations for the array.

Example

First we will have the computer read the values that determine the size of the array. Then we will use a nested implied loop to read the values of the array.

Each implied loop has its own set of parentheses and a comma separates the list from the index. During execution, the value of I starts at 1 and the inner loop index J varies from 1 through N. Then I becomes 2 and J varies again from 1 though N. This process is repeated until I exceeds the value of M. When implied loops are nested, the outer loop index is not incremented until the inner loop index reaches its maximum value.

```
        DIMENSIØN A(10,10)
        READ (5,100) N, M, ((A(I,J), J=1,N), I=1, M)
    100 FØRMAT (2I3/(10F5.3))
```

To illustrate how the computer will read values into the array A, suppose we have the following data punched on cards. The first data card contains

The second data card contains

The variables read contain the following values

$$N = 2$$
$$M = 3$$
$$A(1,1) = 1.3$$
$$A(1,2) = -6.8$$
$$A(2,1) = 1.5$$
$$A(2,2) = 2.1$$
$$A(3,1) = 3.0$$
$$A(3,2) = 12.4$$

Example

Study Table 11.1 and note the variations of the first READ statement. Notice the different orders in which the variables are read. Assume $N = 2$ and $M = 3$.

Table 11.1

READ Statement	List Order
READ(5,100) N, M, ((A(I,J), J = 1,N), I = 1,M)	A(1,1) A(1,2) A(2,1) A(2,2) A(3,1) A(3,2)
READ(5,100) N, M, ((A(J,I), I = 1,N), J = 1,M)	A(1,1) A(1,2) A(2,1) A(2,2) A(3,1) A(3,2)
READ(5,100) N, M, ((A(I,J), J = 1,M), I = 1,N)	A(1,1) A(1,2) A(1,3) A(2,1) A(2,2) A(2,3)
READ(5,100) N, M, ((A(J,I), J = 1,N), I = 1,M)	A(1,1) A(2,1) A(1,2) A(2,2) A(1,3) A(2,3)
READ(5,100) N, M, ((A(I,J), I = 1,M), J = 1,N)	A(1,1) A(2,1) A(3,1) A(1,2) A(2,2) A(3,2)

Example

This example will illustrate another use of a nested implied loop. Suppose we want to read a table with 20 entries. The form of the table is given below.

Identification number	Price			
	Pint	Quart	½Gallon	Gallon
1256	2.50	4.85	9.45	17.50
2412	3.50	5.75	10.65	19.25
1234	.	.	.	.
4132	.	.	.	.
.	.	.	.	.
.	.	.	.	.
.	.	.	.	.

The values are punched on cards as follows.

Identification number	columns	1–4
pint price		5–9
quart price		10–14
½ gallon price		15–19
gallon price		20–24

We want to store the identification numbers in a one-dimensional array called IDNUM, dimensioned at 20. The prices will be stored in a two-dimensional array called PRICE, dimensioned by the array declarator PRICE(20,4). We will use a nested implied loop to read the values.

```
      DIMENSIØN IDNUM(20), PRICE(20,4)
      READ (5,100) (IDNUM(I), (PRICE(I,J), J=1,4), I=1,20)
  100 FØRMAT (I4,4F5.2)
```

The diagram in Table 11.2 shows how the values are read during execution as the values of the indices I and J change.

Table 11.2

			J		
		1	2	3	4
I = 1	IDNUM(1)	PRICE(1,1)	PRICE(1,2)	PRICE(1,3)	PRICE(1,4)
I = 2	IDNUM(2)	PRICE(2,1)	PRICE(2,2)	PRICE(2,3)	PRICE(2,4)
I = 3	IDNUM(3)	PRICE(3,1)	PRICE(3,2)	PRICE(3,3)	PRICE(3,4)
I = 4	IDNUM(4)	PRICE(4,1)	. . .	. . .	. . .
	.	.	.	.	.
	.	.	.	.	.
I = 20	IDNUM(20)	PRICE(20,1)	PRICE(20,2)	PRICE(20,3)	PRICE(20,4)

Example

Note that in this example the DØ loop instructs the computer to execute the READ statement twice, since the value read for N is 2. The READ statement says to read 4 numbers since the value read for M is 4.

```
      DIMENSIØN A(5,5)
      READ (5,100) N,M
      DØ 10 I = 1,N
          READ(5,110) (A(I,J), J = I,M)
   10 CØNTINUE
  100 FØRMAT (2I2)
  110 FØRMAT(5F10.1)
```

Data card 1:	columns	1–2	contains	02
		3–4		04
Data card 2:	columns	1–10	contains	7.2
		11–20		−3.8
		21–30		6.0
		31–40		1.5
		41–50		blanks
Data card 3:	columns	1–10		2.5
		11–20		−1.3
		21–30		8.1
		31–40		6.3
		41–50		blanks

The values assigned to the variable names are:

$$N = 2$$
$$M = 4$$
$$A(1,1) = 7.2$$
$$A(1,2) = -3.8$$
$$A(1,3) = 6.0$$
$$A(1,4) = 1.5$$
$$A(2,1) = 2.5$$
$$A(2,2) = -1.3$$
$$A(2,3) = 8.1$$
$$A(2,4) = 6.3$$

Example

Compare this example to the previous one and suppose $N = 2$ and $M = 4$. The inner DØ loop is executed 4 times and the outer DO loop is executed 2 times. Hence, the READ statement is executed a total of 8 times. Even though the FØRMAT says that a maximum of 5 numbers may be read from a card, the READ statement says to read just one from each card. Since the READ statement is executed 8 times, we would need 8 data cards for the array A instead of 2 cards as in our previous example.

```
      DIMENSIØN A(5,5)
      READ (5,100) N,M
      DØ 20 I = 1,N
         DØ 10 J = 1,M
            READ (5,110) A(I,J)
 10      CØNTINUE
 20   CØNTINUE
100   FØRMAT (2I2)
110   FØRMAT (5F10.1)
```

Exercises

1. Write a statement which will save space for the following variables:
   $F(1,1),F(1,2),F(1,3),F(2,1),F(2,2),F(2,3)$

2. In what order are the following variables written?

   DIMENSIØN K(4,2)
   .
   .
   .
   WRITE (6,100) ((K(I,J), I=1,4), J=1,2)

3. How many numbers does the following READ statement say to read? How many data cards will be read by the DØ loops?

   ```
         DØ 20 I=1,5
            DØ 20 J=1,5
               READ (5,10) A(I,J)
   20    CØNTINUE
   10    FØRMAT (5F10.0)
   ```

4. How many numbers does the following statement say to write? How many lines will be written?

   ```
         WRITE (6,40) (X(3,M), M=1,30)
   40    FØRMAT (10X, 10F10.4)
   ```

5. Using the statements

> READ (5,10) (A(I), (B(I,J), J=1,3), I=1,2)
> 10   FØRMAT (8F10.0)

specify the card columns from which a variable is read. A(1) read from columns ＿＿＿＿, etc.

6. In what order are the following items stored? How many items are in the array A?

> DIMENSIØN A(2,3)
> READ (5,10) A
> 10   FØRMAT (5X, F5.0)

7. Convert the following flowchart segment into FORTRAN. Assume the variable has been dimensioned. What is this flowchart doing?

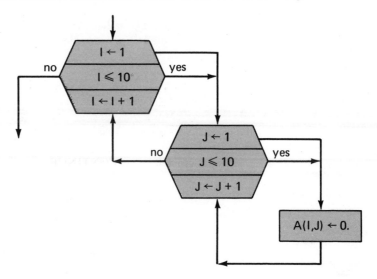

Program Assignments

1. Four postal employees work one week (five days) and put in the hours shown:

	Day 1	Day 2	Day 3	Day 4	Day 5
Worker 1	8.0	8.5	9.5	8.0	8.5
Worker 2	8.0	8.5	10.0	8.0	9.0
Worker 3	8.0	9.0	9.0	9.0	8.5
Worker 4	7.3	8.0	8.2	6.5	0.0

Read in their hours as a table (a two-dimensional array) named WØRK. Assume there is one row per input card. Calculate the total hours worked by each person and the total hours worked by everyone during the week. Write out the results and the input data.

2. As head programmer for the registrar's office, you need to write a program that will classify the number of university students by sex and class standing. Store the information in a table called CLASS. The codes to be used are

freshman	1
sophomore	2
junior	3
senior	4
graduate	5
male	1
female	2

The data is on cards with the following format:

Columns	1–20	student's name
	21–29	social security number
	35	sex
	40	class

Output: On a new page center the following title

STUDENT CLASS INFORMATION

and print the table CLASS with the values found for each entry and the totals. For example,

	FRESHMAN	SOPHOMORE	JUNIOR	SENIOR	GRADUATE	TOTALS
MALE	2	1	3	3	2	11
FEMALE	1	2	3	1	2	9
TOTALS	3	3	6	4	4	

3. Compute and print for each student in the class his average score on four tests, the class average score on each of the four tests, and an average score of the class averages on the four tests. The latter is called the grand average or the grand mean. There will be a maximum of 50 students to process.
   Each data card contains

the student's number	columns	1–3
test score 1		5–7
test score 2		10–12
test score 3		15–17
test score 4		20–22

Output:
a. On the first page print the following headings. Then print the input data.

STUDENT   TEST1   TEST2   TEST3   TEST4

b. On the second page print the students' averages under the following headings.

STUDENT   AVERAGE

c. The third page should list the class average on the four tests and the grand mean.

4. Write a program to perform matrix multiplication and addition with a maximum dimension of 10×10. The input data consists of an $n \times n$ matrix A and an $m \times m$ matrix B. Check to see if $m = n$. If so, then produce a matrix

C = A + B and a matrix D = A × B. If $m \neq n$, write a message saying that the matrices cannot be added or multiplied.

The i,j entry of C is given by the formula

$$c_{ij} = a_{ij} + b_{ij}$$

where a_{ij} and b_{ij} are the i,j entries of matrices A and B, respectively. The first subscript indicates the row and the second subscript indicates the column in which the element appears in the matrix.

The i,j entry of D is given by the formula

$$d_{ij} = a_{i1}b_{1j} + a_{i2}b_{2j} + \cdots + a_{in}b_{nj}$$

or

$$d_{ij} = \sum_{k=1}^{n} a_{ik}b_{kj}$$

Output the matrices A, B, C, and D with appropriate labeling.

The input consists of the values for *n*, the a_{ij} entries of the matrix A, *m* and the b_{ij} entries of the matrix B. Each a_{ij} and b_{ij} is a 2-digit *integer*. The input will be on cards in the following form:

card 1:	n	columns 1–2
card 2:	a_{11}	1–2
	a_{12}	3–4
	a_{13}	5–6
	.	.
	.	.
	.	.
	a_{1n}	
card 3:	a_{21}	1–2
	a_{22}	3–4
	.	.
	.	.
	.	.
	a_{2n}	
	.	
	.	
	.	
card n+1:	a_{n1}	1–2
	.	.
	.	.
	.	.
	a_{nn}	
card n+2:	m	1–2
card n+3:	b_{11}	1–2
	b_{12}	3–4
	.	
	.	
	.	
	b_{1m}	

etc.

5. The southeastern regional manager of the Detroit Motor-Car Company collects data weekly from each of his dealers. The maximum number of dealers at any one time has been 10. Each dealer sells 7 different models made by the DMC. Each dealer's weekly report consists of a punched card containing the number of cars of each model on hand.

It is your job to process two consecutive weeks' reports and determine:

a. The total number of cars of each model in stock in the southeastern region at the end of the first week.
b. The total number of cars of each model in stock in the southeastern region at the end of the second week.
c. The number of cars of each model sold by each dealer during the week.

The data is in the following form:

> first's week's report
> dummy card (dealer code number 00)
> second week's report

The format of each dealer's report is:

dealer code number	columns 1–2
quantity of model 1 on hand	3–4
2	5–6
.	
.	
.	
quantity of model 7 on hand	15–16

Output:

> First week's report data
> Second week's report data
> The three sets of numbers calculated by your program

6. A friend of yours has just developed a compatability test which he wants to use to start MATCH—A Computerized Dating Service. All he needs is for you to write the computer program.

 The input data will be on cards. The first part of the data deck will be results from the men's questionnaires. There will be a maximum of 10 cards. The format of each is:

name	columns 1–18
response to question 1	21
.	.
.	.
.	.
response to question 10	30

All responses are integers. To separate the first part of the data deck from the second part is a card with a 0 in column 80.

 The second part of the data consists of the women's results. Their cards are in the same format as the men's and there should be a maximum of 10 cards.

 The program is supposed to print all the possible dates for all the men. A date should be arranged if the man and the woman agree on at least 8 of the 10 questions. What will you do if a man has no date? This is quite possible since there will be such a limited number of women participating in the dry run.

11.3 Variables with Three Subscripts

The maximum number of subscripts of a FORTRAN variable name is 3. The rules for using a variable with 3 subscripts are similar to those with 1 or 2 subscripts. The variable must be dimensioned; the subscripts are enclosed in parentheses and separated from one another with commas. For example,

DIMENSIØN PLANE (2,3,5)

The variable name is PLANE and the number of storage locations reserved is $2 \times 3 \times 5 = 30$. Let us study an example of a problem in which 3 subscripts are used.

Example

The central weather bureau station receives data from each of its 50 branches throughout the state. At the end of the month it wishes to report the high and low temperatures for each day of the month and the stations reporting them. The input data will be of two types:

> Card 1:
> number of days in the month   columns   1–2
> name of month   3–12
> Card 2–end:
> date   1–2
> weather station number   6–7
> high temperature for that date   12–14
> low temperature for that date   16–18

The dummy data card will contain a −1 in colunms 1–2.

Our output should be in the form of a report:

TEMPERATURE SUMMARY FOR THE MONTH OF XXXXXXXXXX				
DAY	HIGH TEMP.	STATIØN	LØW TEMP.	STATIØN
1	60	11	−11	23
2	49	23	0	16
.	.	.	.	.
.	.	.	.	.
.	.	.	.	.

We can store the information from the reporting stations in an array such as

TEMP(I,J,K) meaning TEMP(date,station,temperature)

The first subscript refers to the date being reported, the second refers to the station reporting, and the third to the temperature. There are two temperatures gathered each day. Therefore, we will store the high temperature in TEMP(I,J,1) and the low temperature in TEMP(I,J,2). Thus, the value of TEMP(21,11,2) is the low temperature at station 11 on the 21st day of the month; the value of TEMP(11,21,2) is the low temperature at station 21 on the 11th day of the month. How shall we dimension TEMP? There is a maximum number of 31 days each month; there are 50 weather stations; and there are two temperatures reported each day. Therefore, we will dimension TEMP with the statement

DIMENSIØN TEMP(31,50,2)

and type it INTEGER because the temperatures are integer values

INTEGER TEMP

Figure 11.2 Beginning Flowchart
Segment for Weather
Report Problem

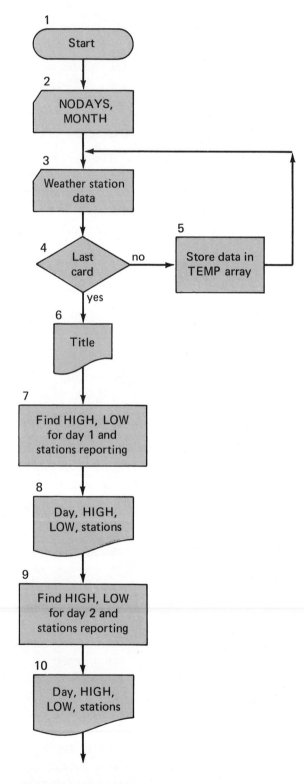

Continue until finished
with last day in month

Let us begin the solution to the problem with the rough flowchart in Figure 11.2. The variable names used are:

NØDAYS — number of days in the month
MØNTH — name of the month
DATE — day of the month reported
STATN — weather station number
HI — high temperature read from the card
LØ — low temperature read from the card
HIGH — high temperature of the day
LØW — low temperature of the day

Figure 11.3 Detailed Flowchart Segment for Storing Input Values in TEMP Array

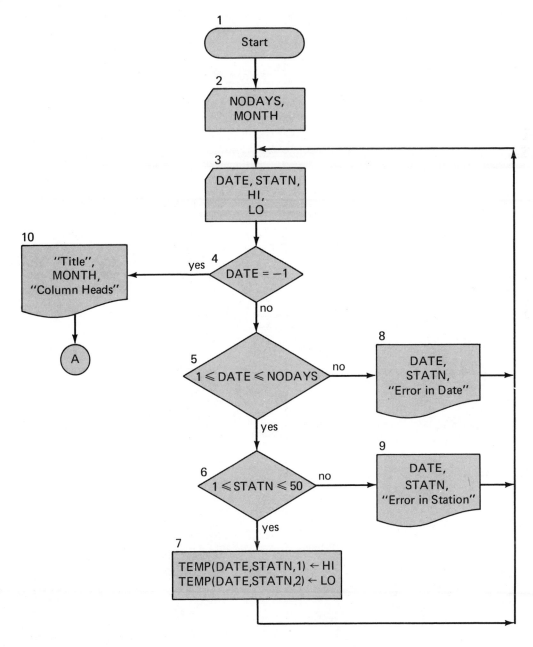

We will now refine the first part of the flowchart which reads in the data (boxes 3, 4, and 5). Before storing the data read into array TEMP, the flowchart includes steps for checking any incorrectly punched cards. See Figure 11.3.

Our next problem is to find for each day the high and low temperatures and the stations which reported them. To simplify the problem let us assume that no two stations had the same high or the same low. The method used is the same one as discussed in Example 2 of section 9.1. We will use the name HSTATN to keep the number of the station reporting the high for the day and LSTATN to save the number of the station reporting the low. We will present the flowchart for day 1 only. See Figure 11.4. Then we will try to generalize the method so that it will work for all the days of the month.

Figure 11.4 Flowchart Segment for Finding HIGH and LOW Temperatures and the Stations Reporting Them for Day 1 Only

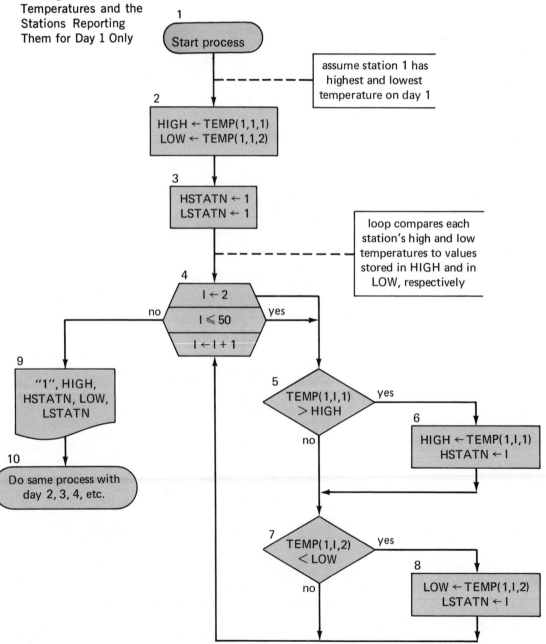

What are the items which make this process find the high and low temperatures for day 1? What would we need to change to make this work for day 2, day 3, and so on? The first subscript of TEMP is the one which specifies the day. If we were to change the flowchart and insert a variable name such as J whenever a 1 appears as the first subscript, we could change J so that J goes from 1 to 2 to 3 to . . . NØDAYS. In other words, we will put boxes 2–8 of the flowchart in Figue 11.4 inside a loop which is controlled by J. The complete flowchart given in Figures 11.5A and 11.5B combines the flowchart segments in Figures 11.3 and 11.4 with the addition of box 11 to control the loop for the days in the month.

Figure 11.5A Final Flowchart Using Three-Dimensional Array for Weather Bureau Problem

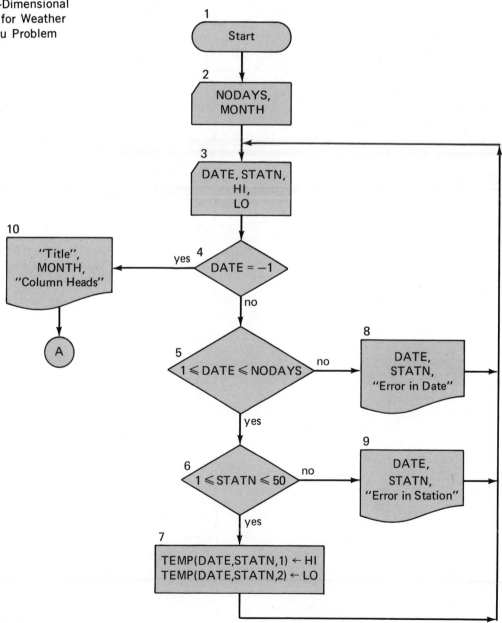

Before writing the program we should decide which variables we want to be *real* and which ones *integer*. In this problem, all variables should be *integer*. This means we need to use a *TYPE* statement to declare DATE, STATN, HI, TEMP, HSTATN, and HIGH as *integers*. All others are integers because their names begin with I, J, K, L, M, or N.

Figure 11.5B Final Flowchart Using Three-Dimensional Array for Weather Bureau Problem (Continued)

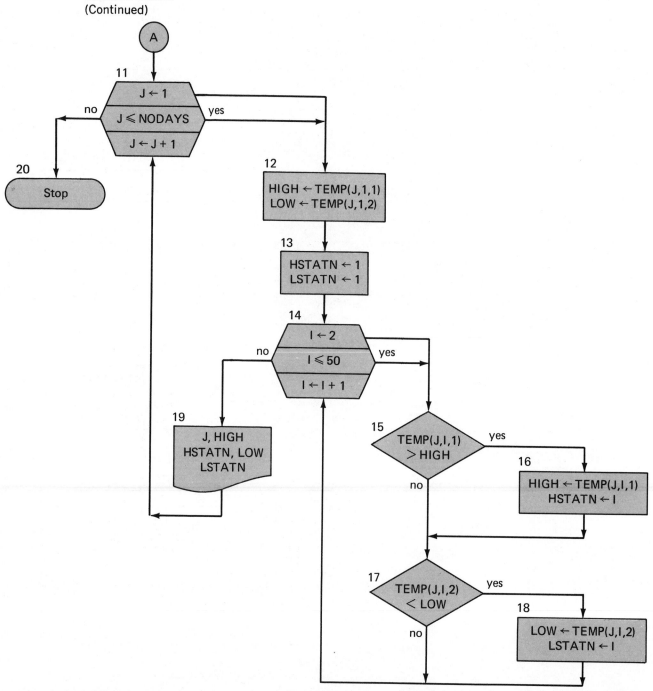

```
C         CENTRAL WEATHER BUREAU REPØRT
          DIMENSIØN TEMP(31,50,2)
          INTEGER DATE, STATN, HI, TEMP, HSTATN, HIGH,
             MØNTH(3)
          READ (5,1000) NØDAYS, MØNTH
1000      FØRMAT (I2,2A4,A2)
   10     READ (5,1030) DATE, STATN, HI, LØ
1030      FØRMAT (I2,3X,I2,4X,I3,1X,I3)
          IF (DATE .EQ. −1) GØ TØ 50
   20     IF (1 .LE. DATE .AND. DATE .LE. NØDAYS) GØ TØ 30
          WRITE (6,1040) DATE, STATN
1040      FØRMAT (10X,I2,5X,I2,5X,13HERRØRbINbDATE)
          GØ TØ 10
   30     IF (1 .LE. STATN .AND. STATN .LE. 50) GØ TØ 40
          WRITE (6,1050) DATE, STATN
1050      FØRMAT (10X,I2,5X,I2,5X,16HERRØRbINbSTATIØN)
          GØ TØ 10
   40     TEMP(DATE,STATN,1) = HI
          TEMP(DATE,STATN,2) = LØ
          GØ TØ 10
   50     WRITE (6,1010) MØNTH
          WRITE (6,1020)
1010      FØRMAT (1H1,44X,24HTEMPERATUREbSUMMARYbFØRb
       .     13HTHEbMØNTHbØFb,2A4,A2/ /)
1020      FØRMAT (27X,3HDAY,13X,10HHIGHbTEMP.,12X,
       .     7HSTATIØN,12X,9HLØWbTEMP.,12X,7HSTATIØN)
          DØ 80 J =1, NØDAYS
             HIGH = TEMP (J,1,1)
             LØW = TEMP (J,1,2)
             HSTATN = 1
             LSTATN = 1
             DØ 70 I = 2,50
             IF (TEMP(J,I,1) .LE. HIGH) GØ TØ 60
             HIGH = TEMP (J,I,1)
             HSTATN = I
   60        IF (TEMP (J,I,2) .GE. LØW) GØ TØ 70
             LØW = TEMP (J,I,2)
             LSTATN = I
   70        CØNTINUE
          WRITE (6,1060) J, HIGH, HSTATN, LØW, LSTATN
1060      FØRMAT (28X,I2,16X,I3,19X,I2,17X,I3,18X,I2)
   80     CØNTINUE
          STØP
          END
```

11.4 Input and Output of Three-dimensional Arrays

We will consider the same cases for input and output of three-dimensional arrays as we did for the input and output of one- and two-dimensional arrays.

Case 1

The specific dimensions of the array are known.

Example

```
        DIMENSIØN  C  (3,2,2)
              .
              .
              .
        READ  (5,100)  C
100     FØRMAT  (10X,F10.2)
        WRITE  (6,100)  C
```

The items in the array C are read and written in the following order in which the first subscript changes more rapidly than the second and the second subscript changes more rapidly than the third.

$$
\begin{array}{c}
C\ (1,1,1) \\
C\ (2,1,1) \\
C\ (3,1,1) \\
C\ (1,2,1) \\
C\ (2,2,1) \\
C\ (3,2,1) \\
C\ (1,1,2) \\
C\ (2,1,2) \\
C\ (3,1,2) \\
C\ (1,2,2) \\
C\ (2,2,2) \\
C\ (3,2,2)
\end{array}
$$

Case 2

Only two of the dimensions of the array are known. The third dimension varies and must be counted by the program.

Example

The general hospital in a large city punches a data card with weekly blood pressure readings for each patient. Blood pressure is taken three times a day, seven days a week. A three-dimensional array called INFØ is used to store the information. The meaning assigned to the subscripts will be

INFØ (patient number, day of week, time of day when blood pressure was taken)

For example, INFØ (10,3,1) contains the tenth patient's blood pressure reading taken on the third day (Wednesday) in the morning. The number of patients in the hospital varies, but the maximum number is 5000. A blank dummy data card is placed at the end of the data cards. (Blanks, when read, are stored as zeros.)

The format of the data card for each patient is:

blood pressure Monday morning	columns	1–3
afternoon		4–6
night		7–9
blood pressure Tuesday morning	columns	11–13
afternoon		14–16
night		17–19

and so on.

To read the data we would have

```
       DIMENSIØN INFØ (5000,7,3)
       I = 1
15     READ (5,100) ((INFØ (I,J,K),K=1,3),J=1,7)
100    FØRMAT (7(3I3,1X))
       IF (INFØ (I,1,1) .EQ. 0) GØ TØ 25
       I = I + 1
       GØ TØ 15
25     N = I − 1
           .
           .
           .
```

The diagram in Table 11.3 illustrates the order in which the values are read, and how the values of I, J, and K change.

Table 11.3

		K		
		1	2	3
I = 1	J = 1	INFØ(1,1,1)	INFØ(1,1,2)	INFØ(1,1,3)
	J = 2	INFØ(1,2,1)	INFØ(1,2,2)	INFØ(1,2,3)
	J = 3	INFØ(1,3,1)	INFØ(1,3,2)	INFØ(1,3,3)
	J = 4	.	.	.
	J = 5	.	.	.
	J = 6	.	.	.
	J = 7	INFØ(1,7,1)	INFØ(1,7,2)	INFØ(1,7,3)
I = 2	J = 1	INFØ(2,1,1)	INFØ(2,1,2)	INFØ(2,1,3)
		.	.	.
		.	.	.
		.	.	.

Case 3

The specific dimensions of the array are variable and are read as part of the data. However, the array must be dimensioned at some maximum amount.

Example

In this example, we use nested implied loops to write out the items in array G. The innermost loop with the index K is completed first; then the loop with the index J is completed; and last the outer loop with the index I is completed. Assume that L = 2, M = 3, and N = 2 and that they have been read previously.

```
       DIMENSIØN G(5,5,5)
           .
           .
           .
       WRITE (6,100) (( (G(I,J,K), K = 1,N), J = 1,M), I = 1,L)
100    FØRMAT (10X, F7.1)
```

The items in the array G are written in the following order:

```
                                G  (1,1,1)
                                G  (1,1,2)
                                G  (1,2,1)
                                G  (1,2,2)
                                G  (1,3,1)
                                G  (1,3,2)
                                G  (2,1,1)
                                G  (2,1,2)
                                G  (2,2,1)
                                G  (2,2,2)
                                G  (2,3,1)
                                G  (2,3,2)
```

We can obtain the same order of items from the following nested DØ loops.

```
        DØ  30  I = 1,L
          DØ  20  J = 1,M
            DØ  10  K = 1,N
              WRITE  (6,100)  G(I,J,K)
10          CØNTINUE
20          CØNTINUE
30    CØNTINUE
```

Exercises

1. How many storage locations are reserved for the array KØN which is dimensioned by

    INTEGER KØN (1000,20,3)

2. Name the variables in the order in which they will be read.

    ```
        REAL  X(2,3,2)
        READ  (5,100)  X
100    FØRMAT  (F7.3)
    ```

3. Design write statements which would produce the following output.

A(1,1,1)	A(1,2,1)	A(1,1,2)	A(1,2,2)
A(2,1,1)	A(2,2,1)	A(2,1,2)	A(2,2,2)
A(3,1,1)	A(3,2,1)	A(3,1,2)	A(3,2,2)
A(4,1,1)	A(4,2,1)	A(4,1,2)	A(4,2,2)

4. What will be computed by the following statements?

    ```
        REAL  Z(3,3,3)
        DØ  10  N = 1,3
          DØ  10  I = 1,3
            DØ  10  J = 1,3
                Z(N,I,J) = 0.
                IF  (I .EQ.  J)  Z(N,I,J) = 1.
10    CØNTINUE
    ```

5. Convert the following flowchart segment to FORTRAN. Dimension all arrays.

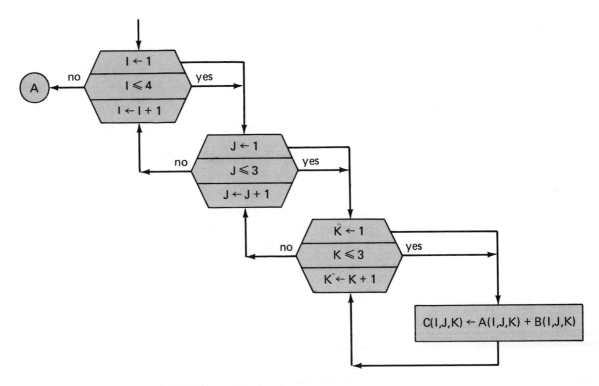

Program Assignments

1. An engineering student has to graph the function

$$f(x,y,z) = x^2 + y - 2z$$

for all integer values of

$$
\begin{array}{ll}
x & \text{between 1 and 3} \\
y & \text{between 1 and 5} \\
z & \text{between 1 and 10}
\end{array}
$$

He needs to find the values of the function for all possible values of x, y, and z. Write a program which will store these values in a three-dimensional array VALUE such that

$$\text{VALUE } (x,y,z) = f(x,y,z)$$

Output the entire VALUE array in the following way.

$$
\begin{array}{l}
\text{VALUE } (1,1,1) = \text{xxxxxxxxx.xx} \\
\text{VALUE } (1,1,2) = \text{xxxxxxxxx.xx}
\end{array}
$$

.
.
.

2. The City Department of Education is tabulating its student enrollment in order to plan for enough classrooms and teachers for next year. For each student there is one card punched in the following form:

name	columns	1–20
sex		21
district no.		23–24
address		26–40
grade		41–42

In the city there are 20 districts numbered 1 through 20. The student's sex is coded as a 1 for boys and a 2 for girls. The school grades are 1–12.

The problem is to determine the number of boys in each grade and district of the city and the number of girls in each grade and district of the city. Write out these totals and label them appropriately.

3. The All-Star Coliseum box office wants to computerize its sales reservations for season tickets. The seats in the coliseum are numbered by row, by seat number and by level. Each of the 25 rows in the coliseum contains 50 seats, and there are 3 levels.

The input to the computer includes one card for each row with the following information:

code for seat 1	columns	1
code for seat 2		2
.		.
.		.
.		.
code for seat 50		50
row number		52–53
level number		55

If code = 1, the seat has been sold. If code = 0, the seat has not been sold. Following these cards is another set of cards which are requests for season tickets. The dummy data card contains a 0 for the level number. Each card has the following format:

level number	columns	1
row number		3–4
seat number		6–7

The program should check the seat requests and see if the seat is taken. If it is, the program should print a message to that effect. If not, the program should mark the seat "sold." The total number of seats sold should be printed at the conclusion of the program.

Chapter 12

Subprograms

12.1 Introduction

All the programs we have studied have been composed of just one unit—the program itself. If we had a large, complex problem to solve, we might want to simplify our work by dividing the problem into several smaller ones. Then we could write several small programs—one for each part of the problem—and test each individual program to see if it works. We could then join together these smaller programs, or **subprograms,** to form one program unit. There would be one program, the **main program,** that monitors the use of the subprograms.

Another reason for writing subprograms is to avoid repetitive processes. If we want to find the average of the numbers in an array A, the average of the numbers in an array B, and the average of the numbers in an array C, we could write the instructions to do the averaging three times—once using A, once using B, and once using C. Or, we could write the instructions once in a subprogram and instruct the computer to use the subprogram once with the data from array A, once with the data from array B, and finally with the data from array C. In programming there are two types of subprograms: functions and subroutines. A function subprogram computes a single valued answer. We have already studied the FORTRAN supplied functions in section 6.4, but in this chapter we will study how a programmer may write his own function subprograms. A subroutine subprogram computes several answers or merely performs a task that the programmer does not wish to include with the instructions of the main program.

12.2 Statement Function

The statement function is similar in use to the FORTRAN supplied functions. The programmer defines the function using a single arithmetic replacement statement. For example, suppose we want to compute the remainder when the value of K is divided by 13. The statement function which will find the remainder is

$$RMN13 \ (K) = K - (K \ / \ 13) \ * \ 13$$

The name of our function is arbitrarily chosen as RMN13. Glancing at this statement, one might think that RMN13 is subscripted by K. But if RMN13 is *not* dimensioned, the compiler assumes that K is the dummy argument of the statement function RMN13. A **dummy argument** is a place holder for the actual argument that will be used in calculation when the function is referenced. The parentheses for (K / 13) are not really necessary but are included to emphasize that the division will be performed first. Let us use the remainder function in solving the following problem.

Example

Read an integer from columns 1–5 of a card. If the number is divisible by 13, print the number. If not, go on to read another card. The dummy data card in the deck contains the number zero. The flowchart solution to the problem is in Figure 12.1.

Figure 12.1 Flowchart Using a Statement Function to Find the Remainder

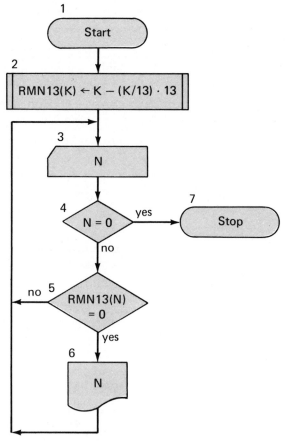

We are using the predefined process symbol, which is shown to the left, to define the statement function RMN13. In the program this symbol converts to a statement which appears before the first executable instruction. This statement is not executed but is used later by the program. In our example RMN13 will be used in an IF statement. The program follows.

```
        RMN13(K) = K − (K / 13) * 13
C       THE ABØVE STATEMENT IS THE FUNCTIØN DEFINING
C           STATEMENT
   10   READ (5,100) N
  100   FØRMAT (I5)
        IF (N .EQ. 0) GØ TØ 20
        IF (RMN13(N) .EQ. 0.0) WRITE (6,110) N
        GØ TØ 10
  110   FØRMAT (10X,I5)
   20   STØP
        END
```

When the computer executes the statement IF (RMN13(N) .EQ. 0.0), the computer must evaluate RMN13(N) before checking to see if the quantity is zero. The value of N replaces K everywhere K appears in the right-hand side of the defining statement. For example, if N = 22, the computation which occurs is

$$22 − (22 / 13) * 13 = 9$$

The value of this entire expression is computed using *integer* arithmetic and is converted to 9.0 because RMN13 is a *real* variable name. Then 9.0 is compared to 0.0 in the IF statement and the value of N is not written.

The dummy argument of the function is named K, an *integer* variable. Therefore, whenever the RMN13 function is referenced, the actual argument given must be an *integer*.

We will study another example of a program with a statement function before stating the rules for the use of statement functions.

Example

We want to determine whether a group of numbers is divisible by either 13 or 17. The data is punched in the following form. The dummy data card signaling the end of the deck contains a zero.

valued to be tested   Columns 1–5

When a number is divisible by either 13 or 17, we want the program to print the number and the divisor.

In the program we can use RMN13 from the previous example and write another statement function RMN17 to find the remainder when a number is divided by 17.

$$\text{RMN17}(K) = K - (K \, / \, 17) \, * \, 17$$

Or we could combine and generalize the two functions into one statement. Instead of writing the specific constants (13 or 17) we could use a variable name in their place. Since this number would be an additional value that must be supplied, we introduce it as another argument L in the defining statement. The new statement function would be

$$\text{RMN}(K,L) = K - (K \, / \, L) \, * \, L$$

We will use the statement function RMN in the flowchart which appears in Figure 12.2 and in the program.

Figure 12.2   Flowchart Showing Statement Function with Two Arguments

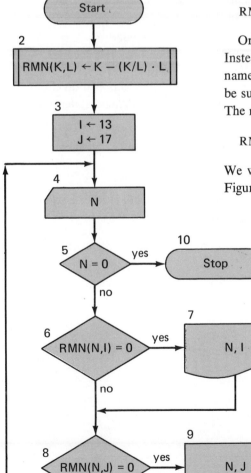

```
C          IN THE STATEMENT FUNCTIØN RMN
C          K IS THE VALUE TØ BE TESTED
C          L IS THE DIVISØR
           RMN(K,L) = K — (K / L) * L
           I = 13
           J = 17
     10    READ (5,110) N
           IF (N .EQ. 0) GØ TØ 20
           IF (RMN(N,I) .EQ. 0.0) WRITE (6,120) N, I
           IF (RMN(N,J) .EQ. 0.0) WRITE (6,120) N, J
           GØ TØ 10
    110    FØRMAT (I5)
    120    FØRMAT (10X,2I7)
     20    STØP
           END
```

Rules for the Use of Statement Functions

1. The general form of the defining statement for the Statement Function is

   fname $(a_1, a_2, \ldots, a_n)$ = expression

   where   fname   is the name of the function. It must be a valid FORTRAN variable name.

   $a_1, a_2, \ldots, a_n$ are simple variables which are the dummy arguments of the function.

   expression   is the expression containing only:
   constants
   non-subscripted variables
   references to FORTRAN supplied functions
   references to previously defined statement functions

2. The statement function must precede the first executable statement of a program and must follow any specification statements.

3. When the statement function is referenced, the list of actual arguments must agree in order, *type,* and number with the argument list of the statement function. For example,

   $F(X,Y,I) = X^{**}I + Y$

   Use 1:

   $Z = F(B,A,2)$

   This will compute $B^2 + A$. In order to compute $A^2 + B$ we would need to write

   $Z = F(A,B,2)$

   Use 2:

   $Q = F(I,K,3)$ *incorrect*

   The arguments I and K do *not* agree in mode with X and Y in the defining statement. Since X and Y are *real* variables, I and K must also be *real* variables.

Use 3:

A = F(XX,YX)   *incorrect*

The original statement function had three arguments. Therefore, each use of this function must contain exactly three arguments.

4. Any expression of the same type as the dummy argument may be used as an actual argument. The expression may be as simple as a constant or a variable. Or it may be more complex and may contain computation to be performed or references to other functions. Following are examples of actual arguments and their corresponding types.

Actual argument	Type
7	Integer
A(3)	Real
Z + B**2	Real
INT (SQRT(X(I)))	Integer

5. The dummy arguments may be the same variable names which appear elsewhere in the program or in other functions defining statements. For example,

```
     F(X) = X * X
     G(X) = 2. * X
10   READ (5,100) X,Y
     Z = F(Y) + G(Y**2)
20   W = X + Z
```

The X in statements 10 and 20 has no connection with the X used to define the statement functions F and G.

12.3 Subprogram Concepts

A subprogram may be classified as a FUNCTION or a SUBROUTINE. One difference between these subprograms is the manner in which they are referenced. A FUNCTION subprogram is referenced in the same manner that statement functions or FORTRAN supplied functions are referenced. A SUBROUTINE subprogram requires a special statement—the CALL statement—to reference it. Both FUNCTION and SUBROUTINE subprograms have names so they may be referenced. In a FUNCTION subprogram the single value computed as an answer must be assigned to the name of the FUNCTION; no value is assigned to the name of a SUBROUTINE.

The first statement in a subprogram is called the **defining statement,** because it specifies whether the subprogram is a FUNCTION or a SUBROUTINE. Part of the defining statement may be a list of arguments. These arguments are variables which may be input to and/or output from the subprogram. The arguments in the defining statements are sometimes called **dummy arguments** because they are place holders for the **actual arguments** that will be used in calculation by the subprogram when referenced.

To contrast the differences between the FUNCTION and SUBROUTINE subprograms we will discuss an example of a program with a subroutine subprogram and then study the same example using a function subprogram.

Example

We want to write a program that will compute the total number of ways of combining N objects taken K at a time. We could use this program if we wished to find the number of different poker hands of 5 cards which could be dealt from a deck of 52 cards. The formula for the number of combinations of N objects taken K at a time is

$$\frac{N!}{K! \, (N - K)!}$$

where N! is read N factorial and is computed by the formula

$$N! = 1 \cdot 2 \cdot 3 \, \cdots \, N$$

For our problem we assume that N is greater than or equal to K and that both N and K are greater than zero. The values of N and K are punched on a card in the following format.

N	columns 1–5
K	6–10

The output will include the values of N, K, and $\dfrac{N!}{K! \, (N - K)!}$.

Since we need to compute three separate factorials—N!, K!, and (N − K)! —we will write a general subroutine which will compute the factorial of any number. We will use the variable name J to represent the number and the variable name JFACT to represent that number's factorial. Therefore, the input to our subroutine is J and the output is JFACT. We will place the variables J and JFACT as arguments in the subroutine defining statement.

The process used to compute J factorial is to start JFACT at 1 and multiply it first by 1, then by 2, then by 3, and so on until we have multiplied it by J. In flowchart form this becomes:

Figure 12.3 Flowchart for Subroutine to Compute N Factorial

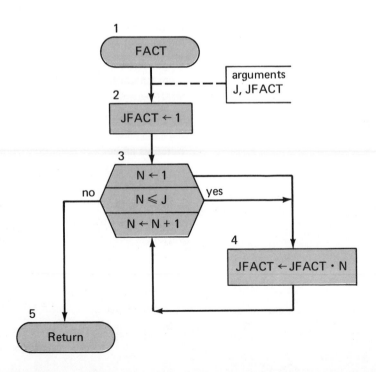

The flowchart for the main program appears in Figure 12.4. The predefined process symbol was used every time the subroutine FACT was referenced. The actual arguments are N and NFACT, K and KFACT, N − K and NMKF.

Figure 12.4 Flowchart for Main Program Using Subroutine FACT

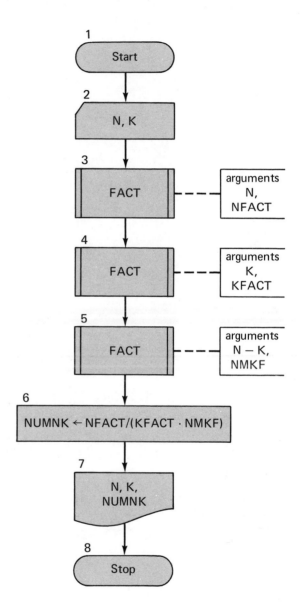

Program 12.1 on page 178 shows the main program with a SUBRØUTINE subprogram following it, because this is the order in which they will appear in the card deck. Since SUBRØUTINE FACT returns only one value to the main program, it could be written as a FUNCTIØN subprogram. Program 12.2 shows how the sample program is written using a FUNCTIØN subprogram.

Note several differences between Programs 12.1 and 12.2.

1. The FUNCTIØN has only one argument, the SUBRØUTINE has two. The variable JFACT which was an argument in the SUBRØUTINE has become the name of the FUNCTIØN. The value computed in the FUNCTIØN must be stored as the value of the FUNCTIØN's name.

Program 12.1	Program 12.2

<pre>C   THIS PRØGRAM USES A SUBRØUTINE
C   AND CØMPUTES THE NUMBER ØF
C   CØMBINATIØNS ØF N ØBJÈCTS TAKEN
C   K AT A TIME
C
C   NUMNK — NUMBER ØF CØMBINATIØNS
C
     READ(5,100) N, K
100 FØRMAT (2I5)
     CALL FACT (N,NFACT)
     CALL FACT (K,KFACT)
     CALL FACT (N–K, NMKF)
     NUMNK = NFACT / (KFACT * NMKF)
C
     WRITE(6,110) N, K, NUMNK
110 FØRMAT (10X,4HNb=b,I5,5X,4HKb=b,I5,
     5X,15HCØMBINATIØNSb=b,I5.)
     STØP
     END
     SUBRØUTINE FACT (J,JFACT)
C   THIS SUBRØUTINE CØMPUTES
C   JFACT — THE VALUE ØF J FACTØRIAL
C
     JFACT = 1
     DØ 100 N = 1, J
       JFACT = JFACT * N
100 CØNTINUE
     RETURN
     END</pre>
	<pre>C THIS PRØGRAM USES A FUNCTIØN
	C AND CØMPUTES THE NUMBER ØF
	C CØMBINATIØNS ØF N ØBJECTS TAKEN
	C K AT A TIME
	C
	C NUMNK — NUMBER ØF CØMBINATIØNS
	C
	     READ(5,100) N, K
	100 FØRMAT (2I5)
	C
	C
	C
	10 NUMNK=JFACT(N)/(JFACT(K)*JFACT(N—K))
	C
	     WRITE(6,110) N, K, NUMNK
	110 FØRMAT (10X,4HNb=b,I5,5X,4HKb=b,I5,
	   . 5X,15HCØMBINATIØNSb=b,I5)
	     STØP
	     END
	     FUNCTIØN JFACT(J)
	C THIS FUNCTIØN CØMPUTES
	C JFACT — THE VALUE ØF J FACTØRIAL
	C
	     JFACT = 1
	     DØ 100 N = 1, J
	       JFACT = JFACT * N
	100 CØNTINUE
	     RETURN
	     END</pre>

2. The SUBRØUTINE is used through a CALL statement. During execution when the CALL is encountered, control transfers to the SUBRØUTINE. Then when the RETURN statement is encountered, control returns to the statement following the CALL. We may picture this as

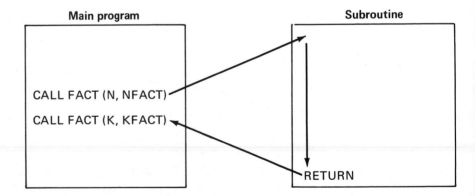

3. The program which uses the SUBRØUTINE (Program 12.1) has three additional variables: NFACT, KFACT, and NMKF, used in calculating NUMNK. These are not necessary in Program 12.2 because the function reference is used in statement 10 to compute NUMNK. Before the computer can divide JFACT(N) by the product of JFACT(K) and JFACT(N–K), it must compute these values. Therefore, the FUNCTIØN is referenced three times. One time the value of N is substituted as the value of J in the FUNCTIØN, and JFACT(N) is computed. Similarly, JFACT(K) and JFACT(N–K) are found. When the FUNCTION returns to the main pro-

gram, it returns to the statement in which it was referenced; so, finally NUMNK can be computed. The following diagram illustrates the way in which a function is referenced.

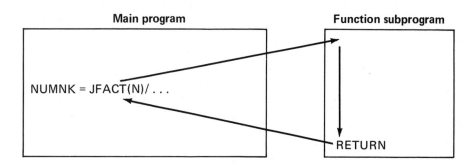

4. The statement number 100 and the variable N are used for different purposes in each main program and corresponding subprograms. The main program and subprograms are separate entities and therefore may use the same numbers and variable names. There is no relationship between statement numbers and variable names in different program units.

12.4 Rules for the Use of FUNCTION and SUBROUTINE Subprograms

Defining the Subprogram

The defining statement of a SUBROUTINE is one of the following:

SUBRØUTINE name
SUBRØUTINE name $(a_1,a_2,a_3, \ldots ,a_n)$

where   name   is the symbolic name of the SUBROUTINE subprogram. It must be a valid FORTRAN variable name.

$a_1,a_2, \ldots ,a_n$ are the dummy arguments

The defining statement of a FUNCTION has the following form:

type FUNCTIØN name $(a_1,a_2, \ldots ,a_n)$

where   type   denotes the *type* of the FUNCTION. It may be omitted. If omitted and the name of the FUNCTION is an *integer* variable name, the value of the FUNCTION is of type *integer*. Similarly, if type is omitted and the name of the FUNCTIØN is a *real* variable name, the value of the FUNCTIØN is of type *real*.

       name   is the name of the FUNCTION. It must be a valid FORTRAN variable name.

$a_1 ,a_2, \ldots ,a_n$ are the dummy arguments of the FUNCTION. They may be variable names or array names. There must be at least one argument.

Referencing the Subprogram

A CALL statement is used to reference a SUBROUTINE subprogram. A CALL statement has one of two forms:

CALL name
CALL name $(a_1,a_2,a_3, \ldots ,a_n)$

where   name   is the name of the SUBROUTINE subprogram
$a_1,a_2, \ldots ,a_n$ are the actual arguments

The reference to a FUNCTION subprogram is of the form:

name $(a_1,a_2, \ldots ,a_n)$

where   name   is the name of the FUNCTION subprogram
$a_1,a_2, \ldots ,a_n$ are the actual arguments

Reference to a FUNCTION subprogram may only appear in the expression of an arithmetic replacement statement or in a relational expression.

Arguments

A *dummy* argument may be:

1. non-subscripted variable
2. array name

An *actual* argument may be:

1. non-subscripted variable
2. array name
3. array element
4. any expression
5. Hollerith constant [1]
6. reference to a FORTRAN supplied function

Terminating

Return Statement.   The form of the RETURN statement is

RETURN

a. A RETURN statement is the last statement executed before leaving a subprogram.
b. A RETURN statement may *not* be the last statement in the range of a DØ loop.
c. More than one RETURN statement is permissible in a subprogram.
d. The RETURN statement returns control to the referencing program. In a FUNCTION subprogram, control returns to the statement containing the function reference. In a SUBROUTINE subprogram, control returns to the first executable statement following the CALL statement.

END Statement.   An END statement must be used to indicate the last physical statement of a subprogram.

---

[1] Hollerith constants are discussed in section 13.5.

Structure

The general structure of an individual subprogram is

a. defining statement
b. instructions
c. RETURN statement which denotes the logical ending of a subprogram
d. END statement which denotes the physical end of a subprogram deck

A subprogram follows the END statement of the main program and precedes the data. If a main program uses several subprograms, they may appear in any order after the main program.

Remarks

a. The actual arguments in the referencing statement must agree in number, order, and *type* with the dummy arguments in the defining statement.
b. When a dummy argument is the name of an array, the corresponding actual argument must also be the name of an array.
c. Since the subprogram is an entity, variable names (except dummy arguments) and statement numbers do not relate to the same name or statement number in the main program or other subprograms.
d. All arrays used must be dimensioned in the subprogram and in the referencing program.
e. One or more RETURN statements must be included in a subprogram.
f. A subprogram may not reference itself.
g. Any subprogram may reference another subprogram. However, if subprogram A references subprogram B, then subprogram B may *not* reference subprogram A.
h. The value computed by a FUNCTION subprogram must be assigned to the name of the FUNCTION in a replacement statement in the subprogram.
i. A subprogram may define or redefine one or more of its arguments. If the values of any of the dummy arguments are changed in the subprogram, the values of the actual arguments are also changed and do *not* return to their original value when control transfers to the referencing program.

12.5 Additional Examples

Example Using Statement Functions

We will now study a sample problem in which we use two statement functions to evaluate formulas. Suppose we want to find the real roots, X_1 and X_2, of three quadratic equations in a program. In general, the 3 different equations may be written as:

$$a_1X^2 + b_1X + c_1 = 0$$
$$a_2X^2 + b_2X + c_2 = 0$$
$$a_3X^2 + b_3X + c_3 = 0$$

The data cards will contain the following values.

card 1:
columns 1–3   number of equations

card 2:
  columns 1–5, 6–10
          and 11–15: values for a_1, b_1, and c_1
card 3:
  columns   "   : values for a_2, b_2, and c_2
card 4:
  columns   "   : values for a_3, b_3, and c_3

We will write the program so that it will find the roots of any number of equations (a maximum of 10). Then, if we later want to find the roots of four equations, our only change will be on the data cards.

We may find the roots by using the formulas

$$X_1 = \frac{-b + \sqrt{b^2 - 4ac}}{2a} \qquad X_2 = \frac{-b - \sqrt{b^2 - 4ac}}{2a}$$

Since we find the expression $\sqrt{b^2 - 4ac}$ in both formulas, we may shorten our work by writing a statement function for the square root of the discriminant ($\sqrt{b^2 - 4ac}$). (The discriminant is defined as $b^2 - 4ac$.) Let the statement function be named RTDIS, and let the dummy arguments be A, B, and C. The defining statement is

  RTDIS(A,B,C) = SQRT(B * B − 4. * A * C)

Another statement function will compute the two roots. The expressions for computing the roots X_1 and X_2 need the values of a, b, and $\pm \sqrt{b^2 - 4ac}$. We can let a dummy argument, DIS, represent the value of the expression $\sqrt{b^2 - 4ac}$. The other dummy arguments will be A and B. The statement function to find one root is:

  RØØT(A,B,DIS) = (− B + DIS)/(2. * A)

If we have just one equation, such as $2.0x^2 + 5.0x − 3.0 = 0.0$, we could use the two statement functions to find its roots, X1 and X2. The FORTRAN statements for doing this are:

  D = RTDIS(2.0,5.0,−3.0)
  X1 = RØØT(2.0,5.0,D)
  X2 = RØØT(2.0,5.0,−D)

The value assigned to D is $\sqrt{5.0 \cdot 5.0 - 4.0 \cdot 2.0 \cdot (-3.0)} = \sqrt{49.0} = 7.0$. The values assigned to X1 and X2 are

$$X1 = \frac{-5.0 + 7.0}{2.0 \cdot 2.0} \quad \text{and} \quad X2 = \frac{-5.0 - 7.0}{2.0 \cdot 2.0}$$

A general flowchart for our problem is shown at the left.

Since we have three sets of equations, we can use three different arrays, A, B, C, to store the coefficients. We can read the values of the coefficients for the first equation into A(1), B(1), and C(1), the values of the coefficients for the second equation into A(2), B(2), and C(2), and for the third equation into A(3), B(3), and C(3). We will have two additional arrays X1 and X2 to store the roots of each of the equations. The flowchart segment for finding the roots of the first equation could be

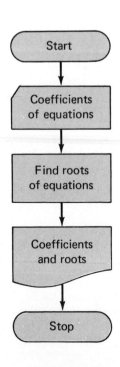

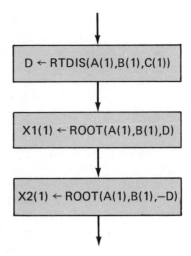

For the second equation, it could be

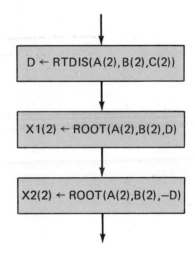

And similarly for the third equation. Note that the only difference between the flowchart segments is the subscript of the variables. Let us use a loop with an index I, that assumes values from 1 to 3 to repeat the execution of the statements.

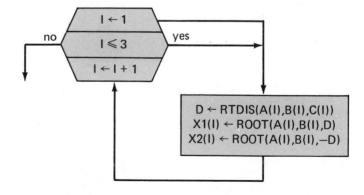

A complete program that allows for handling a maximum of ten equations appears below. Because the first data card contains a value for the number of equations, this value is read first and is assigned to the variable N. In this general program the value of N is used as the upper bound in the implied loops and DØ statement.

```
C        THIS PRØGRAM FINDS THE RØØTS ØF UP TØ 10
C        QUADRATIC EQUATIØNS
         DIMENSIØN A(10), B(10), C(10), X1(10), X2(10)
C        RTDIS AND RØØT ARE STATEMENT FUNCTIØNS
         RTDIS(A,B,C) = SQRT(B*B − 4.*A*C)
         RØØT(A,B,DIS) = (−B + DIS)/(2.*A)
         READ(5,100) N, (A(I), B(I), C(I), I = 1,N)
         DØ 10 I = 1,N
             D = RTDIS(A(I),B(I),C(I))
             X1(I) = RØØT(A(I),B(I),D)
             X2(I) = RØØT(A(I),B(I),−D)
  10     CØNTINUE
         WRITE (6,110) (A(I), B(I), C(I), X1(I), X2(I), I = 1,N)
 100     FØRMAT(I3/(3F5.2))
 110     FØRMAT(1H1,10X,12HCØEFFICIENTS,20X,5HRØØTS//
   .     (1H0,3F10.2,5X,2F10.2))
         STØP
         END
```

Example Using Function Subprogram

We will now consider a problem which uses a FUNCTION subprogram. Suppose we are working with a huge array of data which is collected in an experiment. We now wish to go through this array of real numbers and find out if a 0.0 was recorded. If there was one, our program should go no further, but should print a message that the array contains a zero element and should then stop. However, if no item in the array is zero, we want to check to see if other numbers were recorded in the experiment and find their location in the array. There are at most 1000 numbers from the experiment.

The input data is punched in the following format:

	card 1:		
	columns	1– 4	number of items in array
	card 2:		
	columns	1–10	value of first item in array
		11–20	second
		21–30	third
data for		31–40	fourth
array		41–50	fifth
		51–60	sixth
		61–70	seventh
		71–80	eighth
	card 3 to end of array:		
	uses same format as card 2.		
numbers	columns	1–10	value to check (each number
to			is on a separate card)
check			

The dummy data card contains a −9999.9 in columns 1–10.

The output will be either a message saying there is a zero in the array or a list of numbers checked and their position (subscript) in the array. For example, if we were looking to see if 11.23 is part of the data and $EXPR(21) = 11.23$, then we should print 11.23 and 21.

Our problem asks us to search through the array for zero and for each number on the data card. Therefore, to avoid duplication of work we will write a FUNCTIØN which will compare the value of each element in the array with a given number. If our particular number is in the array, the function will tell

Figure 12.5 Flowchart for FUNC–
TION to Search an Ar-
ray for the Particular
Location of a Number

us the subscript of that item; otherwise the value of the function will be zero.
Figure 12.5 depicts the flowchart for the function subprogram, and Figure 12.6
gives the flowchart for the main program.

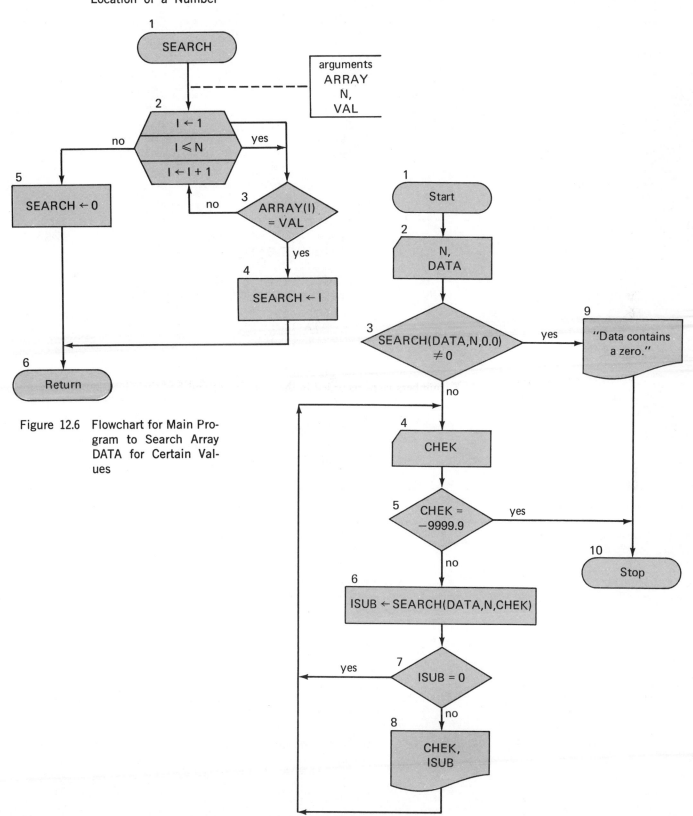

Figure 12.6 Flowchart for Main Program to Search Array
DATA for Certain Val-
ues

Before writing the program and subprogram we should examine our variable names and determine which ones we want to be *real* and which ones *integer*. The *real* items should be

> DATA
> CHEK
> ARRAY
> VAL

The *integer* ones should be

> N
> SEARCH   (since it is the value of a subscript)
> ISUB   (since it is the value of a subscript)

Program 12.3

```
C        THIS PRØGRAM LØØKS THRØUGH A SET ØF DATA TØ
C        SEE IF ØNE ØF THE ITEMS IS ZERØ. IF SØ, THE
C        PRØGRAM STØPS. ØTHERWISE THE PRØGRAM LØØKS
C        THRØUGH THE DATA TØ SEE IF IT CØNTAINS
C        ØTHER VALUES.
C            DATA - ARRAY TØ SEARCH
C            CHEK - VALUE TØ LØØK FØR
C
         REAL DATA(1000)
         INTEGER SEARCH
         WRITE (6,130)
         READ (5,100) N, (DATA(I),I=1,N)
  100    FØRMAT (I4/(8F10.0))
         IF (SEARCH(DATA,N,0.0) .NE. 0) GØ TØ 20
   10    READ (5,110) CHEK
  110    FØRMAT (F10.0)
         IF (CHEK .EQ. -9999.9) GØ TØ 30
         ISUB = SEARCH(DATA,N,CHEK)
         IF (ISUB .EQ. 0) GØ TØ 10
         WRITE (6,120) CHEK, ISUB
  120    FØRMAT (10X,8HVALUEb=b,F12.4,10X,11HLØCATIØNb=b,
        .    I5)
         GØ TØ 10
  130    FØRMAT (1H1)
   20    WRITE (6,140)
  140    FØRMAT (10X,20HDATAbCØNTAINSbAbZERØ)
   30    STØP
         END


         INTEGER FUNCTIØN SEARCH (ARRAY,N,VAL)
C
C        THIS FUNCTIØN SEARCHES AN ARRAY ØF LENGTH N
C        TØ SEE IF IT CØNTAINS THE VALUE VAL. IF IT DØES,
C        SEARCH IS THE SUBSCRIPT ØF THAT ITEM IN THE
C        ARRAY. IF NØT, SEARCH EQUALS ZERØ.
C
         REAL ARRAY(1000)
         DØ 10 I = 1,N
            IF (ARRAY(I) .EQ. VAL) GØ TØ 20
   10    CØNTINUE
         SEARCH = 0
         RETURN
```

```
20    SEARCH = I
      RETURN
      END
```

Note several things in the main program and FUNCTIØN subprogram.

1. The variable name SEARCH is declared an *integer* in both the program and the subprogram.
2. The array DATA which is substituted for the dummy argument ARRAY is dimensioned in the program just as ARRAY is dimensioned in the FUNCTIØN.

Example Using a SUBRØUTINE Subprogram

A teacher gave his class two multiple-choice tests where the answers consisted of one digit (1, 2, or 3). The teacher needs a program that will grade the tests. Each test had a total of 25 questions, worth 4 points each.

> Data Card 1:
>   columns 1–25 correct answers to test 1
>   columns 51–75 correct answers to test 2

For each student there is a data card with the following information:

> columns 1–20 student's name
> columns 21–45 student's answers to test 1
> columns 51–75 student's answers to test 2

The dummy data card contains a zero in column 21.

For each student the output should consist of:

> the student's name
> the grade on test 1
> the grade on test 2

Figure 12.7 on page 188 gives a preliminary flowchart for the problem.

Since the steps for obtaining the results of test 1 or test 2 are the same, we can use a SUBROUTINE subprogram. The SUBROUTINE subprogram will do the following for one test: (1) compare student's answers with correct answers, and (2) compute the total grade.

The SUBROUTINE will be used twice for each student—once to obtain the grade on test 1 and once to obtain the grade on test 2.

In order to compute a student's test grade, the SUBROUTINE must know the correct answers to the test and the student's answers. The main program will read these answers and then pass them as actual arguments to the SUBROUTINE. The subprogram will then compute the student's grade and return it to the main program where the grade will be written.

The flowchart in Figure 12.8 for the subprogram follows the outline given above. The name of the SUBROUTINE subprogram is EVAL, and the variable names used have the following meaning:

> KEY —correct answers
> IT   —answers on a test
> NP —number of points accumulated

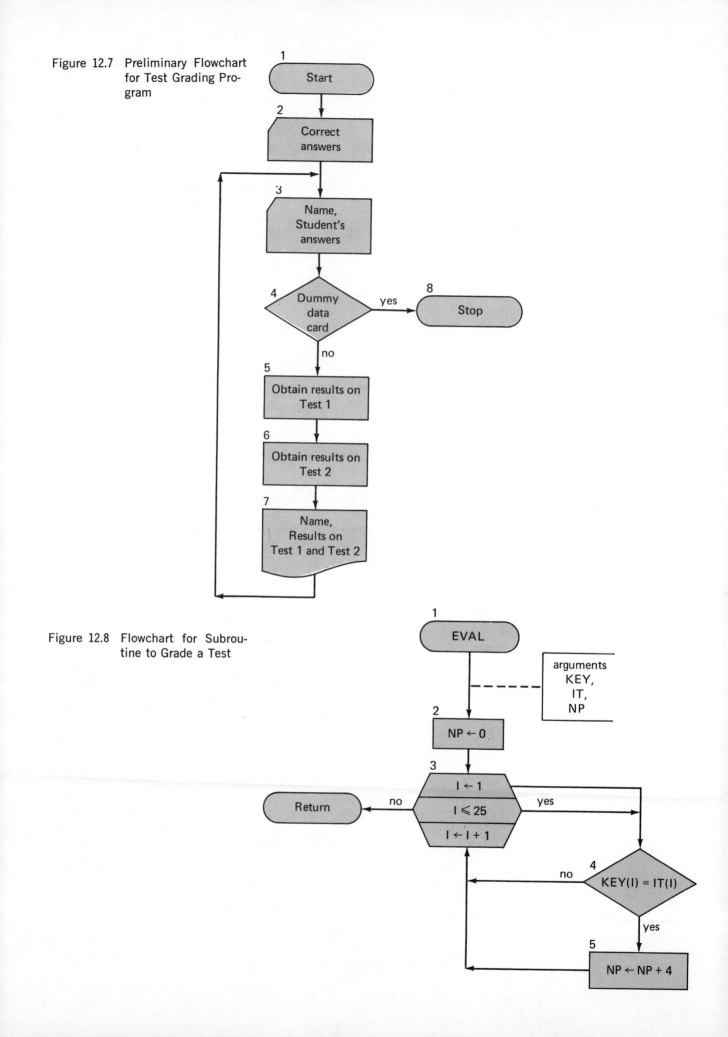

Figure 12.7 Preliminary Flowchart for Test Grading Program

Figure 12.8 Flowchart for Subroutine to Grade a Test

The flowchart in Figure 12.9 is for the main program. The predefined process symbol is used whenever the SUBROUTINE is referenced. The name of the subprogram EVAL is given and then the actual arguments are listed in an annotation box. The following variable names are used in the flowchart.

KEY1	—array containing correct answers on test 1
KEY2	—array containing correct answers on test 2
NAME	—student's name
IT1	—array for student's answers on test 1
IT2	—array for student's answers on test 2
IGRADE	—array for a student's scores on tests
EVAL	—SUBROUTINE subprogram

The FORTRAN program followed by the SUBRØUTINE EVAL is:

```
C        THIS PRØGRAM GRADES TWØ TESTS FØR EACH
C        STUDENT
C
C            KEY1 — CØRRECT ANSWERS TØ TEST 1
C            KEY2 — CØRRECT ANSWERS TØ TEST 2
C            NAME — STUDENT NAME
C            IT1 — STUDENT ANSWERS TØ TEST 1
C            IT2 — STUDENT ANSWERS TØ TEST 2
C            IGRADE(1) — GRADE ØN TEST 1
C            IGRADE(2) — GRADE ØN TEST 2
C
         DIMENSIØN KEY1(25),KEY2(25),NAME(5),IT1(25),
       .    IT2(25),IGRADE(2)
         WRITE (6,90)
         READ (5,100) KEY1, KEY2
    10   READ (5,110) NAME, IT1, IT2
         IF (IT1(1) .EQ. 0) GØ TØ 20
         CALL EVAL (KEY1,IT1,IGRADE(1))
         CALL EVAL (KEY2,IT2,IGRADE(2))
         WRITE (6,120) NAME, (IGRADE(K), K=1,2)
         GØ TØ 10
    90   FØRMAT(1H1,38X,4HNAME,17X,6HTESTb1,10X,6HTESTb2)
   100   FØRMAT (25I1,25X,25I1)
   110   FØRMAT (5A4,25I1,5X,25I1)
   120   FØRMAT (31X,5A4,11X,I3,13X,I3)
    20   STØP
         END


         SUBRØUTINE EVAL (KEY,IT,NP)
C        THIS SUBRØUTINE GRADES A TEST ØF 25 QUESTIØNS
C        EACH QUESTIØN IS WØRTH 4 PØINTS EACH
C            KEY — CØRRECT ANSWERS
C            IT — STUDENT ANSWERS
C            NP — GRADE ØN THE TEST
C
         DIMENSIØN KEY(25),IT(25)
         NP = 0
         DØ 10 I = 1,25
            IF (KEY(I) .EQ. IT(I)) NP = NP + 4
    10   CØNTINUE
         RETURN
         END
```

Figure 12.9 Flowchart for Main
Program to Grade
Students' Tests

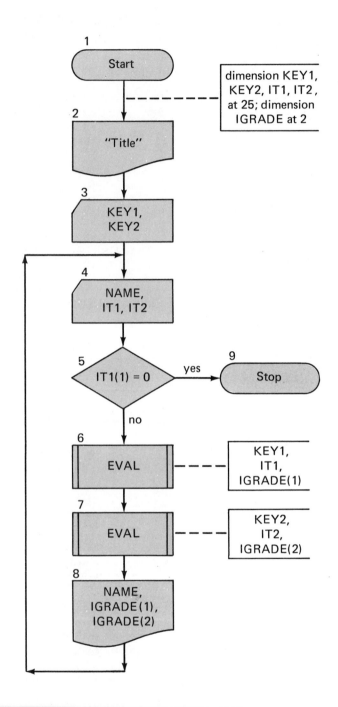

12.6 COMMON Storage

In our previous examples, we passed values to and from subprograms through the use of arguments. Dummy arguments are necessary when we wish to reference a subprogram several times and use different actual arguments with each reference. However, if we always use the subprograms with the same actual arguments, we may place the arguments in a COMMON storage area. This is a special block of memory locations that may be shared by different program units.

Suppose we have a main program which calls subroutine MATCH only once.

```
C        MAIN PRØGRAM
         REAL X(100), Y(100)
         .
         .
         .

         CALL MATCH(X, Y, N, NUM)
         .
         .
         .

         END
```

The subroutine is defined by

```
         SUBRØUTINE MATCH(XS, YS, N, M)
         REAL XS(100), YS(100)
         .
         .
         .
```

We may rewrite the main program and the subroutine to eliminate all arguments. The main program communicates the values to and from MATCH through the use of COMMON storage.

```
C        MAIN PRØGRAM
         CØMMØN X(100), Y(100), N, NUM
         .
         .
         .

         CALL  MATCH
         .
         .
         .

         END
         SUBRØUTINE MATCH
         CØMMØN XS(100), YS(100), N, M
         .
         .
         .
```

The COMMON statement appears in the main program and in the subroutine. It tells how the COMMON storage locations are referenced by both program units. We may picture these COMMON locations with the following diagram. A total of 202 locations are reserved in the COMMON storage area. The COMMON statement not only reserves this space, but also dimensions the arrays. We could have said

```
         DIMENSIØN XS(100), YS(100)
         CØMMØN XS, YS, N, M
```

and all 100 locations of the XS and YS arrays would be in COMMON storage. The subroutine references the first location by using the name XS(1). The main program references the first location by using the name X(1). The name XS(1) cannot be used in the main program to reference location one, and similarly the name X(1) cannot be used in the subroutine to reference location one.

Figure 12.10 Referencing of COM-
MON Storage Loca-
tions

Main program	COMMON storage locations		Subroutine MATCH
X(1)			XS(1)
X(2)			XS(2)
	.		
	.		
	.		
X(100)			XS(100)
Y(1)			YS(1)
Y(2)			YS(2)
Y(3)			YS(3)
	.		
	.		
	.		
Y(100)			YS(100)
N			N
NUM			M

To illustrate how COMMON storage could be used for the communication of variables between subprograms and the main program, we will give part of a program which has just added a subroutine to check the input data to see if it is correct. The data is read into an array KØDE. The values of KØDE should be between 1 and 35. If any element of KØDE is not correct, the subroutine will print the number and its subscript. The subroutine needs to know the values in the KØDE array and the number of elements in the array (NUM). Both the KØDE array and the variable NUM will be placed in COMMON storage.

```
C       MAIN PRØGRAM
C       THIS PART READS IN THE KØDE ARRAY
C       AND CALLS SUBRØUTINE CHECK
        REAL MØNEY, SUM(20,3)
        CØMMØN KØDE(1000), NUM
        READ(5,100) NUM, (KØDE(I), I=1,NUM)
        CALL CHECK
        .
        .
        .

        END
        SUBRØUTINE CHECK
        CØMMØN KØDE(1000), NUM
        DØ 20 I = 1, NUM
            IF (KØDE (I) .GT. 35) GØ TØ 10
            IF (KØDE(I) .GE. 1) GØ TØ 20
10          WRITE(6,100) I, KØDE(I)
20      CØNTINUE
100     FØRMAT(10X, 2I10)
        RETURN
        END
```

It is not necessary to use identical COMMON statements in the program and subprogram. But if we had said

        CØMMØN KDS(1000), NUM

in SUBRØUTINE CHECK, then we would need to write the name KDS everywhere we had used the name KØDE in the *subroutine*. We would *not* need to change the main program.

If we write a program which has several subprograms and uses variables in COMMON storage, probably not every subprogram will use every variable in the COMMON storage area. One subprogram may reference some of the locations; another may reference different ones. In this case, we could divide our COMMON storage area into blocks so that each subprogram will have access to only those locations which it needs. To tell the computer which variables go into which blocks of COMMON storage, we will name each block. Any COMMON block which is named is called **labeled** COMMON storage. In our first examples, because we did not give any name to the COMMON storage area, this area is called **unlabeled** COMMON storage.

For example, study the COMMON statements in the following main program, subroutine and function. There are two COMMON storage blocks: one named FIRST and the other named LAST. The subroutine may reference only the variables stored in the FIRST block and the function may reference only those in LAST.

```
C      MAIN PRØGRAM
       CØMMØN /FIRST/A(10),B(10) /LAST/XY(20)
       . . . . . . . . . . . . . .

       SUBRØUTINE ØNE
       CØMMØN /FIRST/ANS(10),VAL(10)
       . . . . . . . . . . . . . .

       FUNCTIØN TWØ (CHECK)
       CØMMØN /LAST/PRØD(20)
```

Figure 12.11 illustrates the COMMON storage memory locations for the above statements.

Figure 12.11 Referencing of Labeled COMMON Storage Locations

	Main program	COMMON storage location	SUBROUTINE ONE	FUNCTION TWO
FIRST	A(1)		ANS(1)	
	A(2)		ANS(2)	
	A(3)		ANS(3)	
	⋮	⋮	⋮	
	A(10)		ANS(10)	
	B(1)		VAL(1)	
	B(2)		VAL(2)	
	⋮	⋮	⋮	
	B(10)		VAL(10)	
LAST	XY(1)			PROD(1)
	XY(2)			PROD(2)
	⋮	⋮		⋮
	XY(20)			PROD(20)

The COMMON statement may be one of the following two forms.

CØMMØN list
CØMMØN /label₁/list₁/label₂/list₂/ . . . /labelₙ/listₙ

where   each label is any legal FORTRAN name given to the CØMMØN block. It must be enclosed in slashes.

        each list   is any list of variables, array names or array declarators

Rules for the Use of the COMMON Statement

1. The order in which the variables are listed in the statement determine the way in which the storage locations are referenced.

Example

Suppose that the variables A, B, and C of a main program are to share COMMON storage locations with the variables X, Y, and Z of a subprogram. We want A and X to have the same location, B and Y to share another location, and C and Z another location. To obtain the desired relationship the main program would specify

```
C       MAIN PRØGRAM
        CØMMØN A, B, C
```

the subprogram would specify

```
        FUNCTIØN ØNE (TIME)
        CØMMØN X, Y, Z
```

It would *not* be sufficient just to list the variables in a different order. If the subprogram had given

```
        FUNCTIØN ØNE (TIME)
        CØMMØN Z, X, Y
```

then A and Z would share the same location, B and X would share another location, and C and Y another location.

2. The same variable names may be used in the COMMON statements appearing in different programs. As illustrated above, the association is by order in the list and not by name.

3. If several COMMON statements are given in a program unit, they are equivalent to one continuous COMMON statement. The following examples would have the same result in a program.

   a. CØMMØN N, A(10), B(10)
      CØMMØN X(5), W(3)
   b. CØMMØN N, A(10), B(10), X(5), W(3)

4. Unlabeled and labeled COMMON storage may be declared in the same statement. For example, the variables K and N are in unlabeled COMMON locations; SS and TT are in the COMMON block BLØCK1; and the array VAL is in BLØCK2.

CØMMØN K, N /BLØCK1/ SS, TT /BLØCK2/ VAL(30)

5. If a block name is omitted, but two consecutive slashes are given before the list, then the variables in the list are assigned to unlabeled COMMON locations. For example,

CØMMØN /BLØCK1/ SS, TT /BLØCK2/ VAL(30) / / K, N

6. We may reserve storage locations for an array in COMMON storage in one of two ways:

   a. dimension the array using a DIMENSIØN or *type* statement and place the array name in the COMMON statement.

DIMENSIØN B(2000)
REAL MØN(350)
CØMMØN B, MØN

   b. dimension the array with an array declarator in the COMMON statement.

REAL MØN
CØMMØN B(2000), MØN(350)

7. COMMON statements must precede any executable statements, DATA statements, and statement functions.

Examples Using Labeled and Unlabeled COMMON Storage

COMMON storage is used primarily in large programs. Our next example is fairly simple, but its purpose is to illustrate how to establish communication between different program units using COMMON storage. The subprograms in the example are written with the purpose of delegating some of the work to the subprograms. We have not referenced the subprograms more than once with different sets of data as we did in some of our earlier examples.

A large jewelry store has been robbed and the owner wishes to find the amount of his loss. The data cards will contain information from the inventory made before the theft and a new inventory made after the theft. There are 1000 entries in each inventory, so we do not need a dummy data card.

For each type of item in the store a card is punched containing the following information.

identification number	columns	1–5
quantity		6–10
price per item		11–20

Figure 12.12 depicts a preliminary flowchart for our problem.

We will write a subprogram called AMNT to compute the difference between each element in two arrays. The general names A and B are used for the arrays, and the difference between each entry is stored in array DIFF. N is the number of items in each array. After we have found array DIFF, we will call another subprogram to compute the loss. Figure 12.13 gives the flowchart for the subprogram AMNT.

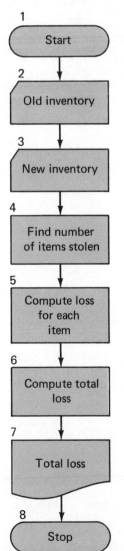

Figure 12.12 Preliminary Flowchart for Finding Total Loss from Robbery

1 Start

2 Old inventory

3 New inventory

4 Find number of items stolen

5 Compute loss for each item

6 Compute total loss

7 Total loss

8 Stop

Figure 12.13 Flowchart for Subroutine to Compute Number of Items Stolen

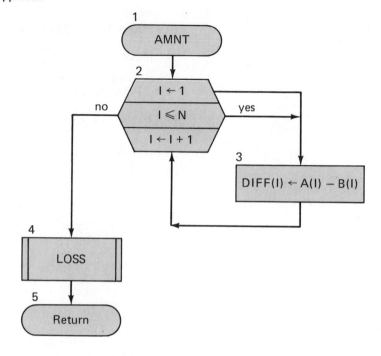

The subprogram called LØSS computes the loss for each item and accumulates them to find the total loss. To compute the loss for each item, we multiply the quantity missing by the price of the item. The general names X and Y
are used for the arrays that are multiplied, and SUM is used to accumulate the
total loss. Figure 12.14 depicts the flowchart for the subprogram LØSS.

Figure 12.14 Flowchart for Subroutine to Compute Total
Loss

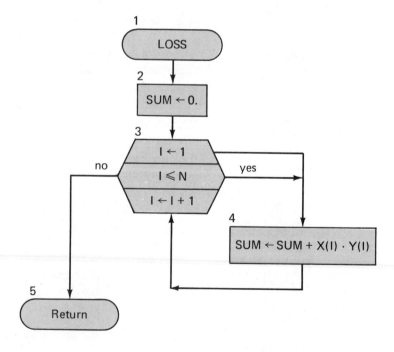

The main program carries out the following steps.

1. Read the data.
2. Call subroutine AMNT (which in turn calls subroutine LØSS).
3. Print the total loss.

The flowchart for the main program appears in Figure 12.15.

Figure 12.15 Flowchart for Main Program of Jewelry Store Robbery Problem

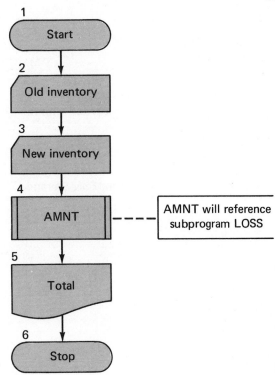

The names of the variables used in the main program are

N　　　　—number of entries in each inventory
QTØLD —array for storing the amount of an item in the old inventory
QTNEW —array for storing the amount of an item in the new inventory
PRICE　—array for storing the price of each item
TØTAL —total loss, value to be printed

The COMMON storage locations reserved between the main program and subprograms are:

N　　　　is read by the main program and used in both subprograms so it will be placed in unlabeled CØMMØN storage.

QTØLD } are read by the main program and correspond with arrays A and
QTNEW } B used in the subroutine AMNT, so they will be placed in a labeled COMMON storage area named BLØK1.

DIFF　　is used by subroutine AMNT and corresponds with array X in subroutine LØSS, so it will be placed in a labeled COMMON storage area named BLØK2.

PRICE　is read by the main program and corresponds with array Y used in the subroutine LØSS, so it will be placed in a labeled COMMON storage area named BLØK3.

TØTAL　is a value written by the main program and corresponds with the variable SUM computed in the subroutine LØSS, and it will be included in BLØK3.

The COMMON statements for each program unit will be

a. C　　　MAIN PRØGRAM
　　　　　CØMMØN N /BLØK1/QTØLD(1000),QTNEW(1000)
　　　　　CØMMØN /BLØK3/PRICE(1000),TØTAL

b.　　　　SUBRØUTINE AMNT
　　　　　CØMMØN N /BLØK2/DIFF(1000)
　　　　　CØMMØN /BLØK1/A(1000),B(1000)

c. SUBRØUTINE LØSS
CØMMØN N /BLØK2/X(1000)
CØMMØN /BLØK3/Y(1000),SUM

Figure 12.16 COMMON Storage Between Main Program and Subprograms

The diagram in Figure 12.16 shows how the locations in COMMON storage are associated with their variable names.

	Main Program	COMMON Storage	Subroutine AMNT	Subroutine LOSS
	N		N	N
BLOK1	QTOLD(1)		A(1)	
	.		.	
	.		.	
	.		.	
	QTOLD(1000)		A(1000)	
	QTNEW(1)		B(1)	
	.		.	
	.		.	
	QTNEW(1000)		B(1000)	
BLOK3	PRICE(1)			Y(1)
	.			.
	.			.
	PRICE(1000)			Y(1000)
	TOTAL			SUM
BLOK2	not used		DIFF(1)	X(1)
			.	.
			.	.
			DIFF(1000)	X(1000)

The FORTRAN main program and subprogram are:

```
C       SAMPLE PRØGRAM USING CØMMØN STØRAGE
C
        CØMMØN N /BLØK1/QTØLD(1000),QTNEW(1000)
        CØMMØN /BLØK3/PRICE(1000),TØTAL
C
        READ (5,100) (QTØLD(I), PRICE(I), I=1,1000)
        READ (5,110) (QTNEW(I), I=1,1000)
100     FØRMAT (5X,F5.0,F10.2)
110     FØRMAT (5X,F5.0)
        N = 1000
        CALL AMNT
        WRITE (6,120) TØTAL
120     FØRMAT (1H1,/////15HTØTALbLØSSbØFb$,F10.2)
        STØP
        END
```

```
      SUBRØUTINE AMNT
      CØMMØN N /BLØK2/DIFF(1000)
      CØMMØN /BLØK1/A(1000),B(1000)
      DØ 10 I = 1,N
         DIFF(I) = A(I) − B(I)
   10 CØNTINUE
      CALL LØSS
      RETURN
      END

      SUBRØUTINE LØSS
      CØMMØN N/BLØK2/X(1000)
      CØMMØN /BLØK3/Y(1000),SUM
      SUM = 0.
      DØ 10 I = 1,N
         SUM = SUM + X(I) * Y(I)
   10 CØNTINUE
      RETURN
      END
```

Example

We will now study a more complicated example which uses COMMON storage. A large parts supply house keeps an inventory of about one hundred different items. When a certain part is ordered, it is necessary to see if the part is in stock. If it is, then an invoice can be sent. If not, the part must be restocked. We wish to write a program to simulate this inventory problem.

The input data will consist of two parts: the current inventory and orders for parts. A dummy data card will separate these two data sets in the card deck and another dummy data card will be at the end of the set of order cards. The format of the data is:

```
inventory cards:
   columns   1–5        part number
            11–18       part name
            21–25       price (XX.XX)
            26–30       quantity on hand
dummy card:
   columns   1–5        −9999
order cards:
   columns   1–5        part number
            11–15       quantity ordered
            21–40       customer's name
dummy card:
   columns   1–5        −9999
```

The output should be a list of items that must be restocked and bills to customers. If an item is not in the stock or an order cannot be filled, a message to that effect should be written.

The flowchart in Figure 12.17 gives the basic structure of the program. There are two subprograms referenced—FILL and NEED.

There are two possible reasons why an order cannot be filled: there is not enough stock on hand, or the part number was incorrect on the order card. We will set up our subroutine FILL so that it will take an order and

Figure 12.17 Preliminary Flowchart
for Program to Send
Invoices and to Obtain
List of Items to be Re-
stocked

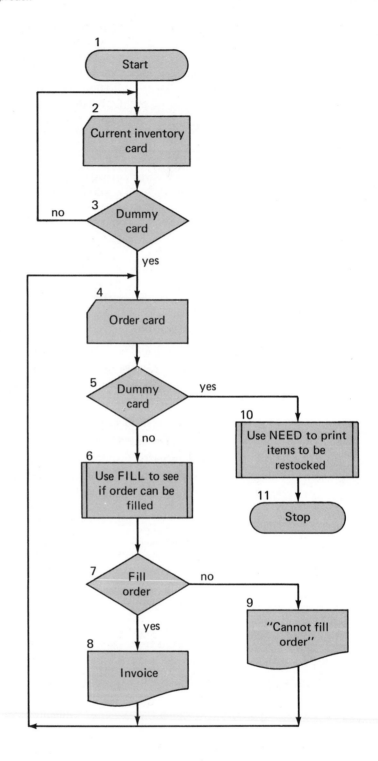

1. determine if the part number is correct. If it is, go on to step 2. If not, set
   KØDE to −1 and return to the main program.
2. decide if there is a large enough quantity of the part to fill the order. If
   there is, set KØDE to 1, reduce the inventory by the amount of parts just
   sold, and return to the main program. If not, set KØDE to 0, save the part
   number of this item in an array of parts to restock, and return to the main
   program.

In summary, the different KØDEs are

$$K\emptyset DE = -1 \quad \text{incorrect part number}$$
$$K\emptyset DE = 0 \quad \text{order cannot be filled}$$
$$K\emptyset DE = +1 \quad \text{order filled}$$

Step 1 of the procedure requires that we search through an array of part numbers in the inventory looking for the part ordered. We have already written a function named SEARCH (see Program 12.3) which will accomplish this task for us. If the resulting value of SEARCH is zero, the part number was not in the inventory. Otherwise SEARCH will tell us the position of the part in the inventory list. That is, SEARCH returns the value of the subscript of the part number in the inventory. This subscript will be stored as the value of ITEM.

Most of the procedure of the program depends upon the way the inventory data is stored in the program. Since we plan to utilize FUNCTI∅N SEARCH with the part numbers, these numbers must be stored in a one-dimensional array. To simplify the rest of the program and to make it easier to follow, we will use the following names for the data in the inventory:

PARTN∅—an array for all the part numbers in stock
NAME —a two-dimensional array of part names
PRICE —a one-dimensional array of part prices
QUAN —a one-dimensional array of the quantity of parts in stock
N —the number of parts in the inventory

We will use these names when referring to the information on an order card:

PAR∅RD —part number ordered
NUM∅RD—number of items ordered
CUST —customer's name

Of these items, the subroutine FILL needs to know the values of PARTN∅, QUAN, PAR∅RD, NUM∅RD, and N. It will compute K∅DE, which signals whether or not the order was filled. If the order cannot be filled, the subroutine will save this part number in an array named REST∅K which will be printed by subroutine NEED at the conclusion of the main program. The variable M will specify the number of items to be restocked. We use M when we are setting up the array REST∅K. We want to store the number of the first part which needs to be restocked in REST∅K(1), the number of the second part to be restocked in REST∅K(2), and so on. In general, we assign the Mth part number to be restocked to REST∅K(M). We will initialize M at 0 and later will increment it by 1 just before a new number is put into REST∅K(M). At any point in the program, M will contain the number of items which have been stored in REST∅K. If we initialize M in the subroutine FILL, then each time that FILL is called, M will be set to zero and each number to be restocked would be placed into location REST∅K(1). However, if we place M in COMMON storage in the main program and in subroutine FILL, then M may be initialized in the main program outside the loop which calls FILL. Subroutine FILL can then increment M each time it is called and M's value will change from 1 to 2 to 3 and so on each time a new number is stored in REST∅K.

We will place the variables in COMMON storage so that they may be used by the main program and the two subroutines. The variables which will be placed in COMMON storage for use by subroutine FILL and the main program are:

PARTNØ
QUAN
PARØRD
NUMØRD
N
M
RESTØK
ITEM
KØDE

The variables which will be placed in COMMON storage for use by subroutine NEED and the main program are:

RESTØK
M

Since both subroutines and the main program make use of RESTØK and M, we will store those in a labeled COMMON storage block named R. All other items used by FILL will be in a labeled COMMON storage block

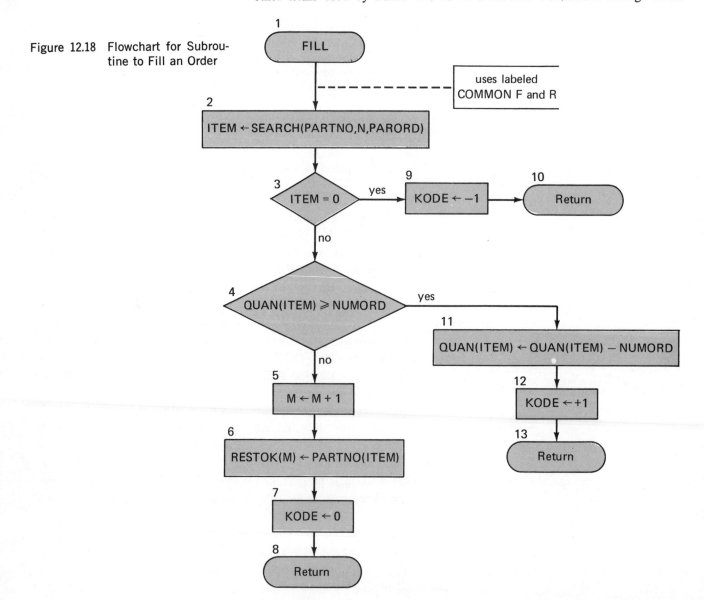

Figure 12.18 Flowchart for Subroutine to Fill an Order

named F. All other arrays used only in the main program will be placed in unlabeled COMMON storage.

The flowcharts in Figures 12.18 to 12.20 are for our subprograms FILL, NEED, and SEARCH, respectively. Figure 12.21 depicts the flowchart for our main program, and the FORTRAN program follows Figure 12.21.

Figure 12.19 Flowchart for Subroutine to Print List of Items to be Restocked

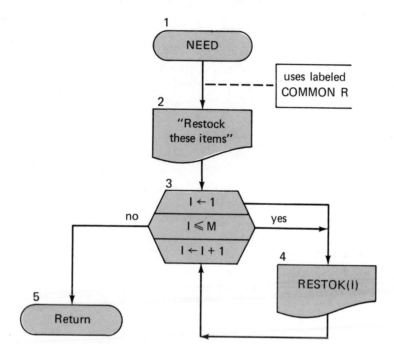

Figure 12.20 Flowchart for Function to Search an Array for a Particular Value

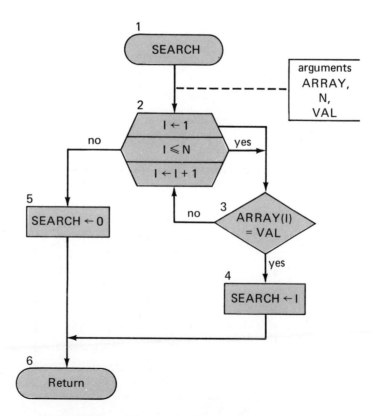

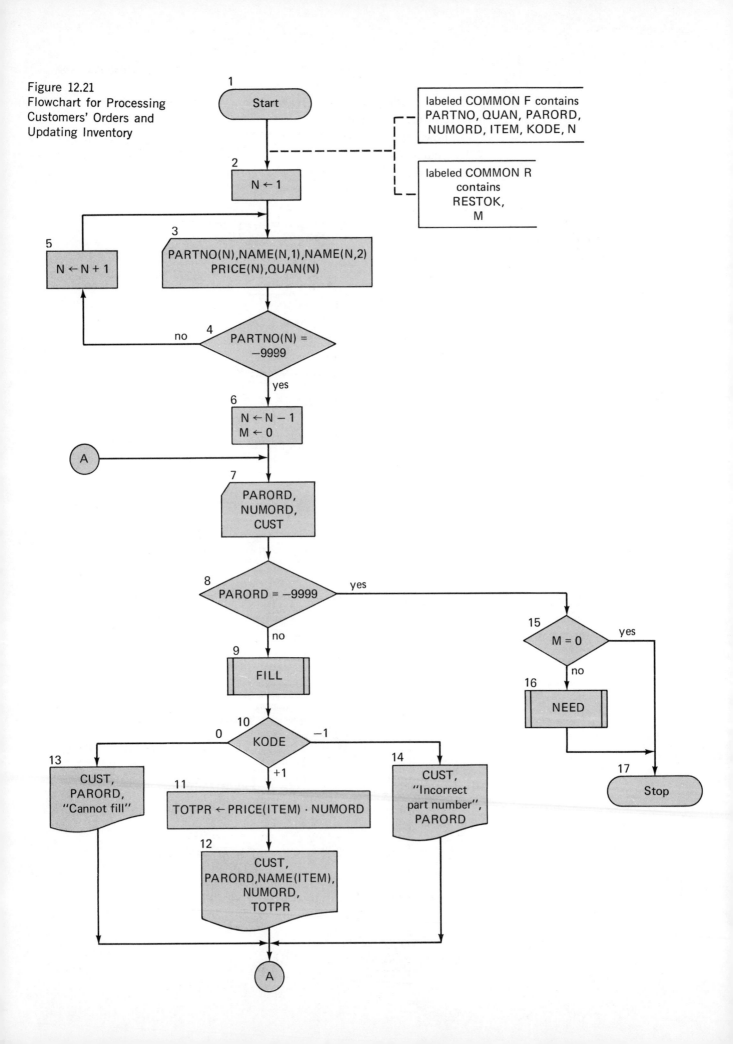

Figure 12.21
Flowchart for Processing
Customers' Orders and
Updating Inventory

```
C        THIS PRØGRAM SIMULATES A PARTS INVENTØRY
C          PRØBLEM
         CØMMØN PRICE(100),NAME(100,2)
         CØMMØN/F/PARTNØ(100),QUAN(100),PARØRD,NUMØRD,
       .  ITEM,KØDE,N
         CØMMØN/R/RESTØK(100),M
         INTEGER QUAN,CUST(5)
         N = 1
   10    READ (5,1000) PARTNØ(N), NAME(N,1), NAME(N,2),
       .  PRICE(N), QUAN(N)
 1000    FØRMAT (F5.0,5X,2A4,2X,F5.2,I5)
         IF (PARTNØ(N) .EQ. −9999.) GØ TØ 20
         N = N + 1
         GØ TØ 10
   20    N = N − 1
         M = 0
   30    READ (5,1010) PARØRD, NUMØRD, CUST
 1010    FØRMAT (F5.0,5X,I5,5A4)
         IF (PARØRD .EQ. −9999.) GØ TØ 80
   40    CALL FILL
         IF (KØDE) 50,60,70
   50    WRITE (6,1020) CUST, PARØRD
 1020    FØRMAT (1H1,10X,3HTØ.,2X,5A4/1H0,10X,
       .  11HPARTbNUMBER,F7.0,1X,12HISbINCØRRECT)
         GØ TØ 30
   60    WRITE (6,1030) CUST, PARØRD
 1030    FØRMAT (1H1,10X,3HTØ.,2X,5A4/1H0,10X,
       .  11HPARTbNUMBER,F7.0,1X,18HCANNØTbBEbSUPPLIED)
         GØ TØ 30
   70    TØTPR = PRICE(ITEM) * FLØAT(NUMØRD)
         WRITE (6,1040) CUST, PARØRD, NAME(ITEM,1),
       .  NAME(ITEM,2), NUMØRD, TØTPR
 1040    FØRMAT (1H1,10X,3HTØ.,2X,5A4/1H0,10X,4HPART,
       .  F7.0,5X,2A4/1H0,10X,8HQUANTITY,I6/1H0,10X,
       .  15HTØTALbPRICEb=b$,F9.2)
         GØ TØ 30
   80    IF (M .EQ. 0) STØP
         CALL NEED
         STØP
         END



         SUBRØUTINE FILL
C        THIS SUBRØUTINE TRIES TØ FILL AN ØRDER
         INTEGER SEARCH, QUAN
         CØMMØN/F/PARTNØ(100),QUAN(100),PARØRD,NUMØRD,
       .  ITEM,KØDE,N
         CØMMØN/R/RESTØK(100),M
         ITEM = SEARCH(PARTNØ,N,PARØRD)
         IF (ITEM .EQ. 0) GØ TØ 10
         IF (QUAN(ITEM) .GE. NUMØRD) GØ TØ 20
         M = M + 1
         RESTØK(M) = PARTNØ(ITEM)
         KØDE = 0
C        NØT ENØUGH PARTS ØN HAND TØ FILL ØRDER
         RETURN
   10    KØDE = −1
C        PARØRD WAS INCØRRECT
         RETURN
   20    QUAN(ITEM) = QUAN(ITEM) − NUMØRD
```

```
                      KØDE = +1
   C                  ØRDER FILLED
                      RETURN
                      END


                      INTEGER FUNCTIØN SEARCH (ARRAY,N,VAL)
   C
   C                  THIS FUNCTIØN SEARCHES AN ARRAY ØF LENGTH N
   C                  TØ SEE IF IT CØNTAINS THE VALUE VAL. IF IT DØES
   C                  SEARCH IS THE SUBSCRIPT ØF THAT ITEM IN THE
   C                  ARRAY. IF NØT, SEARCH EQUALS ZERØ.
   C
                      REAL ARRAY(1000)
                      DØ 10 I = 1,N
                        IF (ARRAY(I) .EQ. VAL) GØ TØ 20
             10       CØNTINUE
                      SEARCH = 0
                      RETURN
             20       SEARCH = I
                      RETURN
                      END


                      SUBRØUTINE NEED
   C                  THIS SUBRØUTINE WRITES THE ITEMS WHICH NEED
   C                  TØ BE ØRDERED
                      CØMMØN /R/STØCK(100),K
   C                  K IS THE NUMBER ØF ITEMS IN THE ARRAY STØCK
   C                  WHICH NEED TØ BE ØRDERED
                      WRITE (6,1000)
           1000       FØRMAT (1H1,19HRESTØCKbTHESEbITEMS///)
                      DØ 10 I = 1,K
                        WRITE (6,1010) STØCK(I)
             10       CØNTINUE
           1010       FØRMAT (7X,F6.0)
                      RETURN
                      END
```

An actual inventory program could be much more complex than this one—
the invoice could print more information, certain price reductions might be in
effect if a large enough quantity were ordered, a part could be put in the RE-
STØK list if its supply were low. Our purpose in giving this example was not
to solve an extremely complex problem, but to illustrate the use of labeled and
unlabeled COMMON storage.

Exercises

1. Write a statement function to compute a person's salary and to pay him
   overtime at $1\frac{1}{2}$ times the normal rate. That is, pay = rate × hours + 1.5
   × rate × overtime. Overtime is hours over 40.

2. A statement function F is defined as $F(X,Y,N) = X**N + X*Y - 7.0$.
   Write a statement that uses the function F to evaluate $(7.3)^2 + (7.3)(6.) -
   7.0$, and stores the value in a variable named VAL.

3. Convert the following mathematical function into a FORTRAN statement function.

$$\omega(\beta) = \sqrt{\sin \beta}$$

4. What will be the values computed for A and B?

```
F(X,Y) = X*X + 2.0*Y − X*Y
A = F(1.0,0.0)
B = F(2.0,3.0)
 .
 .
 .
```

5. All of the following CALLS to subroutine ACT are incorrect. Why?

```
REAL X(50), Y(75), W(50)
INTEGER B(75)
 .
 .
 .

CALL ACT(Z,B,7)
 .
 .
 .

CALL ACT(Z,Y,N,X)
 .
 .
 .

CALL ACT(X,B,M,W)
 .
 .
 .

END

SUBRØUTINE ACT(X,A,N,Q)
REAL Q(50)
INTEGER A(75)
 .
 .
 .

END
```

6. What will be the values of PCT and NWRØNG after subroutine GRADE is referenced by the following CALL statement? Assume NCR = 40.

```
CALL GRADE (50, NCR, NWRØNG, PCT)
 .
 .
 .

SUBRØUTINE GRADE (N, NRITE,RØNG,P)
INTEGER RØNG
P = NRITE * 100 / N
RØNG = N − NRITE
RETURN
END
```

7. If

X(1,1) = 2.	X(1,2) = 3.5	X(1,3) = −6.	X(1,4) = 7.3
X(2,1) = 6.	X(2,2) = 8.	X(2,3) = −1.	X(2,4) = 3.
X(3,1) = 8.	X(3,2) = −2.	X(3,3) = 1.5	X(3,4) = 6.
X(4,1) = 1.	X(4,2) = 0.	X(4,3) = 0.	X(4,4) = 7.

what will be the value of T when T = TRACE(X) is executed?

```
      FUNCTIØN TRACE(X)
      REAL X(4,4)
      TRACE = 0.0
      DØ 10 I = 1,4
          TRACE = TRACE+X(I,I)
   10 CØNTINUE
      RETURN
      END
```

8. Answer TRUE or FALSE.
   a. The statement function may appear anywhere in the program, as long as it precedes the first statement in which it is used.
   b. The last statement in every subprogram is the RETURN statement.
   c. If arrays appear in a subprogram, they must be dimensioned in the subprogram.
   d. Since subprograms are written as separate programs, there is no correlation of variable names and statement numbers between programs.

9. The arguments in a reference to a subprogram must agree in _____, _____, and _____ with those in the defining statement of the subprogram.

Program Assignments

1. Write a subprogram that will delete all zero entries in the array X with N elements and keep the desired entries of X in an array called Y. Write a main program that will do the following:
   a. Read an array A with L elements.
      Read an array Z with M elements.
   b. Use the subprogram written to delete the zero entries in array A and store the others in an array ANEW; and delete the zero entries in array Z and store the others in array ZNEW.
   c. Print out only the arrays ANEW and ZNEW.

2. The observations in a lab experiment are recorded twice a day. Different information is desired depending on a value of an indicator. For a given array write a FUNCTION subprogram in which the answer returned depends on the value of an indicator as follows,

   if indicator = 1 , the sum of the positive numbers is returned
   if indicator = 2 , the sum of the negative numbers is returned
   if indicator = 3 , the sum of all the terms is returned
   if indicator = 4 , the sum of the absolute value of all the terms is returned.

Write a main program that references the FUNCTION subprogram to analyze the morning and afternoon observations. When the morning recordings are punched one per card, the first data card in the set contains the value of the indicator for the set; similarly for the afternoon recordings. A dummy data card containing a 99999999 instead of a data observation separates the two sets of data. Each set has a maximum of 50 observations. The punched cards use the following format:

card 1:	columns 1–3	value of the indicator
card 2, etc.:	columns 1–8	value of the observations.

The output should be on a new page. Center the titles and write the values found by the subprogram and the indicators used. Supply appropriate labeling.

3. In vector analysis, two important operations are the dot product ($\cdot$) and the cross product ($\times$). For vectors $A = (a_1, a_2, a_3)$ and $B = (b_1, b_2, b_3)$ in a 3-dimensional space, we have

$$A \cdot B = a_1 b_1 + a_2 b_2 + a_3 b_3$$
$$A \times B = (\; a_2 b_3 - b_2 a_3, \; a_3 b_1 - b_3 a_1, \; a_1 b_2 - b_1 a_2 \;)$$

Write a subprogram to calculate the dot product, and a subprogram to find the cross product. All input and output is to be made through the main program. For vectors $A = (3, 2, -4)$ and $B = (-2, 1, 5)$ find the dot product and the cross product. For vectors $Z = (5, -3, 2)$ and $V = (4, -1, 5)$ find the dot product. With appropriate labeling write out A, B, A $\cdot$ B, A $\times$ B, Z, V and Z $\cdot$ V.

4. Imagine that you are a programmer for the Institute of Research and Data Gathering. Two different researchers have gone out into the field and have given intelligence tests at random to different subjects. Researcher A reported in with his data already ordered and punched on cards which were in the following format:

card 1:

columns		
1– 5:	number of subjects tested
6–10:	an intelligence test score
11–15:	"
16–20:	"
.	"
.	"
.	"
76–80:	"

card 2, etc.:
same format as card 1 except that a test score is placed in columns 1–5.

Researcher A ordered his scores from low to high when he punched the scores. Researcher B punched his data in the same format as researcher A, and also ordered the scores from low to high. All the scores are *integers*. The data deck is arranged in this manner:

data cards from researcher A
data cards from researcher B

It is your job to produce one list of these scores arranged from *high to low*. Since the original sets of data were ordered it will not be necessary to order the complete data set. Instead use this procedure:

a. Write a subprogram which will reverse the order of the elements in a one-dimensional array. The item which originally was in the first position should end up in the last position and vice versa. Therefore, if the array had been ordered from low to high, this subprogram should change the order so that the array is now ordered from high to low.

b. Merge the two arrays into one array which will maintain the high to low ordering. If NA is the number of items in array A and NB is the number of items in array B, the length of the merged array C should be NC where NC = NA + NB.

The output should consist of the total number of subjects tested and a listing of the array which resulted from combining the first two data sets.

Chapter 13

Additional FORTRAN Statements

13.1 Introduction

Although the FORTRAN statements presented in this chapter are not as commonly used as the statements already studied, these additional statements could be very useful in solving special problems.

13.2 STØP n Statement

The STØP statement may also be in the form

STØP n

where n is an octal [1] number from one to five digits long. The STØP n statement is executable and execution of this statement causes the program to halt.

Most computers will print "STØP n" when the program halts. Therefore, in a program which has several STØPs, this statement could be used to show which of the STØPs caused execution to cease. For example,

```
      DIMENSIØN IA(100)
      READ (5,100) N
100   FØRMAT (I3)
      IF (N .GT. 100) STØP 10
      IF (N .LE. 0) STØP 20
      READ (5,100) (IA(I),I=1,N)
```

The value of N which is read determines how many values of the IA array are read. If the computer prints out STØP 10, the programmer would realize that N is greater than 100. However, if the computer prints STØP 20, then N is either zero or negative.

13.3 Computed GØ TØ Statement

The general form of the computed GØ TØ is

GØ TØ $(n_1, n_2, \ldots, n_k)$, i

where $n_1, n_2, \ldots, n_k$ are the statement numbers of executable statements in the program

  i is an unsigned, non-subscripted *integer* variable. The value of i must be between 1 and k.

The computed GØ TØ statement transfers control to another statement depending on the current value of the variable i. The computed GØ TØ is an executable statement. At execution time the transfer of control is as follows: when the value of the variable i is j, then the next statement executed will be statement number n_j.

---

[1] An octal number is a number in the base 8 number system in which only the digits 0, 1, 2, 3, 4, 5, 6, and 7 are used. See Marilyn Bohl, *Information Processing* (Chicago: Science Research Associates, Inc., 1971).

Example

GØ TØ (4,66,20,5),JUMP

Suppose the value of the integer variable JUMP is 3. When the computed GØ TØ is executed, control transfers to the statement whose number is third in the list, in this example, statement number 20.

13.4 DATA Statement

The general form of the DATA statement is

DATA list$_1$/values$_1$/,list$_2$/values$_2$/, . . . /,list$_n$/values$_n$/

where   list   is a list containing names of variables and/or array elements. If a list contains more than one entry, commas are used to separate the entries.

             values   is a list of valid FORTRAN constants

Rules for the Use of the DATA Statement

1. The DATA statement is non-executable.

2. The DATA statement is used to define initial values of variables or array elements. There must be as many items in each list of variables as there are in the list of values immediately following the list. The values are assigned to the variables during compilation. For example,

DATA A, X, I, PI/3.4, .1, 1, 3.14/

assigns the following values:

A = 3.4
X = .1
 I = 1
PI = 3.14

3. The *type* of the constant and of the corresponding variable must agree. For example,

DATA A,B,C/1,2,3/   *is incorrect*

It must be written,

DATA A,B,C/1., 2., 3./

4. Any subscript which appears in the list must be an *integer* constant. For example,

DATA A(1),A(2),A(3)/1.7, 2.5, −3.86/

5. If consecutive constants in the list of values are identical, they may be written as *n* * constant, where *n* is the number of identical constants. For example,

DATA I, J, K, L, LL/1, 0, 0, 0, 0/

may be written as

DATA I, J, K, L, LL/1, 4 * 0/

6. The following statements have the same effect.

DATA X, Y, PI/0.0, 1.0, 3.14/
DATA X/0.0/,Y/1.0/,PI/3.14/

7. The DATA statements must follow any specification statement (DIMEN-SION, COMMON, *type,* EQUIVALENCE) and precede the first executable statement of the program.

8. No variables in unlabeled COMMON storage may be initialized in a DATA statement. A variable in labeled COMMON storage may be initialized only in a BLØCK DATA subprogram. The general form of a BLØCK DATA subprogram is:

BLØCK DATA
DIMENSIØN and *type* statements
DATA statements
END

For example,

BLØCK DATA
INTEGER QUAN
DIMENSIØN X(15)
CØMMØN /X1/X,QUAN(2),M,MAX
DATA QUAN(1),QUAN(2),MAX,M/23,3,99,0/
END

It is not necessary to initialize all the elements in the labeled COMMON storage block. Also the order of the variables in the DATA statement does not have to be the same as their order in the COMMON statement.

13.5 Hollerith Characters and Constants

Hollerith characters are any of the ANSI FORTRAN characters. Depending on the way they are used, Hollerith characters may appear in three different forms in the FORTRAN language. We find that (1) the characters may be read in; (2) the characters may be printed out; and (3) the characters may form Hollerith constants and be assigned as values to variables. Earlier we studied that (1) when reading in characters we use the A-field specification; (2) when writing out characters we use either the H-field or A-field specification; and in this section we will study that (3) when assigning Hollerith constants as values to variables we use a DATA statement.

The general form of a Hollerith constant is

nHcccc

where   n   is the exact number of characters following the H (including blanks)

cccc   each c represents one Hollerith character. Since we will store each constant in a memory location we will use a maximum of four characters for each constant.[2]

For example,

> 4HMARY
> 3HAb=
> 1H$

To assign Hollerith constants as the values of variables we use DATA statements such as the following.

    DATA MØNEY /1H$/ , EQL /3Hb=b/
    DATA LABL1, CLASS /4HPAGE , 4HITEM/

The values assigned to the variables in storage are

MONEY	$
EQL	b=b
LABL1	PAGE
CLASS	ITEM

When storing Hollerith constants the type (*real* or *integer*) of a variable name is no longer meaningful. Either may be used.

Example

The Personnel Department of a large company wants a list of those men who have a military classification of 1A. There is one card punched for each employee with the information punched as follows

employee name	columns	1–20
classification		26–27

The dummy data card for this problem will not contain numeric information, because we are not reading in numbers. The dummy data card will contain the Hollerith characters ZZ punched in columns 26–27.

The problem is to compare an employee's classification with 1A. If an employee is classified 1A we want the program to write out his name, otherwise the program should go on and process another employee's information. The flowchart for the problem is given in Figure 13.1.

To convert the flowchart into FORTRAN we must know how to compare Hollerith characters. Suppose we write the following IF statement for box 3 of the flowchart

    IF (CLASS .EQ. ZZ) STØP

How will the compiler interpret this statement? CLASS contains Hollerith characters that were read in. But, what about ZZ? The compiler will think that

---

[2] On the IBM 360 and IBM 370 computers, the maximum number of characters which may be stored in one memory location is 4; on the CDC 6000 Series and CDC CYBER 70 computers the maximum is 10.

Figure 13.1   Flowchart for Listing
All Employees with 1A
Draft Status

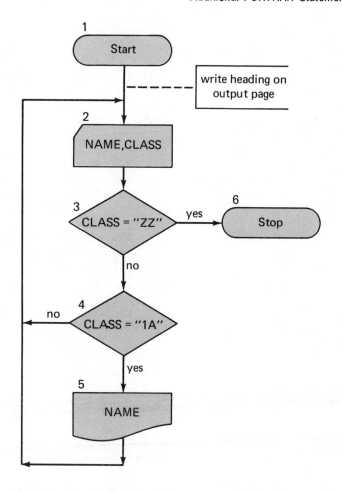

ZZ is a variable name and that it should have a previously defined value. What we really need is a memory location which contains the characters ZZ. Let us store the characters ZZ in a memory location called FINAL. To do this we will use a DATA statement.

DATA FINAL /2HZZ/

In storage this assignment may be depicted as follows

FINAL | ZZ |

The *correct* IF statement is

IF (CLASS .EQ. FINAL) STØP

Similarly, for the question of box 4, we need to store the characters 1A in a memory location. Using a DATA statement let us store 1A in the memory location ØNEA.

DATA ØNEA /2H1A/

Study carefully the following equivalent DATA statements. Any one of them may be used in our program.

1. DATA FINAL, ØNEA /2HZZ, 2H1A/
2. DATA FINAL /2HZZ/ , ØNEA /2H1A/
3. DATA FINAL /2HZZ/
   DATA ØNEA /2H1A/

The complete program is:

```
C        SAMPLE PRØGRAM USING A DATA STATEMENT
C        TØ ASSIGN HØLLERITH CØNSTANTS AS THE
C        VALUE ØF A VARIABLE.
         DIMENSIØN NAME (5)
         DATA FINAL, ØNEA /2HZZ , 2H1A/
C
C
         WRITE (6,200)
     10  READ (5,100) NAME, CLASS
         IF (CLASS .EQ. FINAL) STØP
         IF (CLASS .EQ. ØNEA) WRITE (6,210) NAME
         GØ TØ 10
    100  FØRMAT (5A4,5X,A2)
    200  FØRMAT (1H1,30HMILITARYbCLASSIFICATIØNbØFbb1A///)
    210  FØRMAT (1H0,5X,5A4)
         END
```

13.6 Double Precision Variables and Constants

A double precision value is a real number which occupies two storage locations. It has at least twice as many digits as a real number.[3] This extra precision is needed in some programs to guard against rounding errors which may occur when very large and very small numbers are combined in arithmetic operations.

A double precision constant is written in exponent form using a D instead of an E. For example:

2.376D+7	(2.376×10^7)
6.0D−100	(6.0×10^{-100})
6.0D100	(6.0×10^{100})
3.141592653589D0	

are all double precision constants.

A double precision variable must be typed in a DØUBLE PRECISIØN statement whose general form is

DØUBLE PRECISIØN $a_1, a_2, \ldots, a_n$

where $a_1, a_2, \ldots, a_n$ are variable names, array elements, array declarators, or function names.

In an arithmetic expression a *real* constant or *real* variable may be combined with a double precision constant or variable. When the expression is evaluated, the resulting value is double precision.

Input and Output of Double Precision Values

The FØRMAT specification of a double precision number is

nDw.d

---

[3] On the CDC 6000 Series and CYBER 70 computers a double precision constant may have 29 digits; on the IBM 360 and 370 computers the maximum is 16 digits.

where n   is the number of times the field is to be repeated. If n is 1, it may be omitted.

      w   is the width of the field. w should be at least 7 greater than d.

      d   specifies the number of decimal places to the right of the decimal point.

Input Example

With the following data card in which the numbers are punched right-justified in the field,

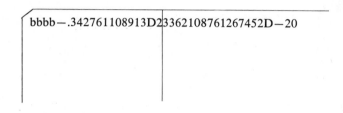

      bbbb—.342761108913D23362108761267452D—20

and the statements

```
     DØUBLE PRECISIØN A,B
     READ (5,100) A,B
100  FØRMAT (D20.12,D20.7)
```

then the values assigned to A and B are

$$A = -.342761108913 \times 10^2$$
$$B = 336210876.1267452 \times 10^{-20}$$

The output of *real* numbers printed under the D-field specification will appear in one of the following forms:

$$\pm.aaa \ldots aD\pm ee$$
$$\pm.aaa \ldots a\pm eee$$

The a's represent the most significant digits of the number, and the e's are the digits in the exponent.

Output Example

Suppose that in storage

$$TERM = .307621186234 \times 10^{-12}$$

With the following statements in a program

```
     DØUBLE PRECISIØN TERM
           .
           .
           .
     WRITE (6,100) TERM
100  FØRMAT (1X,D24.12)
```

the printout will be

bbbbbbb.307621186234D—12

D24.12

FORTRAN Supplied Functions for Double Precision Values

The following list provides the more commonly used functions which have a double precision argument and return a double precision value. Refer to Appendix B for a complete list of FORTRAN supplied functions.

Function Name	Purpose
DSQRT	Square root
DABS	Absolute value
DSIN	Trigonometric sine
DCØS	Trigonometric cosine
DEXP	Exponential ($e^{argument}$)
DLØG	Natural logarithm
DLØG10	Logarithm to the base 10

13.7 Complex Variables and Constants

Since mathematically a complex number has a real part and an imaginary part, in FORTRAN a complex variable will have two real memory locations reserved, one for the real part and one for the imaginary part. The advantage of using complex variables in FORTRAN is that complex arithmetic is defined as usual. A complex variable may be raised to an integer exponent only.

When operations with complex numbers are necessary in a program, the required variables must be typed *complex*. The general form of the *type* statement is

CØMPLEX list

where   list   contains variable names, array names, array declarators, or function names.

For example,

CØMPLEX A,V,B(5)

There will be two storage locations reserved for A, two other storage locations reserved for V, and 10 storage locations reserved for the array B.

Consider another example. To multiply the complex numbers A and B and store the result in Z we could have the following statements.

CØMPLEX A,B,Z

· · · · · · ·

Z = A * B

If A has the value $2 - i$ and B has the value $5 + 7i$ then the value stored in Z is the result of the multiplication $(2 - i)(5 + 7i)$.

The value of a complex variable may be assigned by any of three methods:

1. a READ statement
2. an arithmetic replacement statement
3. a DATA statement

We will discuss each of these methods as well as how to output complex variables.

Input and Output of Complex Values

In FORTRAN a complex variable is considered also a *real* variable. Therefore, the F-field specification is used in the FØRMAT. Two F-field specifications must be allowed for *each* complex number, one for the real part and the other for the imaginary part; similarly for output.

Suppose we want to read in the values for $A = 2 - i$. The data card should be punched giving the value for the real part first and then the value for the imaginary part. For our example, the data card could be punched as follows:

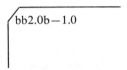

The FORTRAN statements required in the program would be

```
      CØMPLEX  A
      READ  (5,10)  A
  10  FØRMAT  (2F5.1)
      .  .  .  .  .  .
      WRITE  (6,20)  A
  20  FØRMAT  (1H1,2(10X,F5.1))
```

The values printed on the output page would be as follows

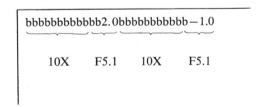

Assignment of Complex Values with an Arithmetic Replacement Statement

To assign the value of $2 - i$ to the complex variable A, the FØRTRAN supplied function CMPLX is used as follows.

```
      CØMPLEX  A
      .  .  .  .  .  .
      A = CMPLX  (2.,-1.)
```

Assignment of Complex Values with a DATA Statement

A complex variable appearing in a DATA statement requires that two values be given. To store the complex number $2 - i$ in A we would have the following statements

```
CØMPLEX A
DATA A/2.0,−1.0/
```

FORTRAN Supplied Functions for Complex Values

To facilitate many of the operations with complex numbers the following functions are available. Refer to Appendix B for a complete list of FORTRAN supplied functions.

Function Name and Arguments	Type of Arguments	Type of Result	Purpose
CMPLX(X,Y)	REAL	CØMPLEX	Value is a complex number. Its real part is X and its imaginary part is Y.
REAL(C)	CØMPLEX	REAL	Value is the real part of C
AIMAG(C)	CØMPLEX	REAL	Value is the imaginary part of C
CEXP(C)	CØMPLEX	CØMPLEX	Exponential (e^c)
CLØG(C)	CØMPLEX	CØMPLEX	Natural logarithm
CSIN(C)	CØMPLEX	CØMPLEX	Trigonometric sine
CCØS(C)	CØMPLEX	CØMPLEX	Trigonometric cosine
CSQRT(C)	CØMPLEX	CØMPLEX	Square root
CABS(C)	CØMPLEX	REAL	Absolute value

13.8 Logical Variables and Constants

Logical constants and variables represent the truth values of true and false. A logical constant is one of the following:

```
.TRUE.
.FALSE.
```

A logical variable must be declared in a *type* statement whose general form is

$$\text{LØGICAL } a_1, a_2, \ldots, a_n$$

where $a_1, a_2, \ldots, a_n$ are variable names, array elements, array declarators, or function names.

A **logical expression** may be a logical constant, a logical variable or an expression formed with logical operators and has the value true or false. The logical operators are:

.ØR. Logical disjunction
.AND. Logical conjunction
.NØT. Logical negation

The general form of a logical expression is:

$$L_1 \text{ op}_1 L_2 \text{ op}_2 L_3 \text{ op}_3 \ . \ . \ . \ L_n$$

where $L_1, L_2, \ . \ . \ .$ are logical variables, logical constants, logical functions, relational expressions, logical expressions, or logical expressions enclosed in parentheses. The logical operator .NØT. may precede any L_i.

$\text{op}_1, \text{op}_2, \ . \ . \ .$ are the logical operators .AND. or .ØR.

If L_1 and L_2 are logical expressions, the logical operators are defined as follows:

.NØT. L_1 is false only if L_1 is true
L_1 .AND. L_2 is true only if L_1, L_2 are both true
L_1 .ØR. L_2 is false only if L_1, L_2 are both false

If op is .AND. or .ØR., then L_1 op op L_2 is never legitimate. The logical operator .NØT. may appear in combination with .AND. or .ØR. only as follows:

L_1 .AND. .NØT. L_2
L_1 .ØR. .NØT. L_2

Hierarchy of Operations

The hierarchy of operations in a logical expression is:

1. Function reference
2. **
3. * and /
4. + and −
5. .LT., .LE., .GE., .GT., .EQ., .NE.
6. .NØT.
7. .AND.
8. .ØR.

Parentheses may be used to change the hierarchy of operations.

Examples

1. The mathematical relationship $b - c \leq a \leq b + c$ may be written

   B − C .LE. A .AND. A .LE. B + C

2. The logical relationship $P \rightarrow Q$ (P implies Q) may be written in two ways

   .NØT. (P .AND. .NØT. Q)
   .NØT. P .ØR. Q

Logical IF Statement

The value of a logical expression may be tested in an IF statement of the form

   IF (logical expression) S

where S is an executable statement.

The executable statement, S, must *not* be another logical IF statement or a DØ statement. (The DØ statement is explained in Chapter 10.) The logical IF statement acts in the following manner:

1. If the relational expression is true, S is executed. Then, if S is not a statement that transfers control, the next statement executed is the one immediately below the IF statement.
2. If the relational expression is false, control goes to the next statement below the IF statement, without executing statement S.

For example,

IF (X .GT. 0.0 .AND. Y .GT. 0.0) QUAD = 1.

Logical Assignment Statement

The general form of the logical assignment statement is

logical variable = logical expression

Example

```
LØGICAL  X,Y,Z
X = .TRUE.
Y = .FALSE.
Z = X .AND.  Y
```

Then Z = .FALSE. For Z is true only if both X and Y have true values.

Example

```
LØGICAL  RANGE1, RANGE2
A = 10.0
B = 3.0
RANGE1 = 1. .LE. A .AND. A .LE. 25.
RANGE2 = B .LE. 0.
```

Then   RANGE1 = .TRUE.
and   RANGE2 = .FALSE.

Example

```
LØGICAL  T, F
T = .TRUE.
F = .NØT. T
```

Then   F = .FALSE.

Input and Output of Logical Variables

The format specification for a logical variable is

nLw

where n is the number of times the field is to be repeated. If n is 1, it may be omitted.
        w is the width of the field.

The information punched in an input field must consist of optional blanks followed by a T or F followed by optional characters. The first T or F encountered determines the value of true or false for the variable. An all blank field is considered false. In output, a T or an F will be printed left-adjusted followed by w − 1 blanks.

Input Example

```
        LØGICAL  A,B,C,D,E
        READ  (5,100)  A,B,C,D,E
100     FØRMAT  (2L1,L3,L1,L2)
```

```
TFTAPbbT
```

makes

```
A = .TRUE.
B = .FALSE.
C = .TRUE.
D = .FALSE.
E = .TRUE.
```

D is false because an all blank field is considered false.

E is true because the first non-blank character is a T.

Output Example

```
        LØGICAL  LIØN,TIGER
        LIØN = .TRUE.
        TIGER = .FALSE.
        WRITE  (6,20)  LIØN,TIGER
20      FØRMAT  (1H0,L5,L2)
```

The output page will be

```
TbbbbFb
‿‿‿ ‿‿
 L5  L2
```

13.9 E-field and G-field Specifications

The E-field Specification

For input and/or output of *real* variables expressed as a number multiplied by a power of 10, the E-field specification is used. The general form of the E-field is

nEw.d

where n denotes the number of times the field is to be repeated. If n is 1, it may be omitted.

   w is the total width of the field. w should be at least 7 greater than d.

   d is the number of decimal places to the right of the decimal point.

Input of Real Values with Exponent. Suppose the following values are to be read:

$$a = 1.643 \times 10^{25}$$
$$b = .0000001 = 1. \times 10^{-7}$$
$$c = 5.4235 \times 10^{3}$$
$$d = .33 \times 10^{2}$$

Using exponent notation (E-notation) where the letter E takes the place of the number 10, these numbers may be written as

$$a = 1.643E25$$
$$b = 1.E-7$$
$$c = 5.4235E3$$
$$d = .33E+2$$

The values are to be punched in the following columns.

columns		
1–10	the value	1.643E25
11–15	the value	1.E−7
16–25	the value	5.4235E3
26–33	the value	.33E+2

All numbers *must be* right-adjusted in the field. The data card would appear as follows.

The READ and FØRMAT statements would be:

      READ (5,10) A,B,C,D
   10 FØRMAT (E10.3,E5.0,E10.4,E8.2)

Note that the letter E and the exponent are included in the total width given for a number. The third number punched on the data card does not have a decimal point punched, but because the E-field specification is E10.4, the correct value of 5.4235E3 is stored for C.

Output of Real Values with Exponent. Real numbers printed under the E-field specification will appear in one of the following forms:

±.aaa . . . aE±ee
±.aaa . . . a±eee

The a's represent the most significant digits of the number, and the e's are the digits in the exponent.

Example

Suppose that in storage

$$A = 423.041245$$
$$B = -9843695.001$$
$$C = 0.00521346$$

using the statements

```
      WRITE  (6,120)  A,B,C
120   FØRMAT  (1H0,5X,E11.4,3X,E15.9,E15.4)
```

the printed output will be

bbbbbbb.4230E+03bbb−.984369500E+07bbbbbb.5214E−02

| 5X | E11.4 | 3X | E15.9 | E15.4 |

The G-field Specification

A more general specification for the input and/or output of real values is the G-field specification. This specification combines the features of the F- and E-field specifications. With the G-field specification, an input value may be punched as for the F specification or as for the E specification. Similarly, depending on its magnitude, the output value may appear as if it were written with an F specification or it may contain an exponent as in the E specification.

The general form of the G-field is

nGw.d

where   n   denotes the number of times the field is to be repeated. If n is 1, it may be omitted.

        w   is the total width of the field. w should be at least 7 greater than d.

        d   is the number of decimal places to the right of the decimal point.

Input of Real Values with G-field.   Suppose a data card is punched with the following values

bbbbbbbb.1251251E−05bbb4000000b1234567.000000

and we use the following READ and FØRMAT statements

```
      READ(5,100)  VAL, SET, XAY
100   FØRMAT  (8X,G12.7, G10.3, G15.6)
```

the values assigned to the variables will be

```
VAL = .000001251251
SET = 4000.000
XAY = 1234567.000000
```

Output of Real Values with G-field.   The output of a real value requires that the width of the field w include four positions for an exponent of the form

E±ee. Depending on its magnitude the real value to be written will appear as a value written with an F specification or as a value written with an E specification. Let M be the magnitude of our real constant. The following table gives the correspondence between M and the specification used.

Magnitude of Real Value	Specification Used
$0.1 \leq M < 1$	F(w–4).d, 4X
$1 \leq M < 10$	F(w–4).d–1, 4X
.	
.	
.	
$10^{d-2} \leq M < 10^{d-1}$	F(w–4).1 , 4X
$10^{d-1} \leq M < 10^d$	F(w–4).0 , 4X
Otherwise	nEw.d

Suppose that in storage the variables have the following values

VAL = .1251251
SET = 4000.0
XAY = 1234567.00

using the statements

```
      WRITE(6,150) VAL, SET, XAY
150   FØRMAT (5X, G20.7, G10.3, G15.6)
```

the output page will be

bbbbbbbbbbbb.1251251bbbbbb.400E+04bbbb.123457E+07

| 4X | G20.7 | G10.3 | G15.6 |

13.10 Variable FØRMAT

Usually a programmer determines how the data is punched and specifies this in the FØRMAT statements in the program. If a program is to be used with different data sets and each set is punched differently, the FØRMAT specification in the program must be changed before each data set is used with the program. Each change implies that the program must be compiled again. To avoid compilation of the program each time, a variable FØRMAT may be used.

Rules for the Use of Variable FØRMATS

1. The FØRMAT specifications, including left and right parentheses, are either read under an A-field specification or defined in a DATA statement. The specification must be stored in an array.
2. The READ or WRITE statement using the variable FØRMAT will reference *not* a statement label but the name of the array where the format is stored.

Example: Reading in a Variable FØRMAT

The specification is (2X,2F6.3,I5,E12.6,F9.3,2E20.7) and is punched in columns 1–31 of the data card.

```
      DIMENSIØN IFØRM (8)
      READ (5,10) IFØRM
10    FØRMAT (8A4)
```

The specification is stored as

IFØRM (1)	(2X,
IFØRM (2)	2F6.
IFØRM (3)	3,I5
IFØRM (4)	,E12
IFØRM (5)	.6,F
IFØRM (6)	9.3,
IFØRM (7)	2E20
IFØRM (8)	.7)b

Example: Defining a Variable FØRMAT in a DATA Statement

```
      DIMENSIØN VAR(2), DBL(3)
      DATA VAR(1),VAR(2) /4H(1H1 , 4H,I5)/
      DATA DBL(1),DBL(2),DBL(3)  /4H(1H0 , 4H,F5. , 2H1)/
```

The specification is stored as

VAR(1)	(1H1
VAR(2)	,I5)
DBL(1)	(1H0
DBL(2)	,F5.
DBL(3)	1)

The following examples use the variable FØRMATs described above.

a.   READ (5,IFØRM) A,B,N,E,X,ZIP,ZAP

This produces the same result as if the following were in the program

```
        READ  (5,100)  A,B,N,E,X,ZIP,ZAP
100     FØRMAT  (2X,2F6.3,I5,E12.6,F9.3,2E20.7)
```

```
   b.   WRITE  (6,VAR)  N
        WRITE  (6,DBL)  X
```

3. The statement label and the word FØRMAT are *not* included as part of the input.
4. After the variable FØRMAT specification is stored in the program, a subsequent input or output statement in the same program can refer to the FØRMAT specification.
5. The name of the array representing the FØRMAT must be dimensioned. (See the examples in item 2 above.)

Example: Using a Variable FØRMAT

Suppose the items of a real array A with 200 elements are to be printed in a column. Only 25 items are to be printed double-spaced on each page.

We need two different carriage controls: 1H1 to go to a new page and 1H0 to double space the items. If we use the array IFMT to store the variable FØRMAT, we can then change the contents of IFMT(1) as needed. We would have either

IFMT(1) | (1H1 | or   IFMT(1) | (1H0

The data card with the rest of the variable FØRMAT specification would be punched as follows

```
,10X,2HA(,I3,3H)b=,5X,F10.4)
```

The following program gives only the statements needed to illustrate the use of the variable FØRMAT for our example.

```
        DIMENSIØN  IFMT(8), LINE(2), A(200)
        DATA LINE(1)/4H(1H1/ , LINE(2)/4H(1H0/
        READ  (5,100)  (IFMT(I), I = 2,8)
100     FØRMAT  (7A4)
        .  .  .  .  .  .  .

        K = 1
        DØ 30  I = 1,200
        IF (I .LT. K) GØ TØ 20
        IFMT(1) = LINE(1)
 20     WRITE  (6,IFMT)  I,A(I)
        IF (I .NE. K) GØ TØ 30
        IFMT(1) = LINE(2)
        K = K + 25
 30     CØNTINUE
```

13.11 EQUIVALENCE Statement

The EQUIVALENCE statement is a non-executable specification statement which permits two or more variables in the same program to share storage.

The form of the EQUIVALENCE statement is

EQUIVALENCE (list$_1$), (list$_2$), . . . , (list$_i$)

where   list$_1$,list$_2$, . . . ,list$_i$ are lists of variable names and/or array element names.

In specifying the lists the following must be observed:

1. Each list is enclosed in parentheses, and the items in the list are separated by commas. Each list must have at least 2 items.
2. The subscript of the array element may be any number less than or equal to the dimension of the array declarator.

Examples

a.   EQUIVALENCE (A,B), (X,Y,Z)

Causes the variables A and B to share the same location, and causes X, Y, and Z to refer to the same location.

b.   DIMENSIØN A(3), B(3)
      EQUIVALENCE (A(1),B(1))

Causes A(1) and B(1) to share the same location, A(2) and B(2) to share a location, and similarly A(3) and B(3).

c.   DIMENSIØN X(10), Y(5)
      EQUIVALENCE (X(6),Y(1))

In storage the association of variables sharing a location is:

X(1)		
X(2)		
X(3)		
X(4)		
X(5)		
X(6)		Y(1)
X(7)		Y(2)
X(8)		Y(3)
X(9)		Y(4)
X(10)		Y(5)

Rules for the Use of the EQUIVALENCE Statement

1. An EQUIVALENCE statement must appear before any statement function definition, DATA statement, or executable statement in the program unit.

2. Unlike DIMENSIØN or *type* statements, subscripts in EQUIVALENCE statements do *not* assign dimensions to the arrays.
3. If two variables or array elements are used in an EQUIVALENCE statement, only one may appear in a CØMMØN statement in the program.
4. Dummy arguments that appear in a FUNCTIØN or SUBRØUTINE may not appear in an EQUIVALENCE statement.
5. The name of a FUNCTIØN or a SUBRØUTINE subprogram may not appear in an EQUIVALENCE statement.
6. Variables of different modes should *not* be equivalenced to each other if the program uses them in the same section. Suppose the following statements are found in a program.

```
EQUIVALENCE (A,I)
A = 3.0
DØ 10 M= I,5
.  .  .  .  .  .  .

10   CØNTINUE
```

The initial value of M will *not* be 3. No value had been assigned to I, so it is undefined.
7. Variables of different modes could be placed in an EQUIVALENCE statement if they are used in different sections of the program. For example,

```
EQUIVALENCE (A,I)
A = 13.0
CALL SØLVE (A)
.  .  .  .  .  .  .

I = 10
DØ 10 M = 1,50,I
```

Appendix A

Reference to FORTRAN Statements

This appendix gives in alphabetical order the general form of the FORTRAN statements discussed in the text and the rules for using each statement. Each statement is classified as a non-executable, an executable, and/or a specification statement. The reference at the end of each statement refers to the chapter and section in the text where the statement is discussed. For example, 11.2 means Chapter 11, section 2.

Arithmetic IF (See IF (Arithmetic))

Arithmetic Replacement Statement—Executable

Form: FORTRAN variable name = FORTRAN arithmetic expression

This statement is used to give a value to the variable on the left-hand side of the equal sign.

Rules for forming an Arithmetic Expression

1. A simple arithmetic expression contains constants and/or variables separated by an arithmetic operation symbol. The symbols used in FORTRAN and the operations they represent are:

Symbol	Operation
+	addition
—	subtraction (or negation)
*	multiplication
/	division
**	exponentiation

2. Two operation symbols may *not* be written one after another in the expression. The two asterisks (**) representing exponentiation are considered one symbol.
3. An expression may begin with a plus sign or a minus sign but no other operation symbol.
4. Other arithmetic expressions may be formed by enclosing a simple arithmetic expression in parentheses. This expression in parentheses may then be combined with other variables and/or constants and/or expressions in parentheses. The variables, constants, and expressions in parentheses are introduced in order to compute the correct mathematical value of a formula.
5. All variables and/or constants in an expression must be of the same *type*. The exceptions are: an expression of any *type* may have an *integer* exponent; a *real* or *double precision* expression may have a *real* or *double precision* exponent; *double precision* or *complex* expressions may contain *real* expressions.

Rules for an Arithmetic Replacement Statement

1. The variable on the left-hand side of the equal sign must be a valid FORTRAN variable name.
2. The expression on the right-hand side of the equal sign must be a valid FORTRAN arithmetic expression.
3. The arithmetic expression does not have to be of the same *type* as the variable on the left-hand side of the equal sign. However, if the expression is *complex,* the variables must also be *complex.*

Reference 5.3

Block Data Subprogram—Non-executable

Form: BLOCK DATA

This statement is the first statement of a block data subprogram which is used to give initial values to variables in labeled common blocks. The subprogram may contain only *type* statements, COMMON, DATA, DIMENSION, and EQUIVALENCE statements.

Not all variables in the common block need to be initialized, but the block must be completely defined through the use of *type* and dimension statements. Variables in more than one common block may receive values in a single block data subprogram.

Reference: 13.4

CALL Statement—Executable

Forms: CALL name
          CALL name $(a_1, a_2, \ldots, a_n)$

where   name   is the name of a SUBROUTINE subprogram
         $a_1, a_2, \ldots, a_n$ are actual arguments

The CALL statement is used to reference a subroutine subprogram. When the CALL statement is executed, control transfers to the subroutine and the statements in the subroutine are executed.

The actual arguments must agree in order, number, and *type* with the corresponding dummy arguments in the subroutine. An actual argument may be one of the following:

1. Non-subscripted variable
2. Array name
3. Array element
4. Any expression
5. Hollerith constant
6. Reference to a FORTRAN supplied function

Reference: 12.4

Comment Statement—Non-executable

To insert comments in a program, the letter C is punched in column 1 of each card containing a comment. The message may be written in columns 2 through 80.

Reference: 4.2

Continuation Statement—Executable

A FORTRAN character other than a blank or zero must be punched in column 6 of a card to tell the compiler that the statement on that card is a continuation of the statement on the preceding card.[1] The character in column 6 is not part of the FORTRAN statement.

Reference: 4.2

COMMON Statement—Non-executable, Specification

Forms: COMMON list
  COMMON $/label_1/list_1/label_2/list_2/$ . . . $/label_n/list_n$

where list may contain simple variable names, array names, or array declarators. Commas are used to separate elements in the list. There is no comma at the end of the list.

  label is any valid FORTRAN variable name. It becomes the name of the COMMON block. If a label is omitted, the list following it will be in unlabeled common storage.

A common block name may appear more than once in a COMMON statement or statements. If it does, all elements mentioned will be stored in the same common block in the order in which they are listed in the COMMON statement.

Reference: 12.6

Complex Type Statement—Non-executable, Specification

Form: COMPLEX list

where list may contain simple variable names, array names, function names, and/or array declarators. Commas are used to separate elements in the list. There is no comma at the end of the list.

This statement is used to type variables as complex variables; therefore they will have complex values. Two storage locations will be reserved for the value of each complex item, one for the real value and one for the imaginary value.

Reference 13.7

CONTINUE Statement—Executable

Form: CONTINUE

---

[1] A given FORTRAN statement may extend to as many as 19 continuation cards on the IBM 360/370, CDC 6000 Series, and CYBER 70 computers.

The CONTINUE statement acts as a no operation. That is, when it is executed, no operation is performed and control proceeds to the next executable statement in the program. It is often used as the last statement in a DO loop.

Reference: 10.2, 10.3

Data Initialization Statement—Non-executable

Form:　DATA list$_1$/values$_1$/,list$_2$/values$_2$/, . . . /,list$_n$/values$_n$/

where　list　contains simple variables and/or array elements. If the list contains more than one entry, commas are used to separate the entries.

values　contains signed or unsigned constants (including Hollerith constants). If there is more than one constant, commas are used to separate them. Each constant may be preceded by $n*$, where n is an integer constant. Using $n*$ in front of a constant is the same as writing the constant n times.

A data initialization statement is used to give an initial value to variables or elements in arrays. There must be as many items in each list of variables as there are in the list of values immediately following the former list. The first variable is assigned the first value; the second is assigned the second value, and so on. None of the variables or array elements may be in unlabeled common storage.

Reference: 13.4

DIMENSION Statement—Non-executable, Specification

Form:　DIMENSION $a_1(n_1), a_2(n_2), \ldots, a_k(n_k)$

where　$a_1, \ldots, a_k$　are array names

$n_1, \ldots, n_k$　are subscript declarators. Each n_i may be 1, 2, or 3 unsigned integer constants separated by commas. If the n_i is only one constant, no comma is used inside the parentheses.

Each $a(n_i)$ defines an array. If the n_i is one constant, the array is one-dimensional; if the n_i is composed of 2 constants, the array is two-dimensional; if the n_i is 3 constants, the array is three-dimensional.

During execution the value of the subscript(s) of an array element must be positive and may not exceed the value of the subscript declarator.

Reference: 9.2

DO Statement—Executable

Forms:　DO $n\ i = m_1, m_2, m_3$
　　　　　DO $n\ i = m_1, m_2$

where n is the statement label of the last statement in the loop. The last statement may not be a GO TO, arithmetic IF, RETURN, STOP, DO, or a logical IF containing any of these.

i is the index parameter. It must be an unsigned, non-subscripted integer variable name.

m_1 is the initial value of the index. It may be a positive integer constant or a non-subscripted integer variable name whose value is positive.

m_2 is the upper bound value of the index. It may be a positive integer constant or a non-subscripted integer variable name whose value is positive.

m_3 is the increment to the index. If m_3 is equal to 1, it may be omitted. If m_3 is omitted as in the second form, it is assumed to be 1. The increment may be a positive integer constant or a non-subscripted integer variable name.

The range of a DO loop consists of the statements from the first statement following the DO statement through the statement labeled n.

When a DO statement is executed, the following happens:

1. The index is assigned its initial value (m_1).
2. All the statement in the range of the DO loop are executed.
3. After the last statement of the loop is executed, the index is incremented by the value of m_3. The new value of the index is compared to m_2. If its value is less than or equal to m_2, then control returns to step 2.

    It is possible that the last statement of the loop may not be reached because of a GO TO or an IF statement which transfers control out of the loop. If this happens, the index retains its current value and we say that the loop has not been completed.
4. If the value of the index is greater than m_2, the DO loop is said to be satisfied and control transfers to the first executable statement following the last statement in the range of the loop. The value of the index parameter is no longer defined at this point.

Reference: 10.2

Double Precision Type Statement—Non-executable, Specification

Form: DOUBLE PRECISION list

where   list   may contain simple variable names, array names, function names and/or array declarators. Commas are used to separate the names in the list. If there is only one item in the list, no comma is used.

This statement is used to make variables or functions into ones which will have double precision values. Two memory locations will be reserved for each value; therefore, the value may contain approximately twice as many digits as a value which is not of type double precision. All double precision numbers are *real* numbers, not *integers*.

Reference: 13.6

END Statement—Non-executable

Form: END

This statement may *not* have a statement label. It is the last statement in a program or subprogram and denotes the physical end of that program unit.

Reference: 6.3

EQUIVALENCE Statement—Non-executable, Specification

Form: EQUIVALENCE (list$_1$),(list$_2$), . . . ,(list$_n$)

where   list   may contain variable names and/or array elements. There must be at least two elements in each list. Commas must be used to separate elements in the list.

The EQUIVALENCE statement causes all the entries in each list to share the same storage location. This means that the location may be referred to by several different names.

When two variables or array elements share storage as the result of an EQUIVALENCE statement, both names may not appear in COMMON statements.

Reference: 13.11

FORMAT Statement—Non-executable

Form: *n* FORMAT($s_1, s_2,$ . . . ,s_k)

where   *n*   is a statement label
$s_1,$ . . . ,s_k are format specifications

The FORMAT specification may be separated by commas, slashes, or a series of slashes. The slash is used to denote the end of a record, such as the end of a card or the end of a printed line.

Any part of the FORMAT may be repeated by enclosing that part in parentheses and placing an integer in front of the left parentheses. This integer specifies the number of times that part is to be repeated.

Reference: 6.3, 8.2, and 8.3

FORMAT Specifications

The following list explains the various FORMAT specifications which may be used.

I/0 of Characters

nAw

where   n   is the number of times the specification is to be repeated. If n is 1, it may be omitted.

w   is the width of the field.[2]

Reference: 9.4

I/0 of Double Precision Values

nDw.d

where   n   is the number of times the field is to be repeated. If n is 1, it may
be omitted.

w   is the width of the field. w should be at least 7 greater than d.

d   specifies the number of decimal places to the right of the decimal
point.

Reference: 13.6

I/0 of Real Values with Exponent

nEw.d

where   n   is the number of times the specification is to be repeated. If n is 1,
it may be omitted.

w   is the width of the field. w should be at least 7 greater than d.

d   is the number of decimal places to the right of the decimal point.

Reference: 13.9

I/0 of Real Values without Exponent

nFw.d

where   n   is the number of times the field is to be repeated. If n is 1, it may
be omitted.

w   is the width of the field.

d   is the number of decimal places to the right of the decimal point.
It must be included even if it is zero.

Reference: 6.3, 8.2, and 8.3

I/0 of Real Values with/without Exponent

nGw.d

where   n   is the number of times the field is to be repeated. If n is 1, it may
be omitted.

w   is the width of the field. w should be at least 7 greater than d.

d   is the number of decimal places to the right of the decimal point.

Reference: 13.9

Output of Messages

nHccc. . .ccc

[2] On the IBM 360 or 370 computers, the maximum number of characters which may
be stored in one memory location is 4; on the CDC 6000 Series and CYBER 70 computers the maximum is 10.

where   n   is the exact number of characters ccc. . . .c to be written.

ccc. . . .ccc   are letters, numbers or special characters (including blanks) to be written. Blanks must be counted when they appear in an H-field specification.

Reference: 6.3

I/0 of Integer Values

nIw

where   n   is the number of times the field is to be repeated. If n is 1, it may be omitted.

w   is the width of the field.

Reference: 6.3, 8.2, and 8.3

I/0 of Logical Values

nLw

where   n   is the number of times the field is to be repeated. If n is 1, it may be omitted.

w   is the width of the field.

Reference: 13.8

I/0 of Spaces to Skip

nX

where   n   is the number of spaces to skip.

Reference: 6.3, 8.2, and 8.3

FUNCTION Subprogram Defining Statement—Non-executable

Form: type FUNCTION name $(a_1, a_2, . . . , a_n)$

where   type   denotes the type of value computed by the function. It may be REAL, INTEGER, COMPLEX, DOUBLE PRECISION, or LOGICAL.

name   is the name of the function. It must be a valid FORTRAN variable name.

$a_1, a_2, . . . , a_n$ are the dummy arguments. They may be simple variable names or array names. There must be at least one argument.

The defining statement must be the first statement in the FUNCTION subprogram. The name of the function must be assigned a value in at least one statement of the subprogram. When a RETURN is executed in the subprogram, the current value of the name becomes the value of the function.

The function name may not appear in any non-executable statement in the subprogram except in the defining statement. The dummy arguments may not appear in a COMMON, DATA, or EQUIVALENCE statement in the subprogram.

Reference: 12.4

GO TO Statement (Unconditional)—Executable

    Form: GO TO n

where n is a statement label

After this statement is executed, the next one executed is the one labeled n. We say that control is transferred to statement n.

Reference: 6.3

GO TO Statement (Computed)—Executable

    Form: GO TO $(n_1, n_2, \ldots n_k)$, i

where $n_1, n_2, \ldots, n_k$ are statement labels
         i is an integer variable. When this statement is executed, the value of i must be between 1 and k.

This statement causes control to transfer to a statement depending upon the current value of the variable i. At execution time if the value of i is 1, the next statement executed will be n_1. If i has the value 2, the next statement executed will be n_2. In general, when the value of the variable i is j, then the statement executed next will be statement number n_j.

Reference: 13.3

IF (Arithmetic)—Executable

    Form: IF (arithmetic expression) n_1, n_2, n_3

where n_1, n_2, n_3 are statement labels.

When this statement is executed, the arithmetic expression is evaluated first. If its value is negative, the next statement executed is the one labeled n_1. If its value is zero, control transfers to statement n_2. If its value is positive, control transfers to statement n_3.

The arithmetic expression is discussed in the arithmetic replacement statement.

Reference: 6.3

IF (Logical)—Executable

    Form: IF (logical expression) S

where   S   is any executable statement except a DO statement or another logical IF.

The simplest form of a logical expression is called a relational expression and is of the form

$$a_1 \text{ op } a_2$$

where a_1, a_2 are arithmetic expressions (discussed as part of the arithmetic replacement statement).

op   is one of the following relational operators:

.EQ.	equal to
.NE.	not equal to
.GT.	greater than
.LT.	less than
.GE.	greater than or equal to
.LE.	less than or equal to

Other logical expressions may be formed by combining relational expressions, logical variables, logical constants, and logical functions with logical operators. A logical variable is one which has been declared in a *type* statement and has the value of true or false. The logical constants are .TRUE. and .FALSE. .

The logical operators are as follows:

.OR.	logical disjunction
.AND.	logical conjunction
.NOT.	logical negation

The general form of a logical expression is:

$$L_1 \text{ op}_1 \ L_2 \text{ op}_2 \ L_3 \text{ op}_3 \ldots L_n$$

where $L_1, L_2, \ldots, L_n$ are logical variables, logical constants, logical functions, or logical expressions enclosed in parentheses. The logical operator .NOT. may precede any L_i.

$\text{op}_1, \text{op}_2, \ldots$ are the logical operators .AND. or .OR.

The logical operator .NOT. may appear in combination with .AND. or .OR. only as follows:

$$L_1 \text{ .AND. .NOT. } L_2$$
$$L_1 \text{ .OR. .NOT. } L_2$$

The logical IF statement is executed in the following manner:

1. The logical expression is evaluated. The resulting value is either true or false.
2. If the logical expression's value is true, the statement S is executed. Then, if S is not a statement which transfers control, the next statement executed is the executable one immediately following the IF statement.
3. If the logical expression is false, control proceeds to the next executable statement below the IF, without executing statement S.

Reference: 6.3, 13.8

Integer Type Statement—Non-executable, Specification

Form: INTEGER list

where list may contain variable names, array names, function names, and/or array declarators. Elements in the list are separated by commas. There is no comma at the end of the list.

This statement makes all the elements in the list of type *integer*. When defined, they will have *integer* values.

Reference: 9.3

Logical IF (See IF (Logical))

Logical Type Statement—Non-executable, Specification

Form: LOGICAL list

where   list   may contain variable names, array names, function names, and/or array declarators. Commas are used to separate the entries in the list. There is no comma at the end of the list.

This statement declares all elements in the list to be of type logical. This means that their values will be either true or false.

Reference: 13.8

Logical Assignment Statement—Executable

Form: logical variable = logical expression

where   logical variable   has been typed in a logical *type* statement
        logical expression   follows the rules discussed under the logical IF statement.

This statement is used to assign a value to a logical variable.

Reference: 13.8

READ Statement—Executable

Form: READ (u,n) list

where   u   is the unit number of the input device
        n   is the statement number of the FORMAT referenced by the READ statement.
        list   may contain variable names, array names, array elements, and/or implied loops. The elements in the list are separated by commas. There is no comma at the end of the list.

This statement receives values from the input device and assigns them to the elements of the list in the order that they are given.

Reference: 6.3, 8.2, and 8.3

Real Type Statement—Non-executable, Specification

Form: REAL list

where   list   may contain variable names, array names, function names and/or array declarators. Elements in the list are separated by commas. There is no comma at the end of the list.

This statement makes all elements in the list of type *real*. When defined, they will have real values.

Reference 9.3

RETURN Statement—Executable

Form: RETURN

A RETURN statement is used to return control to the referencing subprogram. It is the last statement executed before leaving a subprogram. More than one RETURN statement is permissible in a subprogram. When the RETURN statement is encountered in a SUBROUTINE subprogram, control returns to the statement following the CALL statement. In a FUNCTION subprogram, control returns to the statement in which the function was referenced.

Reference: 12.4

STOP Statement—Executable

Form: STOP

This statement is used to cease execution of a program. It may appear anywhere in the program, and there may be more than one STOP statement in a program.

Reference: 6.3

STOP *n*—Executable

Form: STOP *n*

where   *n*   is an octal number [3] from one to five digits.

Execution of this statement causes the program to halt. Most computers will print "STOP *n*" when the program halts.

Reference: 13.4

Subroutine Subprogram Defining Statement—Non-executable

Forms: SUBROUTINE name
         SUBROUTINE name $(a_1, a_2, \ldots, a_n)$

where   name   is the name of the subroutine. It must be a valid FORTRAN variable name.

   $a_1, a_2, \ldots, a_n$ are the dummy arguments. They may be simple variable names or array names.

---

[3] An octal number is a number in the base 8 number system in which only the digits 0 through 7 are used.

The defining statement must be the first statement in the subroutine subprogram. The dummy arguments may not appear in a COMMON, DATA, or EQUIVALENCE statement in the subprogram.

Reference: 12.4

Statement Function Defining Statement—Non-executable

Form: name $(a_1,a_2, \ldots ,a_n)$ = expression

where   name   is the name of the function. It must be a valid FOR-TRAN variable name.

$a_1,a_2, \ldots ,a_n$ are simple variable names which are dummy arguments of the function.

expression   is an expression containing only
                                        constants
                                        non-subscripted variables
                                        reference to FORTRAN supplied functions
                                        references to previously defined statement functions

The statement function must precede the first executable statement of a program and follow any specification statements. Any expression of the same type as the dummy argument may be used as an actual argument. The expression may be as simple as a constant or a variable. Or it might be more complex and contain computation to be performed or a reference to other functions.

Reference: 12.2

WRITE Statement—Executable

Forms: WRITE (u,n)
           WRITE (u,n) list

where   u   is the unit number of the output device.

       n   is the statement number of the FORMAT statement referenced by the WRITE statement.

    list   may contain variable names, array names, array elements, and/ or implied loops. The elements in the list are separated by commas. There is no comma at the end of the list.

This statement causes the output device to receive the output. If there is a list, the values of the variables in the list are transferred from memory to the output device. If the FORMAT contains only H-field and X-field specifications, then no list is needed in the WRITE statement.

Appendix B

FORTRAN Supplied Functions

Definition, Number of Arguments	Name	Example	Type of Argument	Type of Function
Absolute Value $|a|$ (1)	ABS	Y=ABS(X)	Real	Real
	IABS		Integer	Integer
	DABS		Double	Double
	CABS		Complex	Complex
Arctangent arctan(a) (1)	ATAN	Z=ATAN(B)	Real	Real
	DATAN		Double	Double
arctan(a_1/a_2) (2)	ATAN2	P=ATAN2(X,Y)	Real	Real
	DATAN2		Double	Double
Choosing Largest Value Max(a_1,a_2, ...) ($\geq$2)	AMAX0		Integer	Real
	AMAX1		Real	Real
	MAX0	I=MAX0(K,J)	Integer	Integer
	MAX1		Real	Integer
	DMAX1		Double	Double
Choosing Smallest Value Min(a_1,a_2,...) ($\geq$2)	AMIN0		Integer	Real
	AMIN1		Real	Real
	MIN0	N=MIN0(I,K)	Integer	Integer
	MIN1		Real	Integer
	DMIN1		Double	Double
Complex: Express Two real Arguments in Complex Form $a_1 + a_2 \sqrt{-1}$ (2)	CMPLX	COMPLEX Z Z=CMPLX(A,B)	Real	Complex
Obtain Conjugate of a Complex Argument (1)	CONJG	COMPLEX C,D C=CONJG(D)	Complex	Complex
Obtain Imaginary Part of Complex Argument (1)	AIMAG	COMPLEX E A=AIMAG(E)	Complex	Real
Obtain Real Part of Complex Argument (1)	REAL	COMPLEX A X=REAL(A)	Complex	Real
Cosine cos(a)* (1)	COS	X=COS(Y)	Real	Real
	DCOS		Double	Double
	CCOS		Complex	Complex
Double Precision: Express Single Precision Argument In Double Precision Form (1)	DBLE	DOUBLE PRECISION A A=DBLE(X)	Real	Double
Obtain Most Significant Part of Double		DOUBLE PRECISION Z		

Definition, Number of Arguments	Name	Example	Type of Argument	Function
Precision Argument (1)	SNGL	B=SNGL(Z)	Double	Real
Exponential e^a (1)	EXP DEXP CEXP	Y=EXP(X)	Real Double Complex	Real Double Complex
Fix Conversion from real to integer (1)	IFIX	J=IFIX(A)	Real	Integer
Float Conversion from integer to real (1)	FLOAT	A=FLOAT(K)	Integer	Real
Hyperbolic Tangent tanh(a) * (1)	TANH	Y=TANH(X)	Real	Real
Logarithm — base 10 (1)	ALOG10 DLOG10	R=ALOG10(T)	Real Double	Real Double
Logarithm — natural log (1)	ALOG DLOG CLOG	B=ALOG(C)	Real Double Complex	Real Double Complex
Positive Difference $a_1 - Min(a_1,a_2)$ (2)	DIM IDIM	P=DIM(A,B)	Real Integer	Real Integer
Remaindering: Remainder of $\frac{a_1}{a_2}$ (2)	AMOD MOD DMOD	I=MOD(K,N)	Real Integer Double	Real Integer Double
Sine sin(a) * (1)	SIN DSIN CSIN	Y=SIN(X)	Real Double Complex	Real Double Complex
Square Root (1)	SQRT DSQRT CSQRT	Z=SQRT(Y)	Real Double Complex	Real Double Complex
Transfer of Sign(a_1,a_2) Sign of a_2 times $|a_1|$ (2)	SIGN ISIGN DSIGN	X=SIGN(A,B)	Real Integer Double	Real Integer Double
Truncation Sign of a times largest integer $\leq |a|$ (1)	AINT INT IDINT	I=INT(A)	Real Real Double	Real Integer Integer

* a is in radians.

Index